TRIBUTES

E. H. GOMBRICH

TRIBUTES

Interpreters of our cultural tradition

Phaidon · Oxford

Phaidon Press Limited, Littlegate House, St Ebbe's Street, Oxford
First published in volume form 1984
This edition © 1984 by Phaidon Press Limited

British Library Cataloguing in Publication Data
Gombrich, E. H.
  Tributes.
    1. Culture
    I. Title
    306   HM101
  ISBN 0-7148-2338-4

Printed in Great Britain at The Pitman Press, Bath

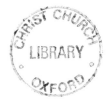

Contents

Preface

'*Let us now praise famous men, and our fathers that begat us.*' The injunction from *Ecclesiasticus* which is so often read out at commemorative functions could have served as a motto for this seventh volume of my collected essays published by the Phaidon Press. True, 'the fathers that begat us' to whom I was proud to pay tribute on sundry occasions are not physical forebears, but our spiritual ancestors to whom we owe the ideas and values which are woven into the fabric of our intellectual life. I have attempted to name some of these ideas and achievements in the titles and subtitles I have given to the individual pieces and thus to point to the common framework that encloses them all. I know that in referring to these illustrious figures collectively as 'interpreters of our cultural tradition' I have done less than justice to their individual contributions, but in casting around for a suitable term I found that the accidents of linguistic usage made the choice of a general subtitle unexpectedly tricky.

An interpreter of the Law is known as a jurist, an interpreter of the Scriptures a theologian; a physician might be called an interpreter of symptoms, and perhaps a scientist an interpreter of natural phenomena. In the Renaissance the term '*umanista*' or humanist was coined to describe the students and interpreters of classical texts and this meaning still adheres to the term in English academic parlance. On the other side of the Atlantic 'humanists' and the 'humanities' have acquired a wider connotation, which would have suited me well but which would have conflicted with English university traditions, where students of language, literature and history are combined in the Faculty of Arts, there being no generic terms for individual members of such faculties. It was no doubt in deference to this diversity of terminology that the American Academy of Arts and Sciences asked me to devote my bicentennial tribute to 'The Arts and Humanities'. I hope that my use of this address as an introductory essay will help clarify for the reader what

I mean by the interpreters of our cultural tradition, or what I have called there the guardians of memory.

To be sure, our Western culture is rooted in the humanities in the stricter sense of the term, and as recently as a generation ago was still generally seen to be so rooted. Despite their great diversity in origin and outlook, nearly all the figures here represented received a grounding in the classics. The curriculum of the German and Austrian Gymnasiums attended by Lessing, Hegel, Freud, Warburg, Kris, and Kurz did not differ widely from that of the high school in Holland frequented by Huizinga, the classical high school to which George Boas went in America, the English public school where I. A. Richards was educated or the various schools attended by Dame Frances Yates during her intense if irregular schooling. The odd man out here is Lord Leverhulme, the self-made industrialist, but he, if anyone, had absorbed the values which his Foundation still serves. In what used to be called the Republic of Learning there are as many mansions as there are in heaven. In referring to 'our' cultural tradition while writing in an adopted language, I was really thinking of that Republic, which has always extended far beyond the frontiers of a single country. And just as passports have always been ignored in that community, it will be seen in the following pages that its members also ignored the conventional boundaries drawn in the universities around the so-called disciplines. The ease with which these minds of distinction were able to move into new fields of learning is in itself an object-lesson which should not be lost on the reader.

I confess, in fact, that it was not piety alone which prompted me to place these tributes before a wider public. I had an ulterior motive in introducing such a varied selection of scholars and critics to the non-specialist reader. I did so to exemplify the nature and value of branches of learning which are in danger, almost everywhere, of being squeezed out of higher education. I did not want to remain wholly silent while the meagre funds available to the universities for these studies are increasingly diverted to specialized courses in science and technology.

I hope that I cannot easily be accused of lacking respect for these vital pursuits; in fact I stressed in the Preface to my preceding volume of essays (*The Image and the Eye*) how greatly I valued the interest which scientists have shown in my work. Of course it is not the scientists who lack an appreciation of our cultural tradition, but a certain type of politician. It appears to be fatally easy to curry favour with the philistines by speaking superciliously of useless subjects of research. How indeed can the hard-pressed taxpayer be expected to appreciate what is at stake? There are, alas, a good many countries in the world where the universities have been more or less reduced to vocational schools and where neither the libraries nor the teaching staff are any longer able to serve the interpretation and continuation of cultural traditions. One soon feels this absence in the quality of life, the boredom and hedonism which threaten the very fabric of civilized existence.

The closing of the Platonic Academy in Athens in AD 529 by the Byzantine Emperor Justinian is generally considered one of the milestones on the road to the Dark Ages. Our academies are not yet being closed, they are simply condemned to atrophy through lack of funds. It will certainly be easier to destroy them than to inaugurate a new Renaissance.

There is little chance of persuading those who seem impervious to argument in these matters. All one can try to do is to change the climate of opinion, if ever so slightly. If any one of the readers of this volume who is also a taxpayer should come to feel that the men and women here described should, after all, be allowed to find successors it will have served its real purpose.

With the exception of my Darwin Lecture of 1979 given at Cambridge University, which is here published for the first time, these texts were originally printed without illustrations, but I gladly accepted the suggestion of Simon Haviland of the Phaidon Press to add a number of explanatory pictures. Each of the tributes to individuals is preceded by a portrait and a brief biographical outline. A few essential bibliographical indications will be found at the beginning of the notes to these chapters. Three of the pieces (on Hegel, Freud, and Warburg) were originally presented in German. In view of my conviction that no translation can be more than an approximation, frequently involving a choice between two 'evils', I need hardly explain why I felt tempted further to revise the translation of my Hegel lecture which had appeared in *Architectural Design* and to prefer my own versions even to the existing standard translations of Sigmund Freud's writings.

In conclusion I should like to thank Diana Davies for her help in preparing the texts for publication and in compiling the index.

London, August 1983   E. H. G.

Focus on the Arts and Humanities

Ladies and Gentlemen, the programme you hold in your hands is printed in characters we derive from the Phoenicians, modified by the Greeks, the Romans and by Carolingian scribes whose forms were taken up in the Italian Renaissance; the numerals have reached us from ancient India via the Arabs; the paper on which it is printed is an invention of the Chinese which came West in the eighth century, when the Arabs took Chinese prisoners who taught them the art of paper-making. The term Friday, of course, comes from the substitution of a Teutonic goddess, Frigg, for the ancient goddess Venus; or rather for the planetary deity to which one of the seven-day cycle was assigned in late antiquity, the cycle we call the week.

I wanted to remind you of the extent to which we are the heirs of many and diverse civilizations to make my first point: that within the life of the mind I regard the humanities as representing the faculty of memory, the memory of our culture. This, I know, is a somewhat old-fashioned view, though it is not so long ago that it was taken for granted. The history of the term in its various applications has been admirably traced in a fine essay by Ronald S. Crane, *The Idea of the Humanities*,[1] which absolves me from the need to pursue the matter at length. *Humanitas* meant to the ancient world roughly anything that

One of a series of addresses delivered as part of the Bicentennial Programme, 'Unity and Diversity: The Life of the Mind', at the American Academy of Arts and Sciences in May 1981. The Commentators were: Meyer Abrams, Class of 1916 Professor of English, Cornell University; Frank Manuel, University Professor of History, Brandeis University; David Pingree, Professor of the History of Mathematics, Brown University; and Seymour Slive, Gleason Professor of Fine Arts and Director of The William Hayes Fogg Art Museum, Harvard University.

distinguished man from beast, and so the notion became identified with what we might call civilized values. Since nobody doubted that these values had first been realized and established by classical culture, it was the memory of this culture which the humanities were expected to keep alive.

I believe that among the arguments which have undermined this conviction some are valid, others invalid. The identification of our civilization with civilization as such is certainly open to the charge of what is nowadays called ethnocentricity, and perhaps also élitism. I hope I have shown in my opening words how impossible it would be to isolate our culture from others, but I also believe that this interconnectedness can best be surveyed from a given vantage point. I have chosen the here and now because it is the here and now from which we look back in time. If we lose our memory we lose that dimension which gives depth and substance to our culture.

There is a fable by James Thurber about the seal who was so opinionated that whenever the Great Seal of the United States was mentioned, he thought he was meant. I am a trifle less conceited, and so I can only surmise that the choice of the Academy fell on me because of my lifelong association with a well-known centre of humanist studies, The Warburg Institute, now part of the University of London. Over the entrance to that Institute you can read in Greek characters the word which its founder wanted to be inscribed there, MNEMOSYNE, Memory, the mother of the Muses.

In Aby Warburg's time the traditional interpretation of the humanities had already come under attack and it was for that very reason that he wanted to re-examine the question of what it was that our culture remembered of the ancient world.[2] Surely not only civilized values, but also darker impulses which endangered the dominance of reason. It is a pity that his insistent question '*Was bedeutet das Nachleben der Antike?*' (What is the significance of the classical heritage?) was translated on the Institute's arrival in England as the Classical Tradition; but, after all, the research and the publications of the Institute refute any too narrow interpretation of that misleading formula. What is distinctive of its work, I believe, is not any particular method of research, but an awareness of the unity of civilization; the determination not to be deterred by what Warburg called the frontier guards of the so-called disciplines. As an historian of art he was led through the study of a Quattrocento fresco cycle to the history of Arabic astrology, and his successor Fritz Saxl to that of medieval scientific manuscripts. Research on *The Architectural Principles in the Age of Humanism*[3] led Rudolf Wittkower to the Renaissance theory of music; her interest in Giordano Bruno made Frances Yates write her *Art of Memory*;[4] the subject of *European Clocks and Watches in the Near East* prompted Otto Kurz to uncover a fascinating chapter in

East-West diplomacy;[5] and D. P. Walker came to write his book on *Spiritual and Demonic Magic from Ficino to Campanella*[6] through his work on Renaissance Platonism. I know that the colleagues who kindly accepted my invitation to join this discussion have found that they too could not be confined within the conventional limits of academic departments while reinforcing and cultivating our cultural memories.

I confess that I miss a full awareness of the role of these cultural memories when I am confronted with those powerful intellectual movements which offer to explain the workings of culture in terms of economic or psychological mechanisms. Several of these anti-historical trends have taken their cue from the switch of interest in linguistics from diachronic to synchronic studies. The undeniable insights yielded by this shift of emphasis have raised the hope among some of our colleagues that we would soon be able to discard the study of individual facts such as I have mentioned at the outset, for a new and all-embracing science of man. I emphatically lack both the knowledge and the time to enter here into polemical arguments, but I must at least substantiate this observation. A quotation from Claude Lévi-Strauss's book on *The Savage Mind* may serve that purpose: '. . . it would not be enough to reabsorb particular humanities into a general one. The first enterprise opens the way for others . . . which are incumbent on the exact natural sciences: the reintegration of culture in nature and finally of life within the whole of its physio-chemical conditions.'[7]

I should like to suggest as a second point for our discussion that if we wholly surrender to this pressure we might contribute to what I propose to call the dehumanization of the humanities. Not that it is hard to account for this pressure. The memory which our culture preserves of the past is depressingly fragmentary, distorted, and incoherent in the fortuitous survival of evidence; there is so very much we should like to know and will never know, so very little we can be sure about. No wonder that dreams and myths often take over where facts are elusive, no wonder, in other words, that to the critical eye much of the humanities looks like the indulgence of subjectivity and that the search has arisen for more objective criteria. Libraries could be filled with books and articles addressing themselves to this problem. I do not pretend to have read even a fraction of the best, but in any case my hour would be over before I had enumerated their titles. I must ask to be forgiven, therefore, if I continue as I started, choosing an egocentric vantage point. I can only speak of my personal experience, however limited, during the fifty years or so that I have looked out into that scenery, even at the risk of repeating what I may have told elsewhere.

I did not start life as a Doubting Thomas. I was attracted to art history as a

schoolboy in Vienna when I read such authors as Max Dvořák, who convinced
me that the art of the past offered an immediate and exciting access to the
mind of bygone ages. When I began my studies in the late 1920s, the
anticlassical movements of contemporary art had focused attention on former-
ly neglected periods, notably late antiquity and sixteenth-century Mannerism,
which offered endless opportunities for fresh research. It so happened that an
early assignment under my teacher Julius von Schlosser confronted me with
an ivory carving attributed to the Dark Ages. I found them dark indeed.
Reading the rivalling hypotheses about stylistic developments in the seventh
and eighth centuries I admired the ingenuity and learning of my elders who
had convinced themselves that they knew what type of art came from
Alexandria, from Antioch, from Byzantium, Rome or Armenia, but I was
worried about their criteria of evidence. I still remember the afternoon when I
decided to sit down and write on a sheet of paper the rock-bottom facts of
what we call securely dated manuscripts or other works during the period. I
probably missed a few, but in any case the paper showed so many blank areas
that I wondered whether this was more than a learned guessing game, with no
prizes for the winners. In the event I extricated myself by suggesting that my
little piece did not come from the Dark Ages at all, but from a slightly later and
better documented period,[8] but I decided to withdraw to the safer field of
sixteenth-century Mannerism.

  Choosing as my subject Raphael's famous pupil Giulio Romano,[9] I was
confronted with a similar perplexity. There is not one document telling us
what the young man in his teens did in Raphael's busy workshop, but this did
not seem to deter famous authorities from pronouncing exactly which figure
or group in his master's oeuvre was really painted by him and which by other
named assistants. I have never surmounted this second crisis of confidence; I
suppose I would not have had any talent for the games of attribution, but I
also lacked enthusiasm for an activity which so often has to make up in
self-assurance for what it lacks in evidence. But my probing did not stop
there. Research took me to the well-stocked archives of Mantua and although
I did not make any spectacular discoveries there, I learned what I should
always have known, that the past was not peopled by abstractions but by men
and women. I found it hard to credit them all with that spiritual predicament
Dvořák and others had found expressed in the style of Mannerism, and I cast
around for alternative explanations of the style, including the demands and
expectations of Giulio's princely patron, the spoilt and pleasure-loving
Federico Gonzaga, about whom we know a good deal from the documents. I
have been wary of collectivism ever since.

  I fear that this account of my intellectual odyssey threatens to sound a little like Voltaire's *Candide*, and I must confess that not even in moving to the Warburg Institute did I find the best of all possible worlds. I was much attracted to the novel game of iconology, the fitting of texts to images, but much as I enjoyed it, I also discovered that the scope it offers for reckless subjectivism endangers our contact with historical realities.

You will not be surprised at my confession, therefore, that I have always been a somewhat uneasy humanist. I was aware, as we all have been, of the great strides meanwhile made by the sciences and most of all by their standards of objectivity. Ernst Kris[10] had initiated me early into the type of question a psychologist might ask of the history of art when he invited me to join him in research into the history of caricature. He wanted to test the hypothesis that portrait caricature could only arise in European art when unconscious fears of image magic were held in check. Whether or not such a hypothesis can be tested, it was the type of question which opened up new vistas to me.

The aspect of psychology I naturally found of immediate relevance to my field of study was the psychology of visual perception. Not that it had played no part in our studies; on the contrary, ways of seeing, ways of perceiving, were frequently referred to by critics and historians alike, but I found it worthwhile to consult recent books and articles and ask whether the traditional assumptions were still accepted. I found they were not, and though I could not hope to master the methods and results of a diverse and flourishing science, I felt able, rightly or wrongly, to use what I had learned to ask an historical question, the question of why art—I should have said, naturalistic representation—had a history at all; in other words, why what we find in certain periods of the history of art like that of ancient Greece or the Renaissance, resembles a learning process and has always been so described. I proposed in *Art and Illusion* (1960) that when the social function of images is expected to serve illusionism—whatever we may mean by this slippery term—that goal can only be reached by trial and error, by the slow and systematic modification of schematic images till they match the motif they are meant to represent. I suggested in another book, *The Sense of Order* (1979), that the same need for a step-by-step development pertains also in the field of the decorative arts, however far down they may reach into the subsoil of psychological and biological needs.

You need not fear that I shall now proceed to dwell on an exposition of my hypotheses. I merely want here to recommend my brain-children as law-enforcement officers. For one of the many things I have learned from the writings of Karl Popper is the possibility of expressing any scientific hypothesis in the form of an exclusion, such as 'there can be no movement exceeding the speed of light', or 'there can be no *perpetuum mobile*'. The value of this inverse formulation of the so-called natural laws is that it is easily seen that one proven instance of contravention disposes of the hypothetical law. It is this risk which makes science exciting.

Likewise, if you could prove to me that Frans Hals was a pupil of Cimabue I would have to pack up. But I hope we can go a little further even than that. If I am right, for instance, that the correct rendering of the human body cannot be learned overnight, we might take care not to explain the absence of such naturalism as an act of free will, or, as the jargon has it, as a manifestation of spirituality. That freedom of choice that enables a twentieth-century artist to render or reject appearances in the interest of his expressive needs was not always available to masters of the past. Hence my early misgivings about the expressionist interpretation of style could now be underpinned by the psychology of image-making.

But the third point which I wish to make here is that such an importation of science, in other words, the search for objective findings, can only take the humanist a certain part of the way. It can and should narrow the scope of the purely subjective, but it cannot and must not eliminate subjectivity as such, for elimination would amount to that dehumanization of the humanities of which I have spoken. I believe such a dehumanization is neither desirable nor possible, for the humanities are after all about human beings. Not that I attach much importance to such etymological arguments, but even without them it is clear that we are dealing with the products of men made for men—always including women. They exist in one way or another to elicit a human response—pleasure, fear, instruction, understanding, admiration, veneration, to mention but a few. Any such response, however general, is not in my interpretation an objective but a subjective fact, it is a kind of experience to which we have privileged access because we are also human.

It is fashionable to dismiss any appeal to human nature as naïve, particularly if it is based on introspection. But however much responses might differ, if the sense of sight did not belong to human nature, the visual arts would not have developed, and if we could not hear there would be no music. It is a moot point whether anyone born blind could become an art historian or anyone born deaf a musicologist, but such an undertaking would surely be as bizarre as a good food guide compiled by computers. They might test food for its ingredients and check the application of recipes, but how could they pronounce on creative innovations?

There is indeed a journal entitled *Computers and the Humanities*, in which I sampled an article entitled 'Toward a Syntactic Differentiation of Period Style in Modern Drama: Significant Between-Play Variability in 21 English Language Plays'.[11] I was relieved to see that the author, Rosanna Potter, started with a *caveat* which supports my position:

> Even after the statisticians have performed their magic and told us which variables differentiate best between plays, which variables correlate highest, which lowest, and which are more reliable, still literary criticism in the strictest sense awaits. It may be a little less likely to fall into impressionistic fallacies, but it must still be firmly rooted in our sensibility as good readers.

Thank heaven for that. The good reader is not yet redundant.

But if I hold that the subjective response must be and remain at the heart of the humanist enterprise, why do I also sympathize with the search for objective criteria, including, if it must be, those established by computers? The answer is, of course, that subjectivity does not mean that anything goes, that we are totally free to feel or dream as the spirit moves us. We aim at the right response, and though this notion is fraught with difficulty it will be my task to justify it. I hope I have made a beginning by pointing at the constraints which set limits to our imagination. Just as science can eliminate a wrong explanation, a false hypothesis, so the disciplined humanist can rule out a false reading, a misunderstanding. His well-trained policemen can gently warn the unwary against the slippery slopes of self-indulgent emotionalism and suggest a more careful and more rewarding use of what I should like to call the controlled imagination. This is the point I tried to make in the conclusion of the final chapter of *Art and Illusion*, but I am not sure how many of my readers picked it up. I there referred in a note to the essay by T. S. Eliot on 'The Frontiers of Criticism', but since I did not quote the passage concerned, I here make good the omission:

> There are many things, perhaps, to know about this poem or that, many facts about which scholars can instruct me which will help me to avoid further definite misunderstandings; but a valid interpretation, I believe, must be at the same time an interpretation of my own feelings when I read it.[12]

His formulation helps me to draw attention once more to scholarship rather than science. It seems to me to be the strength and weakness of scholarship that it concerns itself with the particular and not with the general. From its strength it derives the possibility of proofs, which are denied to the general propositions of science outside mathematics, but it pays for this strength by the random character of its evidence, which I have mentioned before. What is the use of being able to prove something that nobody wants to know?

By proof I here mean the same as the conclusive evidence which would be accepted in a conscientious court of law, or, if you like, in detective fiction. There are many degrees of such proofs, some of which may stand in need of mutual support, but others which not even the greatest sceptic would reject. The work of scholars has often been compared with the solution of jigsaw puzzles, and in such puzzles of sufficient intricacy the demonstration of a fit can be so compelling that it cannot be evaded. Papyrologists may be able to demonstrate that two fragments of a torn scroll fit not only in shape but that the fibres run through in unbroken lines. Medievalists may find a leaf torn from a codex which not only completes the text and the gathering but can also be shown to have left traces of pigment on the opposite page. We have recently experienced the force of a similar argument in disproving a conjecture dear to many scholars on both sides of the Atlantic; I am referring to the Vinland map. Once it had been shown that the parchment on which it was drawn had been taken out of a bound codex and shared the pattern of worm-holes with its other pages, the claims of the alleged document collapsed.

But precisely because such fits are the exception rather than the rule, the scholar notoriously has to go beyond his evidence in the task of making sense of the remnants of the past, whether archaeological, art historical, or textual. I was unfair, therefore, in refusing to play the guessing game about the art of the Dark Ages, for such games have on occasion led to progress by discovering new fits. It is a question of temperament rather than method how much latitude you can tolerate in the reconstruction of the past. Like the patient restorer, the scholar starts from those rock-bottom facts I have mentioned and, I hope, now defined, and carefully tries to fill in the blank areas in between by conjecture and surmise, in other words, by the controlled imagination. To him science is an aid in establishing these little areas of comparative certainty, by means of carbon dating, dendrology or whatever new wizardry may here arise. Other scientific facts he rightly takes for granted without having to spell them out; if he finds charred remains he does not have to say that without oxygen there would have been no fire, or that the material must have been combustible. But while these interpretations of his evidence do not call for comment, the latitude he can and does allow to his imagination deserves, I think, to be examined a little further, for I would maintain that without any latitude we could not continue our studies in the humanities. Even in reading evidence we must mobilize our mind. In *Art and Illusion* I have spoken in this context of the 'Beholder's Share', without which pictures would remain flat areas covered with pigment. When it comes to statements

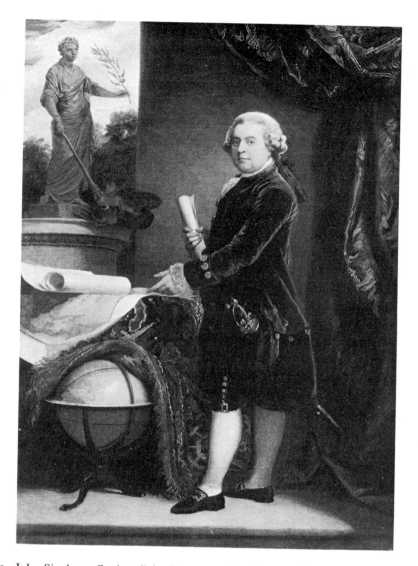

1. John Singleton Copley: *John Adams. c.* 1783. Boston, Museum of Fine Arts

there is something called word-blindness, which demonstrates a corresponding need in our reaction to texts.

Let me return to base and read to you the historical narrative I found in the commemorative pamphlet *A House for the American Academy of Arts and Sciences* (1979). 'The first house of the American Academy of Arts and Sciences was in the mind of John Adams [Fig. 1]. He communicated the idea to the Reverend Samuel Cooper [Fig. 2] at a Harvard Corporation dinner in 1779 in the Philosophy Chamber of the University.'

I know that people differ enormously in the degree to which they visualize what they hear. Introspection suggests to me that I have some elusive image of two eighteenth-century gentlemen conversing at dinner, against a possibly quite erroneous background of a panelled chamber. Assuming that the facts themselves are well established, there could of course be as many ideas of how it actually happened as there are people who take in the information.

Some may conceivably want to elaborate further, even to the point of writing a chapter in an historical novel. They could surely please themselves in describing the scene, the seating order and probably the menu, but they also must respect the known facts. Now the list of the facts which must limit the flights of their imagination is not exhausted by those mentioned in the passage I read. If they are to write tolerable historical fiction they must also avoid what are called anachronisms. They must not make the two diners toast the new Academy in champagne if, as I believe, the ceremonial prestige of the drink dates only from the nineteenth century. You may find this an eccentric example, but I believe that the imaginative reconstructions of past events on the stage, the screen or in novels differ merely in degree from those with which the scholar works. It cannot have escaped your notice that in allowing scope to the latitude of the subjective imagination I am admitting the possibility of a limited plurality of interpretations. As long as they observe the rules and do not clash anywhere with what is known, there can be two or more imaginative readings of a given situation or work, for instance in the writing of biographies. I hope I shall not give offence if I apply this term of latitude to what are called psychobiographies. Our evidence concerning the unconscious conflicts of men and women long dead seems to me so scanty that all we have a right to expect of such books are reconstructions which make sense in terms of what we regard as possible. Maybe John Adams was prompted to found this Academy by an unconscious longing for companionship due to an early childhood trauma. We can never know, and thus we grant this kind of latitude only to authors who are, as we say, really steeped in the period. However intensely the imagination of a genuine humanist may be engaged, he would immediately detect and reject anything that strikes him as a false note. 'Surely,' he would say, 'the table silver is quite wrong for 1779', or 'John Adams could never have used such a word'.

Whence comes this conviction? Of course from long and intense commerce with the monuments and documents of the period. There is no substitute for this immersion in the past, and if I appear to have spoken somewhat slightingly of the connoisseurs of art, I readily grant that they can respond like a sensitive instrument to any forgery pretending to be what it is not. Even such negative assurance needs first-hand familiarity with originals, not

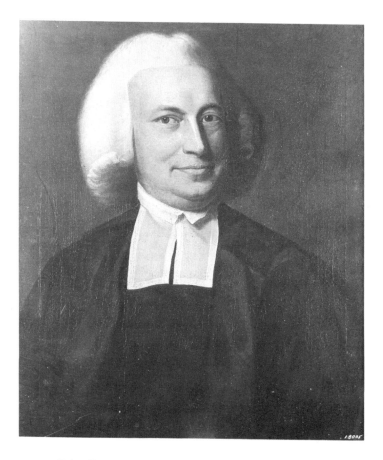

2. John Singleton Copley: *The Rev. Samuel Cooper.* 1769.
Concord, Mass., Ralph Waldo Emerson House

photographs, just as scholars can only feed their constructive imagination on original sources, not on second-hand accounts. Naturally, they read them not in translation but in their original language.

I know that the distinguished colleagues who have honoured me by accepting the invitation to comment on my themes will surely not want to dispute this need, but it might be a good thing if a call could go out from here against the complacent belief that the humanities can be taught in translations.

In the not-too-distant past a humanist was a person who knew classical languages. I do not claim that they are necessarily the only means of entry to our concerns, but given the fact that not only the Romans but also Dante and Erasmus, Milton and Newton wrote in Latin, it is only too likely that the demise of Latin will lead to a grave loss of cultural memory.

In any case, the need to learn languages is not confined to their utility in reading original texts. You cannot possibly know how your own language works if you have never had to grapple with another. What has been aptly called monoglot illiteracy may be detrimental to scientists; in the humanities it can have no place at all. For learning a language is a paradigm, a model for any effort at understanding what is meant by a text, a poem, a piece of music or a ritual. It gives us the first insight into the varieties of human experience by weaning us of the naïve belief that reality is divisible in natural classes and categories to which we only need to affix a name, a name we can look up in a dictionary if we happen not to know it.

It is language which imposes categories on our flux of experience, but it could not function as a versatile tool of communication if the universals with which it operates were not somewhat fuzzy at the edges and sufficiently flexible to serve as metaphors. Again we need not look beyond the printed programme of this meeting. The arts in the title of this academy were primarily intended to be the so-called practical arts such as (I read) 'agriculture, medicine, fire engines, steelmaking'. I take it that in the title of our meeting the coupling of the arts with the humanities shifts the meaning towards the arts in the modern sense of painting, poetry and music.

Few of the words used in our titles could survive translation. 'The Life of the Mind' is immediately intelligible in English, but alas, there is no corresponding category in my native German; you would have to choose between Spirit and Intellect, and neither will quite do. And what would you do with 'Focus'? The word means of course fire, and the metaphor derives from the burning-glass as used in the photographic camera to focus on a motif. There being no such metaphor in German you would have to cast around and try words signifying gaze, eyes, or field of vision—*Blickfeld*—maybe a lesser evil, but an evil all the same.

I should like to suggest as the fourth point of our discussion that there are at least two lessons which the humanist can draw from the daily frustrations and occasional triumphs of the translator—the first is that it is quite possible and even frequent for us to understand an utterance without being able to verbalize it. We know perfectly what a Frenchman means by *esprit*, but we cannot render this meaning in our own language. The second lesson follows from the first; it confirms, in my view, the importance of the boundaries set to our interpretation. What plagues but aids the translator is that he knows pretty well what a word does not mean, and that the true interpretation must be sought within the limits of these negations.

If that is accepted it may well be the case that the humanities have sometimes tried to do the impossible in attempting to express in words what cannot be verbalized. Here, I think, lies the tenuous boundary between the humanist and the critic. The critic is appointed for good or ill to describe his responses. The humanist is under no such obligation. He can use language, as I suggested, to eliminate misunderstanding, to narrow down the task of the controlled imagination, and if he is lucky he may find that in thus tightening the net he has led his readers to a better understanding of his subject, be it a religious or philosophical text, a poem, an image or a piece of music. In this balance of optimism and resignation the humanist does not differ from the scientist, who also knows that there is no such thing as an ultimate explanation but believes—if he follows Popper rather than Kuhn—that he can make progress in suggesting better solutions.[13] To doubt that progress can be made and has been made in the humanities would mean to forget such achievements as the decipherment of the hieroglyphs or of cuneiform, but no student of these texts would claim that there is nothing left there to be interpreted, that we can tell exactly how an Egyptian understood the various prayers and spells he had inscribed in his tomb.

But if you accept that there is a difference between verbalizing and understanding, you have a right to ask what criteria except the negative ones there can be for understanding. I am afraid they are and must remain subjective, but they are none the less real.

The best illustration I can think of does not come from the humanist's workshop but from that of the performing artist, be he an actor or a musician. If he is worth his salt he knows that his first duty is to respect the text, the written words or the notes; it is within these strict limits that he is set the task of so mobilizing his imagination that his performance illuminates every line or bar, through the right inflexion, the right gradation of emphasis, the right tempo and the right accent. Since we shall have the privilege of hearing Rudolf Serkin here tomorrow, I need not enlarge on my conviction that a great performance can be objective and subjective at the same time. Who can deny that there are supreme and less good performances, hopeless ones and inspired ones even within the limits of the prescribed text? It follows that there is latitude but not licence in understanding. There may be different performances of equal validity, but there are certainly many more demonstrably false ones.

But in my view that understanding of which I am speaking cannot be equated with a meeting of minds. What the actor, the musician or the humanist tries to understand is not what Shakespeare or Beethoven thought at the time of writing—that we cannot know and could certainly not verbalize; they want to understand the play or the sonata.

But is not the same true of us listeners, albeit on a much lower level? When we merely hear notes or noises we rightly say that we do not understand the piece. What we mean, I think, is that we cannot form expectations, and thus experience neither surprises nor disappointments. To understand, say, the minuet and trio in a Haydn symphony, means that we are aware of the contrast between the two sections and of their mutual enhancement. We relish the expected change from the more robust minuet to the relaxed and dance-like tune of the trio, and are all the more enchanted the more we realize how the composer has once again invented a fresh and satisfying variant of this simple form, such as Haydn must have done perhaps three hundred times in his oeuvre. To understand here means at the same time to appreciate his wit and originality, or conversely to find that another composer who uses the same convention could not pull it off; Haydn's pupil Beethoven was inspired to develop these contrasts in a new and personal way.

This engendered creativity, of course, is the highest form of understanding, but it, too, rests on the composer's grasp of the potentiality of the form. It is the form which engenders the emotion, not the emotion which is turned into form.

I believe the example illustrates the point forcefully made by Donald Hirsch in his book *Validity in Interpretation*,[14] when he stressed the importance of the genre in the process of interpretation and understanding. The genre, or more generally speaking, any tradition, demands what one might call imaginative participation. We must, as it were, 'get the hang of it' as we can with a game, before we can enter into its spirit.

The member of a culture or subculture is inducted into these traditions from early on and learns to resonate to their manifestations without conscious effort. To the humanist concerned with distant ages or distant lands they present a challenge. But I have never had much patience with the claim that the challenge cannot be met and that we are forever imprisoned in our own language and outlook. The claim rests on the false assumption that understanding is an all or nothing affair. Some alien religions, alien customs or alien styles may make great demands on our understanding, but here as always it is the first step that counts. Even though he may know that he will never be able fully to respond, the humanist will welcome the opportunity of transcending his limitations and widening his imaginative sympathy. If he is lucky he will even succeed in taking his students out of their little selves and their little worlds and convince them that our minds can indeed be stretched. What could be more relevant than this lesson?

I believe that this role I have here attributed to the mental faculties of memory and of the imagination allows me in conclusion to return to one of the central problems of the humanities, the choice of subject. The scientist experiments and observes in order to test a hypothesis which has become a problem to him, and *mutatis mutandis*, the humanist will also single out any evidence which bears on a general point he wishes to make. But where he follows his legitimate interest in particulars he lacks such guidance. He may be able to prove beyond doubt that two potsherds once belonged to the same pot, but if the pot is neither rare nor beautiful he may be confronted with the dread reaction: 'So what?' This reaction, which has sometimes questioned our very right to survive, could never have gained ground, even temporarily, if the humanities had not tried to emulate the sciences in disregarding the question of values. The neglect or even denial of values seems to me the greatest danger in that trend towards the dehumanization of the humanities of which I spoke.

My final point must therefore be that if the humanities are to justify their existence they must continue to occupy themselves with values. It is this concern most of all that distinguishes them from the sciences which include the human species in their purview, be it anatomy, physiology, psychology or, maybe, anthropology. These sciences, if I see the matter correctly, are interested in general laws of organic or mental life. If the humanities are to remain true to their mission, they must tell us more than that. We ask them to show us what man can be.

After all, it is natural to man to seek the limits of human achievement. If that desire were not so universal, there would be no such overriding interest in sport, in world records, or other exceptional feats. I do not know how many in this hall have ever seen a performance of Chinese acrobats. To me it came as a revelation. I did not know that human beings could defy the laws of gravity to that extent and achieve what looks like a state of weightlessness without the slightest sign of strain. We earthbound creatures could not follow them, hence our sense of wonderment.

Certainly, the great achievements in art and in science are of a higher order than mere acrobatics, but in thus illustrating the extension of human capabilities I want to suggest that we should restore to the humanities the sense of wonder, of admiration and also of horror, in other words, a sense of value. That stance of non-involvement, the attitude of *nil admirari* which is too often adopted in the name of scientific detachment seems to me to upset that balance between objectivity and subjectivity which I consider essential.

Common parlance still uses two old terms for striking departures from the human norm, the terms 'genius' for the positive, and 'monster' for the negative deviant. Maybe the traditional humanities concentrated too much on these types at the expense of common humanity. Certainly the monsters, the tyrants and conquerors, loomed too large in our history books, which told us so little about their victims, the ordinary mortals whose villages were burnt

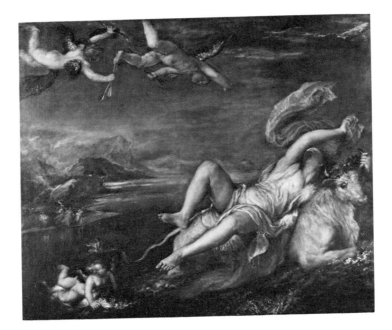

3. Titian: *The Rape of Europa*. 1562.
Boston, Isabella Stewart Gardner Museum

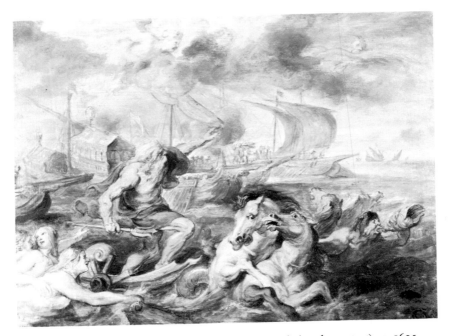

4. Peter Paul Rubens: '*Quos Ego!*' (*Neptune calming the tempest*). *c.* 1635.
Cambridge, Mass., Fogg Art Museum, Harvard University

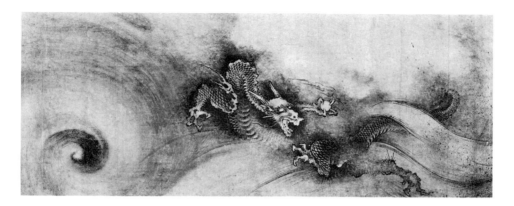

5. Ch'ên Jung: *The 'Nine Dragons' Scroll* (detail). 1244. Boston, Museum of Fine Arts

and whose cities were sacked. The reaction against this bias is much to be welcomed, even though the historian will often have to consult the anthropologist on how to fill in the glaring gaps in our evidence. But when it comes to the geniuses in science, in literature, art and music, I propose that they should never be far from the teaching and the thought of the humanist. Whatever his research, they alone can set standards by offering him continued reminders of the miraculous powers of man. David Hume, you may remember, dealt a mortal blow to the belief in miracles by arguing quite rightly that to prove that they happened we would have first to prove the trustworthiness of our informants. But the miracles wrought by the masters are still among us. You don't have to take anybody's word for it, for there are such marvels here quite within reach: the *Dragon Scroll* in Boston for instance (Fig 5), Titian's *Rape of Europa* at the Gardner (Fig. 3), or the *Quos Ego* by Rubens here at the Fogg (Fig. 4). True, precisely because they are miracles they will forever elude our full understanding, but even to try to understand them better is a rewarding experience, whether your admiration is turned to painting, music, poetry or drama. We need never fear that analysis will kill the experience. How could we, since even Shakespeare has survived his myriad commentators with his magic not diminished but even enhanced?

Ladies and Gentlemen, the only thing I have in common with Shakespeare is that I have small Latin and less Greek. But I still want with your permission to end with a line from that famous chorus of Sophocles' *Antigone* in praise of man. There are many things, the old men chant, which are *deina*, tremendous, awe-inspiring, wonderful, but nothing more *deinos* than man:

Πολλὰ τὰ δεινὰ κοὐδὲν ἀνθρώπου δεινότερον πέλει.

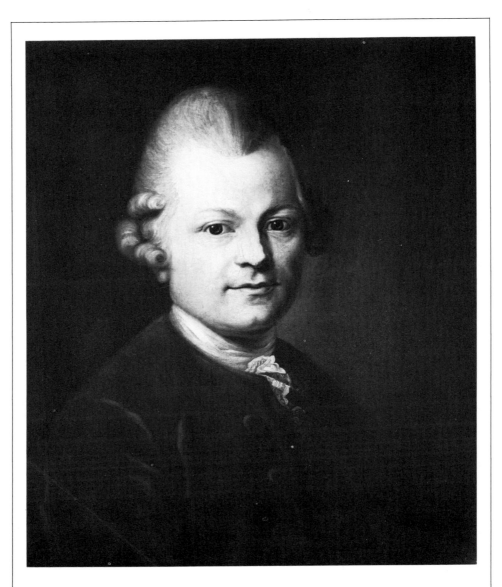

6. Gotthold Ephraim Lessing.
Painting by Anton Graf. Wolfenbüttel, Lessinghaus

Gotthold Ephraim Lessing, critic, author, playwright, and the oldest of the triad of German 'classics'—the others being Goethe (1749–1832) and Schiller (1759–1805)— was born in Kamenz, Saxony, on 22 January 1729, the son of a Protestant pastor. After attending a famous classical grammar school at Meissen he went to the University of Leipzig. From 1748 to 1767 he worked in Berlin as a free-lance writer, except for the period from 1760 to 1765 which he spent as secretary to a Prussian general in Breslau. In 1767 he was invited to Hamburg, where a German National Theatre was to be founded; the venture soon collapsed, but Lessing's critical commentaries, published under the title Hamburgische Dramaturgie, *became famous. From 1770 until his death he was librarian of the ancient library of Wolfenbüttel, near Brunswick. His last years were dominated by the conflict he aroused when he published a posthumous work by the Hamburg Orientalist, Reimarus, denying the truth of the miracles told in the Bible. He died in Brunswick on 15 February 1781.*

The Diversity of the Arts

The Place of the *Laocoon* in the Life and Work of G. E. Lessing (1729–1781)

1. A BORN DEBATER

WHEN I accepted the great honour of being allowed to pay tribute to Gotthold Ephraim Lessing in this lecture series, I did not yet know that my first concern would have to be to insist on the distinction between a master mind and a genius. For Lessing had made it known that if anyone called him a genius, he would give him a box on each ear which would feel like four.[1] You will understand if I shall first have to seek to placate his irascible spirit by quoting that famous self-characterization which occurs in the last issue of the *Hamburgische Dramaturgie* of 19 April 1768 when, at the age of thirty-nine, Lessing looked back on another disappointment of his restless life:

> I do not feel that living spring within me that wells up by its own power, and by its own power gushes forth in such rich, fresh, and pure jets. I must pump it all out of me through pressure and pipes. I should be so poor, so cold, so short-sighted had I not learned somewhat in all modesty to borrow other people's treasures, to warm myself by other people's fires, and to strengthen my eyes with artificial spectacles. Thus I have always felt mortified and annoyed to read or to hear anything to the detriment of criticism. It has been said to suffocate genius, and I flatter myself to derive something from it that comes very close to genius.[2]

Of course this utterance must be seen in its context. During the three years of his association with the new venture of a German National Theatre Lessing had not supplied the troupe with a single new play, as those who had invited the author of *Miss Sarah Sampson* and *Minna von Barnhelm* had no doubt

---

‘Lecture on a Master Mind’ given at the British Academy in May 1956.

expected.[3] Instead he had published a critical weekly in which he lectured the public on the true meaning of Aristotle's *Poetics*. But Lessing's intimate friends had always known that you needed only to expect him to do one thing and he would do another which he considered more important.[4] At this juncture, in fact, nothing could matter more than to show up the inadequacy of the mediocre products which filled the repertoire, by not allowing the public to forget the standards once set by the ancients and exemplified by Shakespeare—the only human being to whom Lessing conceded the title of genius.[5]

In German literary history Lessing is cast in the role of Moses who led his people out of French servitude towards the promised land of *Deutsche Klassik*, which he still saw from afar; the Lawgiver who struck the rock with his rod and lo, water flowed in abundance. But Lessing himself did not believe in miracles. He knew that if the German literary desert was to bloom, water had to be pumped and pumped from somewhere. His quarrel was with those who looked to France for the life-giving tradition. Already in the seventeenth *Literaturbrief* of 1759 he had championed Shakespeare against Corneille.[6] All Europe, of course, looked to England at the time, as the land of enlightenment, freedom and sentiment.[7] But in Germany, which was still almost a literary vacuum, the effect of Lessing's words of power was incalculable. Indeed, if the greatness of a master mind could ever be gauged by his influence alone, I could prove Lessing's claim from my own experience. For in German-speaking countries Shakespeare belongs to the intellectual universe called *Bildung*, French classical drama does not. Most of us were taught at school that French tragedies are frigid and contrived and only of interest to specialists.

How Lessing would have enjoyed campaigning against such a prejudice! For if there is one key to his rich and complex mind, it is his persistent non-conformism. Throughout his life he acted like the Freethinker in one of his earliest plays: 'If my opinions were to become too general, I should be the first to abandon them for the opposite view. . . . I cannot believe that truth can ever be common; as little, indeed, as that there could ever be daylight on the whole globe at one and the same time.'[8]

In Lessing's Germany, of course, opposition to French taste was opposition to majority opinion, backed by all the power and authority of Frederick the Great. It is one of the ironies of history that this fight was to make Lessing a hero, *malgré lui*, of that nationalism he had often and explicitly disowned. Writing to Gleim, who had published *Prussian Warsongs . . . by a Grenadier* (1758), Lessing confessed that he never wanted to be praised as a zealous patriot, 'that is, a patriot who made me forget that I should be a citizen of the world'; indeed, the love of the fatherland seemed to Lessing 'at the most a heroic weakness'.[9]

'I should be ashamed of myself', he said, 'if the idea had even crossed my mind' that no Frenchman could write a moving tragedy.[10] No nation had any intellectual advantage over another. If they had not yet got the perfect tragedy, it was only because they were convinced they had reached perfection already. For this is where the value of criticism lies in Lessing's eyes. Those who called for peace and mutual admiration he reminded that 'disputes alone nourish the spirit of inquiry, prevent prejudice and prestige from ossifying, and painted untruth from masquerading as truth.'[11]

He was always ready himself to submit to that discipline—at least in theory. 'I can only think with my pen on paper', he once explained: 'if my ideas satisfy me in the end, I tear the paper up; if not, I send it to the printers.'[12]

Both in tone and intention Lessing's writings are always a challenge, part of a dramatic dialogue with a real or an imagined opponent. He never writes with Olympian calm. He wants to provoke argument. In the company of friends, we are told, Lessing would take some accepted opinion and assert the opposite, improvising reasons as he went along.[13] When he did not argue he gambled or played chess.[14] His passion for chess, in fact, brought about the most fruitful friendship of his formative years, his association with Moses Mendelssohn, who had been recommended to Lessing as a partner in chess, and became a partner in philosophical argument. In his handling of language for argument Lessing displayed a master mind in that precise meaning of the term in which we speak of a master in chess. I think and hope he might have spared my ears for this assertion.

Lessing enjoyed this mastery, and the exhilaration at the power which language gave him is unmistakable in every line he wrote. Ideas he may have borrowed. This love of the game was his from the start. There is no greater mystery in life than that hallmark of personality which gives to the tone of a writer's voice its unmistakable ring. With Lessing this tone is present in the first letter we have from his hand, written at the age of fourteen, at Christmas 1743. Of course it is polemical. He criticizes his elder sister for not writing to him.

Beloved Sister,

Although I have written to you, yet you have not replied. I am therefore forced to think that either you cannot write or that you do not want to write. I would almost maintain the former; however, I am also ready to believe the latter: you do not want to write. Either is reprehensible.[15]

Cannot you see the proud and still somewhat priggish schoolboy moving his knight and taking his poor opponent between pincers? It remained a favourite trick of his style: 'What do you say to Klopstock's spiritual odes?', he writes to Gleim, fifteen years later: 'if you think badly of them I shall suspect your Christianity, if you think well of them I shall doubt your taste. Which would you rather?'[16]

Sometimes it is a mere pawn of a word which the opponent has incautiously advanced and which becomes the centre of attack, turning the tide in Lessing's favour, as in the opening of that seventeenth *Literaturbrief* to which I have referred: '"Nobody", say the authors of the Bibliothek, "will deny that the German stage owes a large part of its first improvements to Professor Gottsched." I am that nobody, I deny it outright.'[17]

Or the first move in the *Antiquarian Letters* against Klotz:

> Herr Klotz is said to have convicted me of an unforgivable mistake in his book on ancient engraved stones. A reviewer of that book has found it necessary to point this out. Me of a mistake? That is very possible. But an unforgivable one? I should be sorry for that. Not so much for my sake, who committed it, as for the sake of those who do not want to forgive it.[18]

You find the same pouncing on words in the dialogues of Lessing's plays to drive thought and action along. The very first words of *Nathan* are of this kind:

> He's coming! Nathan! God be praised for ever
> That you have now returned to us at last.
> —Yes, Daja, God be praised, but why 'at last'?
> Did ever I intend to come back sooner
> Or could I have? . . .

One of Lessing's last opponents, Pastor Goeze, made Lessing's 'methods in controversy' a special target for his attacks;[19] he complained of his *Theater-logik*, of his use of words and images where only rational arguments should count. Lessing admitted that his style liked to linger on metaphors and that the dramatist's interest in dialogue may have reinforced that natural bent. But what of it? Who says that no one can think clearly and correctly who does not use 'the most literal, the most common, and the flattest expressions'?[20] He would show 'that where he played most with words he yet did not play with empty words'.[21]

Once more we are reminded of *Nathan*, of the delightful scene where the game of chess is actually played on the stage between Sultan Saladin and his

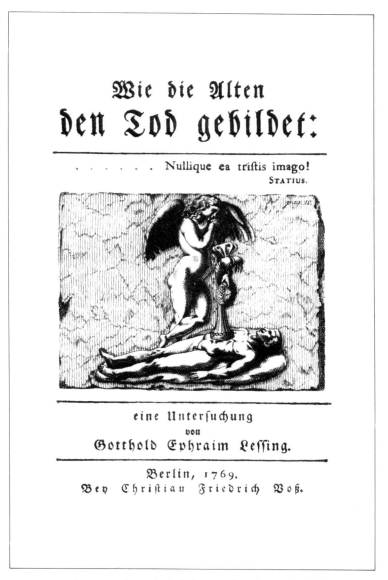

7. Title-page of Lessing's *Wie die Alten den Tod gebildet*
(How the Ancients represented Death). Berlin, 1769

fair sister Sittah. For once the Sultan's mind is not on the game, and as he gives up he is inclined to blame the unformed plain set of pieces 'reminding us of nothing, meaning nothing'.[22]

Lessing always liked to play with pieces rich in associations, and he thought nothing of borrowing them in all modesty from other people's treasures. In recent years this habit of his has increasingly become a stumbling-block to those who want to assess and appreciate his master mind.[23] The more research progresses, the more do we realize that Lessing 'thought in quotations'.[24] But the fact is he was not interested in the knowledge and ideas of the past for their own sake.[25] He repudiated the title of scholar with almost the same vehemence with which he had refused the title of genius:

> I am not a learned man [he wrote in his notes about himself], I never had the intention of becoming one, and I should not like to become learned even if it could happen while I dream. All I have striven for a little was to be able to use a learned book when necessity required it.[26]

When Lessing himself was put in charge of a treasure-house of learning, it was in this spirit that he conceived his duty. The treasures were there for use. 'Whatever has been brought to the knowledge of the world, the world must be enabled to know as accurately and reliably as possible.'[27] What the use might be, was no longer his concern. 'In the world of learning we do well to live and let live. What does not serve us, may serve someone else.'[28]

The narrow specialist who collected only facts and had his head so tightly screwed on that he could not look right or left was for him a figure of fun,[29] but his real wrath was reserved for the adulterator of knowledge, the sloppy scholar who made it impossible to play an honest game. In a way Nicolai was quite right that Lessing indulged in the antiquarian studies, so beloved of the eighteenth century, only as a pastime and to confirm his conviction, not very flattering to us, that the majority of those erudites were charlatans.[30] But so ardent is Lessing's love of integrity and so high his standards that some of these polemics, notably the *Briefe antiquarischen Inhalts*, never translated into English, are among his most enthralling and most readable works. They find their fitting conclusion in that gem of archaeological exegesis which has always been acclaimed as one of Lessing's masterpieces, the little treatise *How the ancients represented death* (Fig. 7), written to correct poor Klotz.[31]

2. THE LAOCOON

In England, of course, it is the *Laocoon*, that grand contest between art and literature, which is by far the best known of Lessing's writings. The idea of such a comparison was very much in the air.[32] Diderot, in his *Letter on the Deaf and Dumb*, which Lessing had reviewed with enthusiasm, had expressed the hope that a critic would take on the problem.[33] It has been shown how much the artfully artless presentation of the *Laocoon* owes to Lessing's favourite critic,[34] and it fits in well with this orientation that he even planned, at one time, to write it in French, since the German language had as yet not been shaped or even created for this type of discussion. It is the measure of Lessing's greatness that he did not succumb to this temptation, that he did take upon himself the trouble of shaping and creating his pieces himself. But the tournament is played by a European team. The first round is against Winckelmann, the German, the second against Spence, the Englishman, the third against the Comte de Caylus, the Frenchman. It is important to keep the dramatic character of the *Laocoon* in mind, because it explains, though it does not always excuse, certain simplifications with which Lessing presents his opponents' views. Their works are held up as examples of a confusion between the means of poetry and of painting, but if you take the trouble to read these authors you will be inclined to acquit them of this particular charge.

> Of the three sister arts of imitation [says Spence] poetry . . . has the advantage over both the others . . . the poet can describe all that either of the others express by shape, or colours; and can farther put the figure into a succession of different motions in the same description.[35]

and Caylus:

> Poetry . . . paints the succession of time . . . and the concatenation of actions; painting . . . can only present to the eyes one happy instance of a striking nature. . . .[36]

Maybe Lessing had forgotten ever having read these passages. But perhaps he did not find them very remarkable in themselves. The distinction these authors elaborate was commonplace in eighteenth-century critical literature, in Shaftesbury, in the Abbé Dubos, and in James Harris. It is a distinction which ultimately, I believe, goes back to Plato's *Cratylus*: between the signs of language such as the word 'horse' which are conventional, and the signs of the visual arts, such as the picture of a horse, which signify naturally. Now, if Lessing's *Laocoon* were only or mainly concerned with this distinction it would owe its fame only to the brilliant presentation of an idea which was neither new nor, as it happens, quite correct. Today we have the means of producing 'natural signs' mechanically with the camera and we have become much more interested in the question how much all representations depend on conventions.[37] The people who know most about that aspect of Lessing's problem are neither artists nor aestheticians, but press photographers who must judge which one of many snapshots of an event is the most telling and the most readable. I very much doubt whether they would confirm Lessing's deductions. Even less would they be interested in the famous controversy whether the marble Laocoon (Fig. 8) shouts or groans. Not even a photograph

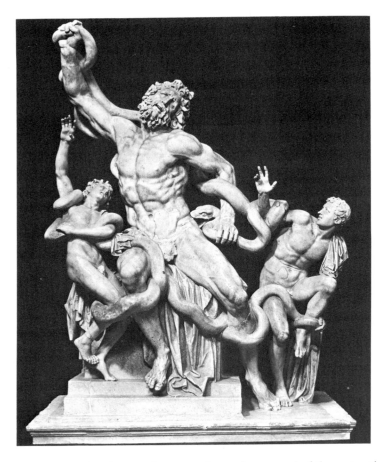

8. Hagesandros and assistants: *Laocoon* prior to the removal of the restorations.
c. 25 B.C. Vatican, Museum

of that ghastly event would necessarily tell us that. Signs being signs, the information they convey will always be selective. Hagesandros and his assistants have concentrated in the Laocoon all the signs for pain and agony which Greek art had evolved over centuries. To ask what noise the poor priest emits is as pointless as to ask after the colour of his hair.

It has often been said that Lessing did not know very much about art.[38] I am afraid the truth may be even more embarrassing to an historian of art who has been charged with the task of celebrating Lessing: he had not much use for art. There is a telling aside in one of his writings against 'superfluous engravings in books', which 'not only fail to assist the reader's imagination but tie it down and thereby mislead it'.[39] He did not mind Ovid being illustrated for the amusement of the public,[40] but let the painters keep their hand from his beloved Homer.

The more one reads the *Laocoon*, the stronger becomes the impression that it is not so much a book about as against the visual arts: 'If Painting is really Poetry's sister', Lessing remarks in it, 'let her at least not be a jealous sister.'[41]

Why this hostility? Can it really have been Lessing's concern with the Horatian tag *ut pictura poesis*, in the sense that he was bored, like most of us, with long descriptive passages? I do not think so; in fact I believe there is a strong argument against this accepted interpretation. Discussing the critics of the *Laocoon* three years after its publication, Lessing writes to Nicolai: 'Not one of them, not even Herder, has the faintest idea what I am driving at.'[42]

3. THE IDEAL OF RESTRAINT AND THE RIGHTS OF PASSION

I am sure we can only grasp this idea if we look at the *Laocoon* in the context of Lessing's work and time. There is one brief but relevant passage in his *Treatise on the Fable*, in which the painter is already put in his place. The test of a good fable, Lessing declares, is that it cannot be illustrated.[43] With one fell blow he destroys the combination of picture and moral which was the essence of the emblem book and had enjoyed such a vogue since the Renaissance. There are strange perspectives opening here, for the emblem fashion was not unconnected with the ancient Platonic conviction that sight is the most noble of the senses and that to see a truth embodied in a symbol comes closest to the highest form of understanding, the way God and His angels see the truth, not through a glass darkly but face to face.[44] To the Platonist such direct intuition is superior to discursive reasoning which proceeds laboriously step by step. Lessing breaks with this tradition. To him a fable condenses not a truth but an argument, which he compares to the demonstrations of science.[45]

I believe it is in this light that we must see his quarrel with Spence and the tradition he embodies. Spence was interested in the emblems and symbols of antiquity. Lessing, I am sorry to say, was not. It is no use, he objects, to compare images with texts if the artist who created the images was not free. 'Superstition overloaded the Gods with symbols . . . works of art which too obviously display the marks of religious convention do not deserve that name, because art is here not practised for its own sake.'[46]

In this passage, which is, I believe, the first formulation of *l'art pour l'art*,[47] art is severely reminded of its business to be beautiful. But the point is that Beauty is *not* Truth. Lessing was not a Platonist. He had once singled out Shaftesbury as the most dangerous enemy to religion because the most subtle,[48] the man, that is, who conceived beauty as divine revelation. Lessing is at pains to drive home the opposite point of view. Greek law, he asserts for instance, enjoined strict censorship on all works of art which were not beautiful.[49] To stifle science in such a way would be criminal, for the human soul is in need of truth. The fine arts, serving our pleasures only, may be subject to the law.

Now visual beauty has quite often to serve Lessing as a foil. In his *Introduction to J. Thompson's Tragedies* of 1756 he had said, 'I would infinitely prefer to have created the most misshapen of men to having made the most beautiful statue of Praxiteles',[50] by which he means that he would much rather have written Lillo's *London Merchant* than Addison's *Cato*.

Here we get hold of the most important strand which may help to unravel the tissue of Lessing's treatise. For that comparison has been traced back to a passage from Dryden[51] in which the cold beauties of French poetry are compared to 'the beauties of a statue but not of a man, because not animated with the soul of poesy which is imitation of humour and the passions.'[52] And this significant contrast Lessing found in the critic whose importance for his cause needs no elaboration, the critic, that is, who first had all but identified Shakespeare with Nature and thus laid the mine which was to blow the whole edifice of classical aesthetic sky-high.

Historically speaking we are here watching the conflation of various traditions: that of the *paragone*, the rivalry of the arts, interweaves with the classic distinction between the sublime and the beautiful,[53] and these categories in their turn are seen in terms of political and national traditions, liberty and tyranny, England and France.[54] Shakespeare is free and sublime poesy, Corneille rigid if beautiful statuary. Nor was this identification entirely unfair. French orthodoxy had indeed defended the authority of the three unities, with reference to the laws of classic painting. 'We are shocked', Voltaire reminds de la Motte, who had wanted to do away with them, 'to observe two events in the same picture . . . did M. Le Brun paint Alexander at Arbela and in the Indies on the same canvas?' Would anyone prefer a medley of events to this 'noble simplicity'?[55]

It was an argument which was almost bound to provoke the rejoinder that poetry differs from painting in medium and subject and to send the critic to such books as Dubos and Harris. But all this might have come to nothing, or to little more than a paragraph in a treatise on the drama which Lessing was preparing in his correspondence with Mendelssohn.[56] It would not have led to the publication of the *Laocoon* in 1766 if a new champion of 'noble simplicity' had not appeared on the European scene in the person of Johann Joachim Winckelmann.

It was in the context of their correspondence on the drama that Mendelssohn referred Lessing to Winckelmann's *Thoughts concerning the Imitation of Ancient Statuary and Painting*, which had come out in 1755.[57] For the first time he found his views on Greek drama countered with an argument from Greek sculpture. Lessing, who had an uncanny sense for intellectual currents, must have scented danger in the air. In Winckelmann he found a manifesto of Platonizing neo-classicism presented with all the enthusiasm of a mystic creed. Shaftesbury's religion of beauty was about to oust the psychological hedonism of Hogarth[58] and Burke.[59] The noble simplicity and majestic calm of Greek statuary was extolled as a great moral force, the true manifestation of the Greek soul.

In one of the notes for the *Laocoon* Lessing expresses the suspicion that it was the ideal of beauty in the visual arts which gave rise to the ideal of moral perfection in poetry—the ideal, of course, of Corneille.[60] Lessing's *Laocoon* opens with a quotation of the very passage from Winckelmann's pamphlet which Mendelssohn had quoted against him, for it was here that Winckelmann commended what he thought was the admirable restraint of Laocoon, who does not shout but controls his pain. 'Laocoon suffers', he says, 'but he suffers like the Philoctetes of Sophocles; his agony touches our very soul, but we would wish to be able to bear agony as this great man does.'

What better opening could Lessing hope for than this absurd half-sentence about Sophocles? Philoctetes notoriously shows his suffering. And why not? Everything that is stoic is undramatic, *untheatralisch*.[61] Self-control may arouse admiration, but admiration is a cold emotion and excludes all warmth of passion.

The polemical reference must be obvious to anyone familiar with Lessing's writings on the drama. It is against Corneille and his ideal of nobility resulting in admiration. That, I submit, is what Lessing was 'really driving at', and why the *Laocoon* had to be written.[62] He feared that in Winckelmann, and in the current that carried Winckelmann to the height of European fame, French classicism, already on its last legs, had acquired an unexpected ally. Winckelmann's great *History of Ancient Art* had appeared in 1764. Lessing attacked it obliquely by politely but persistently questioning its scholarly authority.[63] His motto was 'divide and rule'. You can have your quiet majesty—in statuary. Visual art is not fit for anything better than to give pleasure through beauty. I leave it to you. But leave me the world of passion, action, movement, which is 'the soul of poesy' and for which I have been fighting in German literature.

In the *Laocoon* Lessing erects a high fence along the frontiers between art and literature to confine the fashion of neo-classicism within the taste for the visual arts, where indeed it remained unchallenged till Fuseli discovered the pictorial equivalent to Shakespeare in the rude sublimities of Rembrandt.[64] Lessing never mentioned Rembrandt and would hardly have approved of him. He was quite satisfied with Laocoon remaining silent in cold marble as long as Philoctetes was allowed to roar on the stage till the French puppets were blown into the wings.

Seen in this light, the *Laocoon* continues the work of the seventeenth *Literaturbrief*, or rather it secures its gains against an unexpected threat from the flank which might indeed have swayed the course of German literature. Two years later, in the *Hamburgische Dramaturgie*, Lessing proceeded to the attack. Forced by external circumstances, he changed from a reviewer who concerns himself with the expression of the passions in acting[65] to a critic who argues with increasing acerbity against Corneille and Voltaire. Ostensibly the argument turns round the somewhat barren problem as to whether the French had understood Aristotle's definition of tragedy correctly, or whether Shakespeare did not more truly conform to the demands of the oracle. But why is this definition of Aristotle pushed around on the chessboard? Because it speaks of arousing and purging the passions, and Lessing is concerned once more with preventing any interpretation which would limit the stirring experience of fear and pity and the profound therapeutic effects of vicarious agony.

I doubt whether such persistent and skilful advocacy can be explained solely in terms of the history of ideas which makes Lessing himself only the puppet of impersonal forces. True, these forces worked on him, but he also worked on them, and we shall not get nearer to the core of this extraordinary mind unless we ask what it was that made him, the master of reasoning, into the champion of passion.

There is a tantalizing anecdote, recorded by Lessing's brother, which would make a psychologist prick up his ears. In the early sixties a friend of Lessing's observed him playing faro with such intensity that, though he happened to be winning, he was covered in perspiration. On being warned not to risk his purse and his health, Lessing replied, true to type, that if he had to play in cold blood he would not play at all. 'I have my reasons for playing so passionately. Violent emotion activates the inert machine, drives the humours round, and rids me of a physical anxiety from which I sometimes suffer.'[66]

If Robertson was right that Lessing's interest in Aristotle's medical interpretation of catharsis dates only from his later Hamburg years,[67] the passage would even gain in interest. Lessing took the definition up from Dacier or elsewhere because he knew it to be true.

4. PSYCHOLOGICAL CONFLICTS

What was this passion and this anxiety? I do not want to resort to psychological jargon, which I could not handle with competence, but I do not think we would go far wrong if we called it aggression. Lessing called it the bile, which amounts to the same thing. To diagnose the author of the Vade-mecum for Pastor Lange, the destroyer of Gottsched, the writer of the antiquarian letters against Klotz and of the Anti-Goeze, as an aggressive person is no great feat of psychological insight.[68] We might learn more from one of the most personal documents of Lessing's life, which was found among his papers after his death, a curious, half-ironical monologue which he jotted down during the supreme crisis of his career.[69]

It was the night when Lessing received the order from his sovereign, the Duke of Brunswick, henceforward to submit all his writings to the censor, to prevent the continuation of his quarrel with Pastor Goeze, who had impugned his honour.

> I do not want to get angry [he wrote] or rather, I want quickly, quickly, to get rid of my anger, so that I soon calm down again and do not spoil my sleep, which I am more anxious to preserve than anything in the world. Well, what about it, my dear irascibility? Where are you? Where do you hide? You have free rein. Break loose! Have a good go!
>
> You rogue. Well, you only want to take me by surprise? and since you cannot do that here, because I egg you on myself, and spur you, you want to spite me by being dull and placid?
>
> Well, quickly do what you want to do with me, gnash my teeth, beat my brow, bite my lip.
>
> While I write this, I really do this, and immediately he stands before me, exactly as I knew him—my father of blessed memory. For that was his habit when something started to rankle, and whenever I want to imagine him with special vividness, I need only bite my under lip in the same way; just as, whenever I think of him vividly for whatever reason, I can be sure that my teeth will immediately sit on my lip. . . . All right, my old boy, all right, I understand you, you were such a good man, such a choleric man. . . .

And Lessing remained calm. He submitted to the Duke's order.

We should like to know more about that father who appeared so vividly in his son's mind with that characteristic gesture of trying to restrain his temper. He had been a respected pastor in the small town of Kamenz in Saxony and no mean scholar.[70] We have a record of his antiquarian learning in the Latin thesis he wrote in Wittenberg, *de non commutando sexus habitu*, on the impropriety, that is, of women wearing men's clothes and men women's.[71] If you like, you might find it significant that his son was to write a work of greater fame against the illicit mixture of *genera*. More seriously, it must have been father Lessing's interest in English theological writings, his translations of Tillotson, who was considered the example of a new lucid prose style and of a liberal outlook, which influenced his son.

It fits in well with our expectations that the first literary effort we have of Lessing is a congratulatory address for the year 1743,[72] in which he plays the game of dialectics against his father. The poor pastor was in the habit of saying that things were going from bad to worse, and the clever schoolboy, whom we have already seen wielding the cudgels of logic against his sister, proceeded to prove with arguments from astronomy, history, and the scriptures that one year is exactly like the other. We do not know how the father reacted. Presumably with pride. His son made such marvellous progress at school that his teacher called him a horse that needed double rations of books, not of food.[73] In books Lessing had discovered a weapon against which no authority was proof.

We know from his correspondence that young Lessing never lost his faith in the power of argument against his father. In one letter home he even drops into Latin when he appeals to his father not to share his mother's prejudice against a free-thinking fellow student.[74] We must give father Lessing some credit for his son's abiding faith in reason. Without it he might have become a mere rebel, a rebel against authority, like many a lesser mind. Lessing never denied authority. No critic could ever do that and remain consistent. But he would not accept any authority he had not found in himself.

We are told by Freud that we all learn to master our natural feelings of jealousy by such an act of identification, by making our father an ally, as it were, against those dark forces within ourselves which we have learned to fear.

Maybe Lessing was fortunate in that the image of his father gave him both licence to indulge his aggression and the desire to control his temper. But perhaps a psychologist might see in this combination the cause also of those physical anxieties Lessing complained of. He had learned to bite his lip, to turn his aggression inwards against himself, and only a proper fight could free him of his tension.

Luckily we scarcely need the aid of the psychoanalyst to probe into Lessing's secret. He was his own merciless analyst. He soon learned to turn the formidable weapons of dialectics against his poor self. He pilloried himself in his first comedy as the young conceited scholar who is ashamed of his 'old man's' learning and proves from Hobbes that a son might well beat his father.[75] He wrote the *Freethinker* to prove to his father that he could laugh at his own intolerance.[76] And at the age of twenty he composed the first canto of a poem on religion which, for all its turgid language and old-fashioned metre, is one of the most moving self-examinations of a desperately honest man.[77] In this poem Lessing knocks down pretence and self-deception, and all the soothing things with which he had excused his sins and vices, till the very act of planning this epic on religion is unmasked before our eyes for what Lessing took it to be, the fruit of ambition, worse, the product of envy. The first cantos of Klopstock's *Messias* had appeared, staking a claim for German strains to reach heaven. If Lessing finds himself emulating Klopstock, what else is emulation but envy? *Nacheifern ist Beneiden.*[78]

It would be mean to use such a moving self-accusation in evidence against its author. But if we replace the offensive word envy by jealousy and say that throughout his life Lessing remained jealous of his reputation, jealous of the fame of German letters, we say, I hope, nothing unfair. Most of all we must remember that Lessing had learned to master his aggression by identifying himself with the object of his jealousy. He had found the answer to the riddle: When is a quarrel not a quarrel? When it is for truth. In a fight for truth, he argues in a beautiful passage, 'the losing party loses nothing but errors and can therefore always share in the other's victory'.[79] Once more the game of chess in Lessing's *Nathan* comes to mind, where each partner really sides with the other. If Lessing sometimes borrowed arguments from his opponents' armoury, this may have been the price he had to pay for this curious compulsion.[80]

It accounts, I believe, both for his strength and for his occasional weakness as a playwright. In his plays, too, passion is often transmuted into dialectics, which threatens to disintegrate the conflict. In the fragment *Samuel Henzi* the hero does not clash with tyrannical authority but with his fellow conspirators, who want to proscribe a venerable city father. In *Miss Sarah Sampson* the melodramatic action turns largely on the guilt feelings of the fallen heroine, who craves for punishment from her all-forgiving father. The play, of course, ranks high in the annals of German literature for its middle-class milieu and its emotional tone, but I cannot help feeling that in this only instance where Lessing wanted to open the floodgates of emotionalism his dialogue sounds contrived. He has to borrow passion from other people's treasures—I am told, from Richardson's sentimental best sellers.[81] There is little doubt that the original plan of *Emilia Galotti*, Lessing's most virile play, was conceived as a corrective against this overdose of borrowed emotion. It is the story of Virginia but with a difference. For once more it is the daughter who persuades her father to kill her rather than to expose her to the temptations of her princely pursuer, not, mark you, because she fears violence but because she fears her own hot blood.[82] Strangely enough, a similar tragedy of love for the oppressor underlies even the brittle surface of Lessing's most popular comedy, *Minna von Barnhelm*. It was one of the first plays I saw, but I confess that I never understood its well-concealed plot, which is too often represented as a glorification of the Prussian army.[83] But Tellheim, the hero, is not a Prussian; he is a nobleman from Livonia. It is true he took service in the army of Frederick the Great but, being Lessing's hero, he all but sided with the enemy when he was a member of the occupation force holding down Saxony. Not only did he fix the levies as low as possible; he even advanced part of them himself when a village could not pay. Hearing of this unusual officer, Minna, the daughter of a Saxon squire, broke through convention and prejudice and gatecrashed a party to meet Tellheim. Before the army moved on, the two were engaged, but after the war his letters stopped. When the play opens she has gone in search of her unwilling fiancé only to discover that his un-Prussian activities have aroused suspicion of bribery and that he has been dismissed from the army. Penniless, he wants to release her from her obligations, but she, too, has a story to tell. Her uncle, the count, incensed at her unpatriotic conduct, has disinherited her. Tellheim, hearing that they are now both outcasts, immediately stands by his pledge. Luckily, Minna's story was only a fib and a feint, and all ends well because a disreputable French courtier brings the first news from the palace that Tellheim is rehabilitated. He declines to re-enlist. The sub-title 'Soldier's Luck' can only be a bitter joke. What turns the tragedy into a comedy is mainly that it is the girl who woos and the hero whose sense of honour forbids him to yield. But for a comedy the protagonists show perhaps too much control, too much nobility. When Lessing attacked the stoic ideal in the *Laocoon* he was again turning his criticism against the strongest trend in his own character.

Lessing, as we have seen, could only let himself go in intellectual argument. His anacreontic lyrics are conventional, and even his biting epigrams, beautifully turned as they are, usually borrow their shafts from other people's armoury. His most characteristic creations, I am afraid, lie buried in the rare complete editions of his works; he called them *Rettungen*, rehabilitations, where he takes up with immense learning the case of some obscure figure from the past whose name had been unjustly blackened by official historians. He had discovered, as he remarks with fine self-irony, that 'among scholars the gift to brook contradiction is altogether a gift confined to the dead'.[84] But he also took great care not to take unfair advantage of that discovery: 'Those whom everybody attacks will be safe from me', he once wrote.[85] He preferred to select his culprits from among the great authorities such as Martin Luther, who had maligned the humanist Lemnius without real provocation.[86] It is true he had been repaid in worse coin, but was it not time history apportioned the blame between the two correctly?

It is fitting that Lessing's greatest works of his last years arose out of these activities as an advocate before the Court of Truth. In 1774, at the age of forty-five, as the ill-paid librarian of Wolfenbüttel, he told his brother that he could only drown his increasing depressions by throwing himself 'from one worthless literary investigation into another'. These included such publications as the *Enquiry into the Age of Oil Painting* and on the *Hirschau Stained Glass Windows*,[87] which would suffice to give stature to a specialist. The theatre had lost all interest for him. He was bored and disgusted by it. 'If I need entertainment I shall rather arrange a little comedy with the theologians.'[88]

5. FAITH VERSUS BIGOTRY

It was not to be the mocking comedy of the kind so frequent in the libertine eighteenth century. Lessing was no scoffer like Voltaire. On the contrary, such scoffing always drove him into opposition.[89] He had a profound respect for the great religious thinkers of the past who had grounded their theological system on faith. What he disliked was the well-meaning liberalism of enlightened Christians who wanted to have it both ways and pretended to prove the verities of religion by the light of reason. This Lessing would not have. Once more he insisted on a dividing line, *eine Scheidewand*. Trespassers should be prosecuted. Rational Christians were merely irrational philosophers.[90]

He first puzzled his enlightened friends with a number of publications in which he contrasted the consistency of orthodox beliefs with the fashionable compromisers.[91] Only then did he trail his coat properly by publishing the famous *Fragmente eines Ungenannten*, which he considered an uncompromising and therefore consistent presentation of the rationalist case against miracles and the gospel story. An early admirer of Pierre Bayle and a Pyrrhonist at heart,[92] Lessing was convinced that historical testimony was as much beyond the reach of rational proof as were the articles of faith. He even expected the orthodox faction to thank him for this clarification. But Hauptpastor Goeze jumped into the fray, holding the Lutheran Bible aloft and insisting on submission to the letter. Lessing found himself involved in the wrong battle, and his exasperation explains perhaps the violence of his language. He had wanted to draw the fire of the enlightened theologians and was compelled to argue about issues he had considered settled. It was not the pastor's faith which angered him. It was his pride, his claim to have the monopoly of truth, the one thing Lessing could never abide.[93]

And so he was provoked into that most quoted utterance of his in the

Rejoinder, that the value of a person is not determined by his being in possession of truth, but by his honest efforts to strive after truth:[94]

> If God held in His right hand all truth, and in His left the precious ever-active urge for truth although with the qualification that I would ever and always err, and said to me: Choose, I would humbly grasp His left hand and say: Father, give, pure truth is only for You alone.

In my own words: 'Father, if only you let me go on playing against you I do not demand to win.' For, to return to Lessing's better words, 'it is not the possession of truth but the search for truth that expands the powers of man wherein alone consists his ever-increasing perfection.'

It was a sentence that aroused the particular wrath of Pastor Goeze. What could be more absurd? Why should we expand our powers if truth always eludes our grasp as the water shrinks away from thirsty Tantalus?

> What a consolation for the alchemist [Goeze mocks]. The more they burrow in coal and work in smoke and vapours, the more their powers expand and their perfection grows. How deep would they fall if they ever found the philosopher's stone![95]

I cannot help thinking that Goeze interpreted Lessing's words more profoundly, almost more prophetically, than most of his later commentators. What the pastor did not know or did not want to know was that Western mankind had already made the fateful choice. What else is the creed of the scientist than the conviction that truth is always provisional, hypothetical, and that what matters is the search through which man's powers expand?[96] Alas, his having stumbled upon the philosopher's stone may indeed lead to his fall if it makes mankind turn away from the search for truth.

Lessing was quite aware of the provisional character of all natural science that proceeds by induction.[97] But there is no evidence that this awareness ever dimmed his admiration for a pursuit that had been the first love of his youth. His favourite teacher at school was the science master,[98] and he remained convinced that science, not classics, should form the foundation of education[99]—today, no doubt, he would furiously argue the opposite case. We know that he was prevented from studying medicine by the veto of his parents, who feared the influence of his scientific friend Mylius;[100] and it is significant that in one of his early poems, addressed to Mylius, there is the germ for another *Laocoon* in which poetry, content with 'appearances', was contrasted with science, concerned with truth: Newton is to our age what Homer was to the Greeks; and is he less creative than the poet?[101]

In one of his latest philosophical drafts Lessing discusses the perfectibility of man and his inability to possess the whole truth in terms of Newtonian science which hark back to the *Laocoon* problem.[102]

The soul of man has an infinite capacity for ideas, but being finite it can only obtain them step by step, in an infinite sequence of time. The order in which we absorb these ideas is determined by the five senses. But once more we find sight deposed from its Platonic throne. The eye is the organ responsive to light waves, but may we not one day develop senses for electricity or magnetism which will reveal new beauties and new aspects of reality?

I believe these slightly abstruse excursions into 'science fiction' may throw light even on Lessing's most heatedly discussed treatise, *The Education of the Human Race*, and the links between his religious and his aesthetic convictions.[103] Revelation, he claims, can only unfold in time. There are many strands which went into an elaboration of this philosophy, but the most important, I think, is the ancient doctrine of accommodation, according to which Revelation had to translate the ineffable truth into the symbolic language of the Scriptures. In early notes to the *Laocoon* Lessing refers to the Oriental imagery of the Old Testament and remarks drily that in Northern countries the Holy Ghost would have used different images.[104] As with nations, so with ages. As mankind grows up and reason advances, truth appears in less poetic garb and Revelation takes on new forms. But by its very nature it can never show us the whole. It must always remain provisional at any moment of time, and to claim any of its manifestations, any of its images, as the whole and absolute truth is to misunderstand God's ways with man.[105]

What we can know of God is the moral law that concerns our emotions and actions in this life. The injunction of St. John to his congregation to love each other, therefore, deserves the epithet 'divine' more truly than the much admired Platonic opening of St. John's Gospel, beautiful as it may be.[106]

It was in this conviction that he embarked on *Nathan the Wise*. His polemics had been banned, and he decided to try whether he could still preach from his old pulpit. It is characteristic of Lessing that scarcely ten years after his campaign against Voltaire's plays he adopted the method and message of the great preacher against *le fanatisme*.[107] Jealousy had blossomed into emulation.

Nathan with its operatic plot is, of course, constructed round the fable of the three rings from Boccaccio. I hope I shall not be accused of overplaying my hand if I suggest that it is a story of jealousy resolved. The precious heirloom which the father is always to hand on to his favourite son suddenly appears in three identical versions in the hands of the three rival brothers. In Lessing's adaptation the genuine ring was to have the secret power 'to make agreeable to God and man whoever wore it in that confidence'. They go to court and Lessing's judge dismisses the case for lack of evidence.

> 'My advice is this:
> You take the matter simply as it stands.
> Since each received the heirloom from his father
> Let each of you believe it genuine. . . .
> And when the jewel's power will become
> In your grandchildren's children manifest,
> I summon in a thousand thousand years
> Again them to this court. Then will a man
> More wise than I appear in judgement's seat
> And speak. Now, go.' So said the modest judge. . . .
> Saladin, if you feel yourself to be
> This wiser man of promise—

Whereupon the sultan rushes towards the sage, grasps his hand, and exclaims: 'I who am dust, am nothing? God!'[108]

I have always found this exclamation the most moving moment in the play. The sage has gently humbled the great sultan and reminded him of the human condition. Nathan, whose wife and seven sons have been burnt to death in a pogrom and who yet submitted to God's will and adopted a Christian child, has the right to preach against the presumption of human beings who commit their crimes in the name of truth.

But just as in *Minna*, the tragedy is behind us. There is a resigned serenity in the blank verse of *Nathan* which heralds the classic age of German literature. Lessing thought that the play was more the fruit of polemics than of genius.[109] But with his attention diverted from the abstract problems of the dramatist's art, the spring within him began to flow of its own accord and sometimes gushed forth in real and therefore untranslatable poetry.[110] Take the first line of the Templar's monologue:

Hier hält das Opfertier ermüdet still.[111]

I wonder if there is any line in German drama more irrationally moving than this comparison of the harassed mind with the tired animal on the way to the altar. It is hardly fanciful to read in it something of the terrible lassitude which often overcame Lessing in his last years of solitude. His wife had died in childbirth after a short year of marriage. He died at the age of fifty-two.

It was not only his outward fate which made Lessing's last years tragic.[112] It was that inevitable compulsion to oppose the tide of fashion which made him impatient of the movement of Storm and Stress and that cult of genius and passion he had done so much to promote. Who could have predicted that the author of the seventeenth *Literaturbrief* would be scathing about Goethe's *Werther*[113] and the turbulent *Goetz von Berlichingen*?[114] 'The devil will get my Faust in the end', he said about his long-projected play, 'and I shall get Goethe's.'[115] He did not live to see that Goethe as a real genius was to accept his call to discipline, was even to stage Voltaire's *Mahomet* in Weimar, much to Schiller's bewilderment,[16] and finally to marry Faust to Helena. If it could be shown that the gadfly of Lessing's criticism had its share in driving Goethe from the mists of the Brocken towards Winckelmann's Hellas, this paradoxical feat would be the fitting conclusion to the lifework of a truly Socratic spirit.

I do not think that a master mind need necessarily have a message for this age. Lessing, of course, belongs with all his fibres to the great eighteenth century. But just because he was so thoroughly of his time, his dedicated life refutes those insidious voices who like to tell the writer today that the only way out of the Ivory Tower leads through what they call 'commitment' to a creed, party, or faction. Lessing was always engaged, but never committed. Indeed he wrote:

I hate all people who want to found sects from the bottom of my heart. Because it is not error, but sectarian error, nay, even sectarian truth, which is the misfortune of mankind; or would be, if truth ever wanted to found a sect.[117]

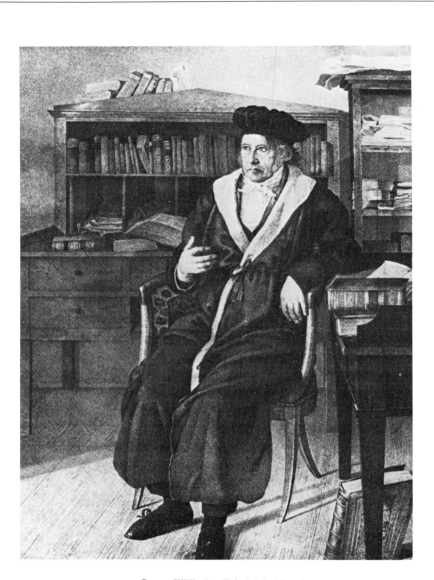

9. Georg Wilhelm Friedrich Hegel.
c. 1830. Lithograph by Julius Ludwig Sebbers

Georg Wilhelm Friedrich Hegel was born in Stuttgart on 27 August 1770, the son of a civil servant of Württemberg. He attended a classical grammar school in Stuttgart then went on to study theology at Tübingen, from where he obtained a degree in 1790. After a period as a private tutor in Bern (Switzerland) and Frankfurt he gained a minor position at the University of Jena in 1801; he there completed his first major philosophical work The Phenomenology of the Spirit *(1806). From 1808 to 1816 he was headmaster of a classical grammar school at Nuremberg. His* Science of Logic *appeared during this period. After a brief spell at the University of Heidelberg, where he published the* Encyclopedia of the Philosophical Sciences *(1817), he accepted a Chair at Berlin University. He became strongly identified with the policies of the Prussian government, publishing in 1821 the* Philosophy of Right and Law. *His lecture courses, which dealt with the philosophies of religion and history, and with the history of philosophy and the arts, were subsequently published from his own notes and those of his students. He died of cholera on 14 November 1831.*

'The Father of Art History'

A Reading of the *Lectures on Aesthetics* of
G. W. F. Hegel (1770–1831)

1. THE DEBT TO WINCKELMANN

Georg Wilhelm Friedrich Hegel should be called the father of the history of art, or at any rate of the history of art as I have always understood it. We are of course accustomed to the idea that sons rebel against their fathers, and if we are to believe the psychologists, they do this because they want, and indeed need, to break away from the overpowering influence of paternal authority. I still believe that the history of art should free itself of Hegel's authority, but I am convinced that this will only be possible once we have learned to understand his overwhelming influence.

The role of the father of art history which I have assigned to Hegel is usually attributed to Johann Joachim Winckelmann; but it seems to me that rather than Winckelmann's *History of Ancient Art* of 1764, it is Hegel's *Lectures on Aesthetics* (1820–9) which should be regarded as the founding document of the modern study of art, since they contain the first attempt ever made to survey and systematize the entire universal history of art, indeed of all the arts. Hegel

---

This lecture was delivered in February 1977 on the occasion of my being awarded the Hegel Prize of the City of Stuttgart. In my opening words I thanked the spokesman of the prize-giving body for his kind words and for having made it easier for me to explain why the honour of the great award had also caused me some embarrassment. 'To some extent,' I continued, 'this applies to all public honours, since the recipient usually knows full well that he is not all that praiseworthy, but I am quite particularly conscious of not being Hegelprize-worthy. After all, criticism of the Hegelian heritage plays no minor part in my writings. Heinrich Heine once spoke of himself as a "run-away Romantic". Maybe I am something like a run-away Hegelian.'

himself looked up to Winckelmann as one who, in his words, 'in the field of art was able to awaken a new organ and to open up totally new methods of approach to the human mind'.[1] But Winckelmann's concept of art was quite different from Hegel's. For him the essence of art lay in the Greek ideal. Just as his predecessor Vasari had written about the rebirth of his artistic ideal, so Winckelmann was concerned with the development of this exemplary art to absolute perfection. At the same time he saw his work as a *Lehrgebäude*, a theoretical treatise, aiming to demonstrate, through the example of Greek art, what beauty was. Hegel, if I may simplify for a moment, incorporated this theory into his philosophical system, but restricted its range of validity. The credit for having given classical shape to sensuous beauty still went indisputably to the Greeks, but Classicism itself only represents one phase of art, as the history of art can no more stand still than history itself.

I would like to try to formulate briefly what Hegel took over from Winckelmann and how he broadened the scope of that static system to form a universal history of art as we know it today. He found three fundamental ideas in Winckelmann which he incorporated into his own structure of ideas. The most important is the firm belief in the divine dignity of art. Just as Winckelmann in his famous hymn to the beauty of the Apollo of Belvedere (Fig. 10) is really celebrating the visible presence of the divine in a work of man, so too Hegel ultimately saw in all art a manifestation of transcendent values. It is a point of view which Plato consciously rejected, but which Neoplatonism brought back into circulation in European intellectual life, for it credits the artist with the ability to behold the Idea itself in its supernatural realm and to reveal it to others. I may perhaps call this metaphysical faith in art *aesthetic transcendentalism*, with the warning that it is not of course to be confused with Kant's transcendental aesthetics. This aesthetic transcendentalism tinged with Neoplatonism certainly appears less pronounced in Winckelmann's approach than it does in the philosophy of his friend and rival, Anton Raphael Mengs, yet Winckelmann's cult of beauty nevertheless draws its justification from there. The second fundamental idea that Hegel took over can be described as *historical collectivism*. By this I mean the role that is assigned to the collective, to the nation. For Winckelmann, Greek art is not so much the work of individual masters as the expression or the reflection of the Greek spirit, with the concept of spirit not yet quite containing the metaphysical overtones that it has in Hegel, but being much closer to Montesquieu's *Esprit des lois*. Thirdly, even in Winckelmann this consummate expression is the end result of a development, in fact of a development whose intrinsic logic is intelligible. The stages of Greek art, the progression of style, led of necessity to what Winckelmann calls the 'beautiful style', passing through the phase of

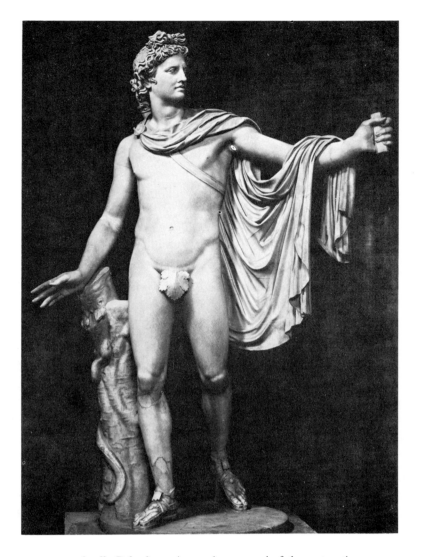

10. *Apollo Belvedere* prior to the removal of the restorations.
4th century B.C. Vatican, Museum

the noble or austere style, and leading inevitably to decline, by making concessions to sensual pleasure. In this third instance we can talk of an *historical determinism* which explains why, for all its perfection, Greek art already bore within it the seeds of its own downfall.[2]

It is clear that this determinism is to some extent incompatible with what Winckelmann felt to be his mission: the call to emulate Greek works and to return to the Golden Age of art. This flaw in Winckelmann's doctrine was all the more evident to his German contemporaries as they were struggling to gain awareness of the independent identity of their national art. Here I am thinking primarily of Herder, but also of Schiller, whose essay, 'Über naive und sentimentalische Dichtung', aims to do justice to the Golden Age of classical Greece, without regarding it as an absolute.

2. THE PHILOSOPHY OF PROGRESS

Those were the years in which this ancient dream of a Golden Age became unexpectedly topical. It seemed as if human reason only needed to take control of the reins to make the dream come true. I am here speaking of the French Revolution, which Hegel also regarded as virtually a cosmic event. 'For as long as the sun has shone in the firmament and the planets have revolved about it,' he says in the *Philosophy of History*,

> man has not been seen to stand on his head, that is on his thoughts, and to construct reality accordingly . . . All thinking beings have celebrated this era . . . an enthusiasm of the spirit filled the world with awe, as though the divine had at last come to a true reconciliation with the world.[3]

I am convinced that Hegel's philosophy, which I would like to describe as *metaphysical optimism*, can only really be understood in relation to this event. Like many of his contemporaries, he looked at the developments preceding the triumph of reason from the standpoint of this climactic event, and even in the stages of natural evolution, from dead matter through plants and the animal kingdom to man, he found confirmation of his theory that the entire historical process was a necessary development leading to the emergence of the self-knowing spirit.

Like other ideas, Hegel had certainly adopted the belief that art plays an important role in this cosmic process from his boyhood friend Schelling. The three sections on the religion of art in Hegel's difficult early work *The Phenomenology of Spirit* (1806) are on the whole couched in such abstract terms that the actual history of art plays no part in them, yet it seems to me that even here, as in the subsequent *Encyclopaedia* (1817), Winckelmann's three fundamental ideas lie behind the abstractions. For here too art is essentially theophany, the unveiling of the divine, and here too it is bound to an historical collective. In Hegel's words, 'the work of art can only be an expression of the Divinity if . . . it takes and extracts . . . without adulteration . . . the indwelling spirit of the nation.'[4] Thus, just as aesthetic transcendentalism and collectivism are raised to the status of dynamic principles, so the logic of development in Winckelmann is elevated into universal determinism. For art also has a part to play in the self-creation of the spirit, which takes place with all the compelling force of a syllogism and thus the history of art is also seen as 'revealing the truth . . . which is manifest in the history of the world.'[5]

The metaphysical optimism proclaimed in these words now necessarily carries with it a further principle, which is no less fundamental to Hegel's conception of the history of art than it is to his interpretation of all other historical events: I am talking about the principle of relativism, which in Hegel's work is a result of the dialectic. As far as the history of art is concerned, this *dialectic relativism*, which is itself again relative, only really first becomes important in the *Lectures on Aesthetics*.

3. THE LECTURES ON AESTHETICS

These lectures, which Hegel gave four times in Berlin, are known to us through the loving reconstruction by his student Hotho, who used Hegel's notes for his lectures as well as the notes that his students took. For this reason perhaps one ought not to weigh each word too carefully, but on the whole they bear the stamp of indisputable authenticity. Like other works of Hegel, they are hardly an easy read. The abstract presentation, of which I do not need to give examples, often becomes abstruse, but when the reader is about to lose patience he is occasionally reconciled by a passage that appears to be rooted in living experience.

Hegel had a genuine feeling for painting, and incidentally for music too, but his knowledge of the actual history of art was so scarce that he let himself be hoaxed into believing that the tomb of Count Engelbert II von Nassau in Breda was the work of Michelangelo. Nevertheless, Hegel had a clear notion of what he called the requirements of scholarship, 'the precise familiarity with the vast realm of individual works of art, both ancient and modern'. According to him scholarship in the field of art also demands, 'a wealth of historical, and also very specialized knowledge, as the individuality of a work of art is related to something individual and thus requires detailed knowledge if it is to be understood and explained.'[6] He speaks with gratitude of the achievement of connoisseurs, yet rightly recalls that they occasionally limit their knowledge of a work of art to its purely external aspects and 'have little notion' of the true nature of the work of art . . . 'not knowing the value of deeper studies . . . they dismiss them.'[7] Naturally these deeper studies were what mattered to Hegel. His aim was to prove the validity of what to him was an essential, comforting belief in universal reason, by showing that the history of art could be perceived in the terms of those steadily evolving principles which in his philosophy determine all events. Even where such an undertaking appears misguided, the reader cannot fail to be struck by the consistency with which Hegel sets about extracting the meaning allotted to every art form, to every age and to every style. This very consistency was necessary in order to help emphasize the real heart of his doctrine, namely the dialectic, which firmly anchored the metaphysical optimism in relativism.

This connection can most easily be explained by again referring to the Classicism of antiquity, which for Hegel culminated in Greek sculpture. For as an art form sculpture stands somewhere between architecture, which is still inextricably bound to matter, and painting, which represents the more advanced process of spiritualization, as its real subject is light—a thought which perhaps stems from Herder.[8]

Of course for Hegel even painting represents only a stage to be passed through before coming to music, which is an almost completely demateral-ized art form, and music must in turn give way to poetry, which deals with pure meaning. The value of all the arts is again, however, relative, as 'art is far . . . from being the highest form of expression of the spirit'; it is dissolved by reflection and replaced by pure thought, by philosophy, as a result of which art belongs to the past.[9]

For Hegel, therefore, the art of antiquity, as Winckelmann had perceived, certainly forms the centre-piece of the true history of art, but its perfection was confined to a limited phase of the life of the spirit, for just as long as it was still possible to represent the gods as visible beings. What precedes the art of antiquity is a less conscious stage: Oriental art. Hegel calls this pre-art (*Vorkunst*) and, following the Neoplatonist Creuzer, he attributes to it a particular form of symbolism which is not yet adequate to the spirit.[10] Hegel had the fortune, or the misfortune, to write about ancient Egyptian art just before the hieroglyphs were deciphered, and thus before the picture of Egyptian civilization was radically altered. For Hegel, Egypt

is the land of the symbol and sets itself the spiritual task of self-deciphering the spirit, without really attaining its end. The problems remain unsolved and the solution which we are able to provide consists therefore merely of interpreting the riddles of Egyptian art and its symbolic works as a problem that the Egyptians themselves left unde-ciphered . . .[11] As a symbol for this proper meaning of the Egyptian spirit, we may mention the Sphinx [Fig. 11]. It is, as it were, the symbol of the symbolic itself . . . recumbent animal bodies out of which the human body is struggling . . . The human spirit is trying to force its way forward out of the dumb strength and power of the animal, without coming to a perfect portrayal of its own freedom and animated shape.[12]

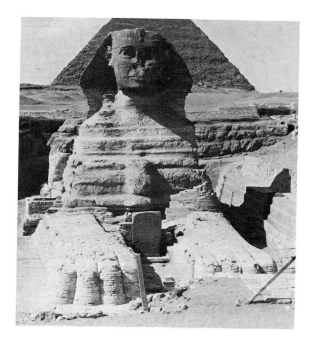

11. *The Great Sphinx of Gizeh. c.* 2700 B.C.

Thus an unexplained monument of art becomes for Hegel a metaphor for the spirit of the entire age. And once firm in his opinion that at that time the spirit, like the Sphinx, remained shackled to the animal, he was also able to state that,

> the Egyptians constructed their towering religious buildings in the same instinctive way in which bees build their cells . . . Self-awareness has not yet come to fruition and is not yet complete in itself, but pushes on, searching, conjecturing, continually producing, without attaining absolute satisfaction and therefore always restless.[13]

It is not difficult to see how much this dramatic picture of the struggling spirit owes to the principle of the dialectic, for it essentially represents a negation of the Classical ideal which Hegel, as well as Winckelmann, saw translated into reality in the art of Ancient Greece. Yet no matter how often Hegel refers to Winckelmann in the passages concerned, he still saw, with remarkable lucidity, that the sixty years which separated him from his model had radically transformed the image of Greek sculpture. The new awareness of the sculpture of Aegina, and above all of the Parthenon, inevitably altered the emphasis.[14] In fact, Hegel is one of the first virtually to dismiss the Belvedere Apollo, with a joke taken from an English journal describing it as a 'theatrical coxcomb', and to describe the Laocoon as a late work already declining into Mannerism.[15] It may be that he did not care much for these works. He had never been to Italy and looked for reasons to explain 'why the sculpture of antiquity leaves us somewhat cold . . . we feel at once more at home with painting . . . in paintings we see something that works and is active within ourselves.'[16]

A crucial point in Hegel's view of history was the idea that sculpture belonged to pagan antiquity and painting to the Christian era, which he called the Romantic age. This construction rested on the coincidence that marble statues survive more easily than paintings. Hegel knew of course that the ancient Greeks held their painters, such as Zeuxis and Apelles, in no less esteem than they did their sculptors, and he was not entirely happy with this interpretation of painting as a subjective, romantic art form. But since, as he cautiously says, the inmost heart of the Greek outlook corresponds more closely 'with the principle of sculpture than with any other art . . . the backwardness of painting in relation to sculpture is only to be expected.'[17] Whatever the truth may be, Hegel's efforts to examine each art form according to its ability to express certain spiritual values led him to describe the painter's medium with a clarity that has rarely been equalled, before or since, in the history of art.

For us, the notion of the 'painterly' is linked with the name of Heinrich Wölfflin, who in his *Principles of Art History* so articulately described the development of style from sculpture to painting. We should recall that Hegel too believed that the sculptural necessarily precedes the 'painterly'. Thus Hegel talks of the plastic-sculptural element in painting and describes the problems of composition in painting in a passage which could almost have been written by Wölfflin:

> The next type of arrangement still remains entirely architectural, a homogeneous juxtaposition of the figures, or a regular opposition and symmetrical conjunction both of the figures themselves and of their attitudes and movements. The pyramidal form of the group is very popular here . . . In the Sistine Madonna [Fig. 12] too this type of grouping is still retained as decisive. In general it is restful to the eye because the pyramid draws together by its apex what would otherwise be a scattered juxtaposition, and gives the group an external unity.[18]

But the painter who, as Hegel says, uses all the means available to him in his art,[19] the 'painterly' painter, finds still more possibilities of development and thus, in the course of the artistic evolution that Hegel exhaustively describes, Dutch seventeenth-century painting virtually becomes an end in itself.

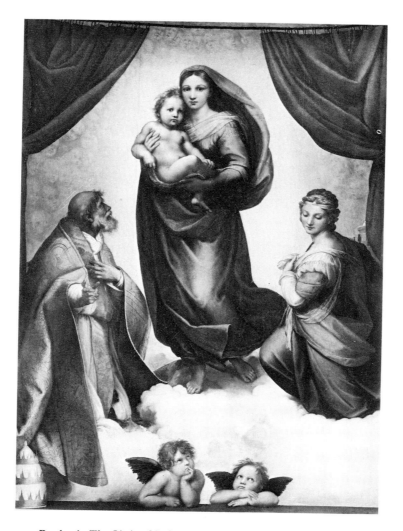

12. Raphael: *The Sistine Madonna*. 1513–14. Dresden, Gemäldegalerie

It would indeed be worthwhile to assemble a small anthology of the passages in which, tired of arid disquisitions, Hegel gives us his spontaneous reaction to painting. The grinding noise of his conceptual mill is silenced, giving way to a real love of the work of art. A brief example must again suffice:

While classical art essentially gives shape in its presentation of its ideal only to what is solid, here we have, arrested and brought before our eyes, the fleeting expressions of changing Nature—a stream, a waterfall, the foaming waves of the ocean, a still life with random flashes of glasses and plates etc, the external shape of spiritual reality in the most specific situations: a woman threading a needle by the light [Fig. 13], a band of robbers frozen in movement, the most transient aspect of a gesture, the laughing and guffawing of a peasant; in all this Ostade, Teniers and Steen are masters . . .[20] But even though heart and thought remain unsatisfied, closer inspection reconciles us. For it is the art of painting and the painter that should delight and thrill us. And in fact if we want to know what painting is, we must look at these small pictures in order to say of this or of that master: now he can really paint . . .[21]

Hegel had been to the Netherlands and was obviously filled with enthusiasm for Dutch paintings. Whereas his description of Italian art is largely based on the fundamental work by Rumohr, which had just been published, his writing here is based entirely on his own observations. There is still perhaps an ideological element in this. The Romanizing sympathies of the Nazarenes had spoiled for many the pleasure in the recently discovered, so-called 'primitive' Italian painters, whereas in Holland Hegel could enjoy the triumph of protestantism both in and through the paintings. 'It would not have occurred to any other people, under any other circumstances, to portray subjects like those that confront us in Dutch paintings as the principal content of a work of art.' Hegel finds the justification for their choice of subjects in 'their sense of a self-earned freedom, through which they have attained well-being, comfort, integrity, spirit, gaiety and even a pride in their cheerful daily life'.[22]

If we like, we can still see even in this glorification of the Dutch people a reflection of Winckelmann's idealizing of the Greeks. And as was the case with Winckelmann, it follows from Hegel's system that such a blossoming bears within it the seeds of its own dissolution. The 'colour magic' of painting brings an inevitable transition to music. When analysing this art form, Hegel also surprises us by showing a lively enthusiasm for Mozart and Rossini, which contrasts strangely with his somewhat laboured attempts at a purely conceptual edifice.

One thing is certain. As far as Hegel was concerned, his aesthetic theory of categories formed an integral part of his total system of philosophy, for, as is stated in the *Aesthetics*,

only the whole of philosophy can be equated with the knowledge of the universe as the *one* organic totality in itself . . . within the crowning circle of this scientific necessity each single part is on the one hand a circle

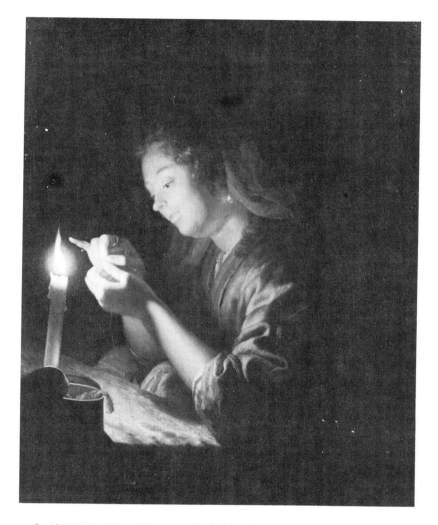

13. Godfried Schalcken (1643–1706); *A Girl Threading a Needle by Candlelight.*
London, Wallace Collection

turning in on itself, while on the other hand it has a simultaneous and necessary connection with other parts—a backwards from which it is derived and a forwards towards which it drives itself, in so far as it fruitfully engenders an 'other' out of itself again, making it accessible to scientific knowledge.[23]

There is obviously something extremely seductive about a system like this, in which every conceivable natural, spiritual and historical phenomenon has its place, and precisely because Hegel was the last and the most consistent person to construct such a system, this philosophy did not lose its effect when the influence of his metaphysics dwindled.

4. DETERMINISM IN ART HISTORY

Hegel's spiritual succession is not confined to philosophers who subscribed to every definition in his *Encyclopaedia*. It is indeed well known that Karl Marx, for example, opposed to Hegel's thesis of the primacy of the spirit the antithesis of the primacy of matter, in order, to use the famous double meaning of the dialectic, both to cancel and to preserve the system (*aufheben*). His is the most influential but by no means the only attempt to secularize, as it were, the Hegelian metaphysics, without thereby sacrificing the synopsis of at least all historical events. In my essay 'In Search of Cultural History',[24] I tried to demonstrate the extent to which the leading champions of art history and cultural history in the German-speaking countries came under the spell of Hegel. The striving to 'reconstruct' the spirit of the age through art runs from Carl Schnaase, through Jacob Burckhardt, Heinrich Wölfflin, Karl Lamprecht, Alois Riegl and Max Dvořák to Erwin Panofsky. Brief as my analysis was, I neither want to nor can repeat it here. One matter however is close to my heart. I do not wish to create the impression that I lack respect for these masters. It cannot be too often repeated that the best tribute that one can pay a scholar is to take him seriously and constantly to reappraise his lines of argument. I would be the last to demand that art and cultural history should give up seeking relationships between phenomena and remain content with listing them. If that had been my aim, I would certainly not have concerned myself with Hegel. What gave me pause was not the belief that it is hard to establish such relationships but, paradoxically, that it often seems all too easy. The gigantic structure of Hegel's aesthetic can itself serve as proof of this observation. Although his virtuosity is evident, we have already seen how, in his interpretation of Egyptian art, he tried to slip from the metaphorical into the factual, and how he relegated a figure like Apelles to the verge of Greek art, to fit in with his construction of the historical sequence of the arts.

Even the professional historian succumbs easily to the temptation to *corriger la fortune*. Ultimately every historical account is, and indeed must be, selective. It is thus natural to confine oneself to what appears to be significant and to neglect that which appears less essential. Karl Popper, the great methodologist of science, has made me sensitive to the dangerous allures of these siren songs.[25] The true scientist does not seek confirmation of his hypotheses; he is primarily on the look-out for contrary examples. A theory which cannot conflict with anything has no scientific content. The danger of the Hegelian heritage lies precisely in its temptingly easy applicability. After all, the dialectic makes it all too easy for us to find a way out of every contradiction. Because it seems to us as though everything in life is really interconnected, every method of interpretation can claim success. Here it depends above all on a plausible point of departure. 'The artist must eat', we read in Lessing and since artists cannot indeed paint without eating, it is certainly possible to base a credible system of art history on the needs of the stomach.

All these attempts at interpretations often make me think of the old anecdote about the farmer who had sold a pig for 300 crowns. He is sitting comfortably in the inn with his sack of coins in front of him. He empties it onto the table and begins to count, 'One, two, three.' He gets to ten, then fifty, then a hundred and begins to yawn—150, 180, 181. Suddenly he sweeps the money together and shoves it back into the sack. 'But what on earth are you doing?' his companions ask him. 'It's been right up to now, so the rest will be right,' the farmer replies.

I do not imagine of course that I am the first or indeed the only art historian who likes to check. On the contrary, I have often asked myself whether today, nearly one and a half centuries after Hegel's death, my polemic against certain interpretations of history is not perhaps a case of tilting at windmills. And yet I have found often enough that it is not windmills that one is charging, but real giants. I have already mentioned five of these giants by their weird names. They are *aesthetic transcendentalism*, *historical collectivism*, *historical determinism*, *metaphysical optimism* and *relativism*. They are all related to the mythical Proteus, since they remain constant in every metamorphosis.

Transcendentalism, the idea of art as revelation, survived in a secularized form. Though no longer the manifestation of the self-realizing spirit, the work of art is still seen as the expression of the spirit of the age, which, as it were, remains visible across its surface. The word 'expression', with its elusive ambiguity, facilitates this transition, enabling the historian to disclose the philosophy of an age, or its economic conditions, behind the work of art. What is common to both methods is the connection with collectivism. The individual work of art is seen in terms of its style, which should now be interpreted as a symptom, a manifestation of class, race, culture or the age.

Determinism now assumes an explicit, or at least implicit, key role in this method. The very essence of the Hegelian heritage lies in the *a priori* conviction that the Gothic style is a necessary result of feudalism or of scholasticism, or that all three phenomena are merely different manifestations of the same underlying principle. Now, it may well be conceded that both direct and indirect connections exist between these disparate phenomena. The question is merely to find the point at which, to use a variation on one of Hegel's favourite expressions, triviality turns into absurdity. Certainly historical determinism has found so many opponents that the question would appear to be settled, if ever a question could be settled. There is no need to make any decision here about the problem of causality, of the validity of natural laws or of free will, in order to refute the idea that the course of history follows a necessary development. Thus the Nobel Prize winner from Göttingen, Manfred von Eigen, emphasized recently that we can accept the validity of the laws of nature without this being a sufficient reason to conclude that history follows an irrevocable and pre-determined course.[26] I often like to compare the multifarious influences that lie behind artistic creation with the influence that climate has on vegetation. No one will deny that this dependency exists, and the fact that the vegetation in turn influences the climate may also recommend the comparison to partisans of the dialectic. It is even possible to learn of variations in the climate from looking at the annual rings of an old tree. And yet the calculation is only of limited validity, for the mutual effect is not produced by these two factors alone; numerous other factors, which cannot be calculated in advance or reconstructed, come into play. It is worth remembering that the chance importation of a couple of rabbits into Australia nearly led to the entire land being completely stripped of vegetation. You cannot get around the reality of chance.

I know of course that in the second edition of the *Encyclopaedia* Hegel explained the famous sentence taken from his Philosophy of Law, 'Whatever is rational (*vernünftig*) is real and whatever is real is rational', to the effect that what he understood by reality was 'not the merely empirical . . . existence mingled with chance but the existence that is inseparable from the concept of reason'.[27] Ultimately, however, this attempt at salvage is based on a circular argument, for if chance does not concern philosophy, then history certainly does not concern it either. For time and time again history bears out the old proverb, '*Kleine Ursachen, grosse Wirkungen*' (small causes, great effects: tall oaks from little acorns grow) – a veritable spell which once and for all lays the ghost of historical determinism.

This really appears so obvious that we have to ask ourselves why people so often resist this insight. Maybe the power of chance hurts our self-esteem. We talk about blind, senseless or stupid coincidence and even find misfortune, both in life and history, easier to bear, if we can regard it as unavoidable fate. How much easier it would be if we shared Hegel's metaphysical optimism, which tries to convince us that ultimately everything is for the best. The wish gives birth to the thought, in whatever way faith in a pre-determined happy ending to the cosmic play may be formulated. Granted that not all determinists are also optimists. Oswald Spengler, for example, who had so much in common with Hegel, prophesied the inevitable decline of the Western world. On the other hand, of course, the essential factor in metaphysical optimism is that there cannot and ought not to be any decline or deterioration which does not pave the way for a higher form of development.

I do not think I am too far wrong if I also describe this relativism as the official dogma, so to speak, of contemporary art historical teaching, in so far as it has embraced determinism. One cannot condemn that which is unavoidable, any more than a geologist can condemn the Ice Age. Certainly it was some time before art historians came to adopt this attitude, which goes far beyond Hegel in its levelling tendency. According to Hegel there is naturally a decline, even if it does serve progress. Today it is considered scientific to eradicate the concept of decline from the art historian's vocabulary wherever possible, so as to allot every era that was once condemned, its rightful place in the chain of development. The vindication of Gothic art in the eighteenth century was accepted even by Hegel. Later, following in the tracks of Burckhardt, Wölfflin reinstated Baroque art, Wickhoff defended Roman art, Riegl the art of late antiquity and Max Dvořák the catacomb paintings and El Greco. Walter Friedländer completely freed Mannerist art from the stigma of decline, and Millard Meiss undertook a positive evaluation of the painting of the late Trecento. At the moment we are even witnessing a revival of respect for French nineteenth-century Salon painting, which until recently was still considered to be the ultimate in kitsch.

I will by no means dispute that we have profited a good deal from all these efforts: we have cast off prejudices and have learnt to look more closely.

I am a peace-loving man and am quite prepared to let each of the five giants have his plaything as long as he limits his territorial claims. I will even concede to metaphysical optimism the reality of a form of progress which links nature with history. We have understood since Darwin that there is no need here for a teleology; only for the cruel mechanism which eliminates the unadapted. Perhaps in the field of art too a chance mutation occasionally leads to a highly promising solution, which in turn leads to further selection. The history of art has been presented in terms of progressive evolution first in antiquity, then in the Renaissance and also by Winckelmann, and what these accounts considered as decline can admittedly also be interpreted in the relativist sense as yet another process of adaptation. But adaptation to what? After all, not every collective, not every group, makes identical demands on artists and on their standards. In connection with this, Julius von Schlosser quite rightly insisted that one should not confuse the real history of art with the history of artistic idioms or styles.[28] Certainly the history of style lends itself rather better to attempts at hypothetical reconstruction than does the phenomenon of artistic mastery. Even the masterpiece cannot come into existence without the favour of fortune, but here I will willingly concede to aesthetic transcendentalism that the highest artistic achievement soars into a sphere which even in principle defies scientific analysis.[29]

5. THE ABDICATION OF ART CRITICISM

The continued topicality of the issues raised by Hegel seems to me unquestionable. But they become burning problems only in connection with the present situation in art. It is necessary here to recall the intrinsic ambiguity of the word 'history', which has also crept into the title of this lecture. Hegel, 'The Father of Art History', may be taken to refer to Hegel's relations to the historiography of art, such as I have discussed them here; but these words may also imply that Hegel influenced the development of art itself, and this, no doubt, is a much weightier question.

We must never forget that the writing of history can in its turn influence the further course of events and it is this feedback—which Hegel would probably have described as 'dialectic'—which accounts for the decisive influence of his philosophy of history. Let us recall that Hegel saw in art not only a reflection of the Divine but also an aspect of the continuous process of creation which passes through the artist.[30] The role which classical antiquity assigned most of all to the poet is therefore attributed to every true artist; he is a seer, a prophet, who is not only the mouthpiece of God but also helps God to achieve His own self-awareness.

Hegel's lectures on the philosophy of history tell us even more explicitly than do those on aesthetics how he conceived the historical role of such a divine mission. It is true that his reflections on what he called 'world historical individuals' refer more immediately to political leaders. He had, most of all, Napoleon in mind, who had overcome the French Revolution and yet preserved its achievements and whom, in a famous letter written after the battle of Jena, he described as 'this world soul'.[31] But when Hegel speaks of great men we are entitled also to include artists; in any case artists would not allow themselves to be excluded. According to Hegel it is the task of what he calls 'these business managers of the World Spirit to be aware of the necessary next step to be taken by their world, to make this step their aim and to devote their energy to this . . . They represent, as it were, the next species which had already been prefigured internally.'[32]

It is obvious that it is not granted to ordinary mortals to recognize and understand this anticipation of the future in the present. There is only one conclusion, therefore, that they can draw from Hegel's philosophy: whatever the World Spirit may be aiming at, it must be something new. Thus the old is being devalued while the unknown and untried at least carries within itself the possibility of harbouring the seeds of the future. To be rejected by his age becomes the very hallmark of genius. The great masters must be ahead of their time, for if they were not they would not be great masters.

Those of us who do not regard the changes of styles, of trends, and of fashions as a revelation of higher purposes must ask ourselves how we can really know what the future will appreciate; indeed we may even wonder why we must assume that the next generation will necessarily have a better taste than our own. But for those who endorse Hegel's metaphysical optimism, the process of selection has been shifted from the present to the future. It is only future success which counts as valid, as a true verdict, the test of the Divine Will. Any criticism of contemporaries becomes theoretically impossible because such criticism always incurs the danger of turning out as blasphemy in the future. All that remains for the critic in the end is to try to see which way the wind blows. As Popper has shown, an even more dangerous giant looms up behind metaphysical optimism: metaphysical opportunism.

Neither Popper nor I have ever wished to assert that the philosophy of progress in art, the theory of the avant-garde,[33] was exclusively inspired and nourished by Hegel's philosophy. And yet I believe that it could be shown what an essential contribution was made by the Hegelian tradition. I have drawn attention elsewhere[34] to a remark by Heinrich Heine, who explicitly derived this consequence for art criticism from Hegel's philosophy. Heine, who regarded Hegel as the greatest German philosopher since Leibniz, placing him above Kant, took issue in his Paris *Salons* of 1831—the year of Hegel's death—with the critics who had censured a painting by Descamps because it was badly drawn. He insisted that 'every original artist, and even more so every artistic genius, must be judged by his own aesthetic standards . . . Colours and shapes . . . are no more than symbols of the Idea, symbols which rise in the mind of the artist when the sacred World Spirit moves it.' Heine speaks of the 'mystical bondage' of the artist, and in view of this lack of freedom any criticism becomes arrogant pedantry.

It is true that in the field of art criticism it took a good deal of time for the critics to admit defeat and thus to arrive at what Hegel would have called the self-abrogation of art criticism. But every successive wave of the artistic revolution of the nineteenth century gave a fresh uplift to optimistic relativism. The belief in progress polarized not only the political world but also the world of art; all that was left was the impetus of the advance and the inertia of the reactionaries. In this constellation it was no longer the task of the critic to criticize, his mission was to assist the good fight of the movement; he became the herald of the new epoch and did his best to turn these prophecies into reality. Remember with what relish the artistic manifestos of the early twentieth century indulged in apocalyptic rhetoric announcing the new dawn, the new era, the new dispensation. Here too Hegel provided the direct inspiration. Eckart von Sydow, in a pamphlet of 1920 on *German Expressionist Culture and Painting*, wrote: 'We may say, with but a few qualifications, that the German Spirit has once more found immediate contact with the World Soul, as in the days of the Middle Ages.'

I do not want to be misunderstood. Such an utterance does not speak against Expressionism, merely against its metaphysical underpinning in aesthetic transcendentalism. I would even go further and admit that a metaphysical faith can indeed inspire an artist or an artistic movement. Nearly all great art is religious and the religious element in Hegel's philosophy also had its inspiring effect. I believe that the historian of the art of our century has to study Hegel much as a student of the ecclesiastical art of the Middle Ages must get to know the Bible. Only in this way can he, for instance, learn to understand the triumphant rise of modern architecture and its present crisis.

Take the words Walter Gropius wrote in 1923 in his article on 'The Idea and the Structure of the National Bauhaus': 'The attitude of a period to the world becomes crystallized in its buildings, for in these both the spiritual and material resources of the age find their simultaneous expression.'[35] Of what kind of expression he dreamt we know from the beautiful speech which he made at the opening of the first exhibition of students' work at the Bauhaus:

> Instead of sprawling academic organizations, we shall witness the rise of small, secret, and self-contained leagues, lodges, workshops, conspiracies, intent on guarding the mystery which is the core of the faith and on giving artistic shape to it until the time when these isolated groups will be fused once more into an all-embracing and vigorous spiritual and religious vision which must eventually crystallize in a great *Gesamtkunstwerk*, combining all the arts. This great communal creation, this cathedral of the future, will in turn illuminate with its radiance even the smallest objects of everyday life.[36]

I hope every reader can sense the intoxicating sweep of these words of a great architect. Intoxication, however, is so often followed by a hangover and we did not have to wait for this very long. In 1976, Sir John Summerson, one of the most outstanding critics and historians of architecture in England, on the occasion of being awarded the Gold Medal of the Royal Institute of British

Architects, spoke of his beginnings in the 1930s as an enthusiastic champion of Modern architecture in England and remarked that he now finds the starry-eyed optimism of some of his articles 'nauseating'.[37] Another of the leading English critics made the frank confession in front of the same forum that during the struggle for Modern architecture he had occasionally praised works which he did not really find so very good, simply because they were modern not reactionary.[38] These confessions are worthy of the highest respect and indeed we must warmly welcome all the debates which take place today wherever architecture is being taught and practised. It is through the encountering of arguments and counter-arguments that we shall learn from the mistakes of the last few decades.

In the visual arts of painting and sculpture such a return to a critical debate will not be quite so easy, for, after all, they lack the practical criteria to which a work of architecture has to do justice. Here the critic is entirely thrown back on himself. Naturally, we must not demand that the critic should have no prejudices and no dreams of the future. But theoretically, he never has the right to operate with the slogans of 'Our Age' and even less of 'Future Ages'.

It was Immanuel Kant who insisted on the stern and frightening doctrine that nobody and nothing can relieve us of the burden of moral responsibility for our judgement; not even a theophany, such as Hegel saw in history. 'For', he writes, 'in whatever way a Being might be described as Divine . . . and indeed manifest itself', this cannot absolve anyone of the duty 'to judge for himself whether he is entitled to regard such a Being as a God and to worship it as such.'[39] It may well be that Kant here demands more than is humanly possible, and yet much would be achieved if the world of art would come to see that Kant was right.

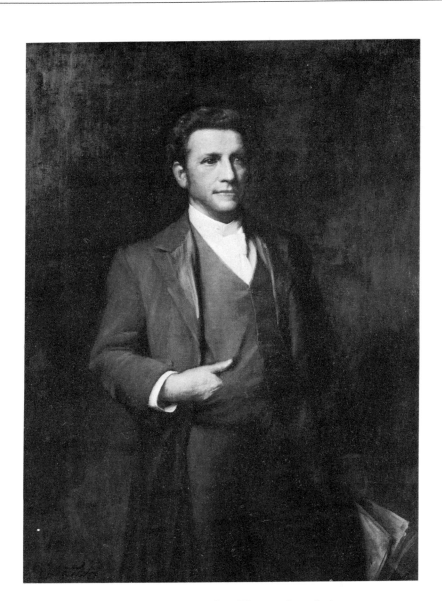

14. W. H. Lever, later first Viscount Leverhulme.
1897. Painting by Samuel Luke Fildes. Port Sunlight, The Lady Lever Art Gallery

William Hesketh Lever, first Viscount Leverhulme, industrialist, philanthropist and art collector, was born in Bolton, Lancashire, on 19 September 1851. He entered his father's grocery business at the age of sixteen and at twenty-one became a partner. In 1884 he patented 'Sunlight Soap', which he began to manufacture in 1885. In 1888–9 he started a new factory and a model village at Port Sunlight on the Mersey, near Bebington, Cheshire, on which he lavished much care. From 1906 to 1910 he was Liberal MP for the Wirral. Having purchased several art collections, he opened Hulme Hall Art Gallery at Port Sunlight. His wife, Lady Lever, died in 1913; the Lady Lever Memorial Art Gallery was opened in 1922. Meanwhile, in 1917, he had entered the House of Lords as Baron Leverhulme of Bolton-le-Moors and since 1922 as Viscount Leverhulme of the Western Isles. He died on 7 May 1925.

Nature and Art as Needs of the Mind

The Philanthropic Ideals of Lord Leverhulme (1851–1925)

1. VICTORIAN VALUES

I SHOULD like to thank the Trustees for the honour they have done me in inviting me to give the Fourth Leverhulme Memorial Lecture. I am most conscious of the fact that it was an act of faith on their part to ask a cloistered historian of art to deal with 'a subject related to the more urgent problems of the day affecting the welfare of society at home and abroad'. I certainly would not have had the courage to accept, if my assignment had been to *solve* any of the more urgent problems of the day. But it is said that diagnosis is half the cure, and I hope you will at least consider my diagnosis a contribution to a problem which profoundly concerned Lord Leverhulme for its effect on the welfare of society. Thus I have ventured to take my cue for the topic and title of this lecture from certain of his statements which I found in the catalogue of the memorable Royal Academy Exhibition, in the spring of last year, dedicated to the Founder of the Lady Lever Art Gallery and Port Sunlight on Merseyside (Fig. 15).[1] These foundations, I discovered, were more than random benefactions, they sprang from a philanthropic conviction which I tried to sum up in my title, the conviction, to put it in Biblical terms, that man does not live by bread alone. 'A child', he wrote for instance, 'that knows nothing of God's earth, of green fields, of sparkling brooks, of breezy hill and springy heather, and whose mind is stored with none of the beauties of nature . . . cannot be benefited by education', and, more concretely, he commends 'semi-detached houses with gardens back and front, in which they will be able to know more about the science of life than they can in a back

The Fourth Leverhulme Memorial Lecture given at Liverpool University in February 1981.

71

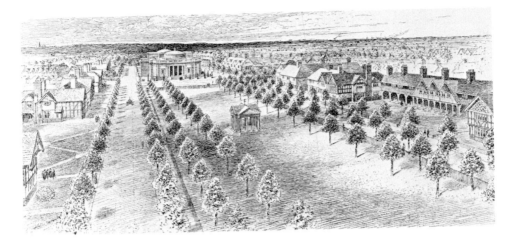

15. Lomax-Simpson: *Port Sunlight: 'The Diamond'*. Reproduced from T. Raffles Davison, *Port Sunlight*, 1916, Pl. 2

slum'. And as with Nature, so with Art. 'Art and the beautiful civilize and elevate', he wrote, 'because they enlighten and ennoble', and this faith, of course, was behind his foundation of the Lady Lever Art Gallery.

The moral earnestness and the unquestioning optimism of these utterances may strike you as typically Victorian, and you will have no difficulty in sensing behind Lord Leverhulme's faith in the benefits of nature and of art the teachings of the great Victorian prophets, notably of course the admonitory voice of John Ruskin, who so frequently exhorted the merchants of England. But today Ruskin's voice only sounds like distant thunder, he may be read for his style, but his message is muted. Two connected notions, or perhaps slogans, have contributed to this dismissal of the ideals which inspired him and also Lord Leverhulme. I mean the charges of élitism and of paternalism. The two are connected, because élitism is alleged to pride itself in the possession of a superior culture, and paternalism adds to this charge the arrogant belief that members of the élite also know better than common mortals do what is good for them. Having promised in this brief hour to discuss what I have called the needs of the mind, I must confront these charges, to which I shall have to return in the end. How can anyone claim to know the needs of the mind and allege that the vast majority of men and women here on earth who have little contact with the beauties of nature and none with art are short of mental sustenance? How can we be sure that we, who have enjoyed some of these benefits, have thereby improved our minds beyond the level of those who have not? I make no such general claim but I am not neutral in this matter. After all, if I had announced the title 'Gossip and

Scandal as needs of the mind', or, perhaps, 'Hunting and Fishing as needs of
the mind', even a convinced relativist might have raised his eyebrows. Such
needs, it is true, might be defended on the general ground that what the mind
requires most is an interest, an occupation. Not all such interests or
occupations are equally desirable from the social point of view and we all
would like to canalize these needs into areas which keep people out of
mischief. Lucky are the people who have an interest which makes them
creative, and twice lucky those who find that their own creations also mean
something to others. I said lucky, not happy, for the satisfaction of the needs of
the mind does not guarantee happiness. In any case it is not with the
exceptional creators in art and in science that I shall be concerned, but with
the minds of men in general.

2. THE FUNCTION OF METAPHOR

Let me thus start with the somewhat dogmatic assertion that among the needs
of the mind the possession of language comes first and foremost. Language is
more than an instrument of communication, more than a set of labels to be
attached to the people and objects which exist in our environment. Language
must be creative to perform its vital functions. The external and the inner
worlds of man are not composed of a number of entities waiting to be named
and described. The multitude of potential experiences is infinite, while
language, by its very nature, can never consist of more than a finite number of
words. It would soon come to the end of its resources if the mind were not able
to create categories, to parcel out this elusive world of ours into convenient
packages to which more or less permanent labels can be attached at will.
Traditional terminology calls the more permanent ones 'universals', the more
movable ones 'metaphors'. Since nature and art are among the richest sources
of metaphor, they answer the needs of the mind, *quod erit demonstrandum*.

There is an example close at hand to give a little more substance to these
generalities. I mean the trademark 'Sunlight Soap' (Fig. 16). Metaphor is
Greek for 'transfer' and according to the traditional interpretation the
qualities of the 'universal' 'sunlight' are here transferred to another 'universal', namely 'soap'.[2] I would prefer to say that the new brand of soap was put
into a parcel together with other things bright and beautiful such as sunlight,
and labelled accordingly. Nobody would have called it 'Night-gloom'.

Any number of similar metaphors testify to this capacity of the mind
consciously or unconsciously to articulate and order the world of experience
by linking it with a natural phenomenon of universal significance—from the
description 'a sunny temperament' to the old song-hit 'You are my sunshine'.

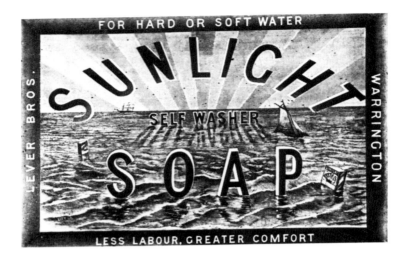

16. Sunlight Soap advertisement from the *Lancashire Grocer*, 1887

So intimately do these impressions of the external world and our emotional response tend to fuse in the mind that we say with the same conviction that the sun is 'smiling'; a metaphor which does not tell astronomers much and has therefore been classed among the so-called 'pathetic fallacies', but which tells the psychologist that the sun and smiles can affect us in a similar way. Without forming such compounds linking our sensory experience with our emotional life we could not communicate our feelings to others—and to ourselves. In short, it is my belief that it is only through this process of creative articulation that the mind becomes wholly mind.

I call it creative, because it seems to me that it is only through naming that these feelings can fully emerge into existence. Animals, no doubt, have many responses which resemble our own; if we hesitate to attribute to them a mind, it is, I submit, because they lack the capacity to code their experience. They can recognize, but they cannot recall, and thus they presumably live only in the present. Without arresting the flux of life and transferring it into the realm of symbols the mind could never achieve self-awareness. It is on these conclusions, as the lawyers say, that I wish to rest my case for the importance of nature and art to the needs of the mind.

3. HAZLITT ON 'THE LANGUAGE OF NATURE'

I propose to call, as my first witness, a great English writer from the period when that love of nature which Lord Leverhulme shared had just become articulate. I am speaking of William Hazlitt and his essay of 1814, entitled

'On the Love of the Country'.[3] It fittingly starts with a quotation from Rousseau, that great prophet of nature who rejoiced when he had moved to Annecy, seeing 'a little spot of green' from his window (Fig. 17). It concludes with the thought that 'for him . . . who has well acquainted himself with Nature's work . . . she . . . always . . . speaks the same well-known language, striking on the heart'. It is a conclusion which suits my case, but the way in which Hazlitt has reached it reminds me of the changes which have meanwhile come over psychology and philosophy. Briefly Hazlitt accounts for this experience in terms of Aristotle's logic and John Locke's picture of the mind. From the first he takes the distinction between the individual and the universal. Human beings, he rightly claims, are individuals, and our attachments here are to particular persons. I am not sure that Casanova or Don Giovanni would necessarily have agreed, but from the moral point of view he was of course right. I am less sure that he is right when he claims that in nature our attachment is always to universals, to classes of features such as fields and lawns rather than to particulars. Surely we can love a particular landscape or even a particular tree, but Hazlitt needs this distinction to explain our love of nature in general, for which he accounts, in the tradition of John Locke, by the association of ideas. 'Thus', he writes, 'if I have once enjoyed the cool shade of a tree, and been lulled into a deep repose by the sound of a brook running at its feet, I am sure that wherever I can find a tree

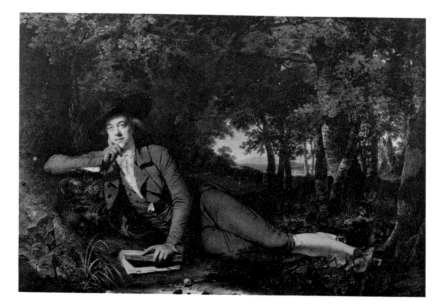

17. Joseph Wright of Derby: *Sir Brooke Boothby in a Landscape, with a volume of Rousseau.* 1780–81. London, Tate Gallery

and a brook, I can enjoy the same pleasure again.' And also, remembering his Aristotle, he asserts that '. . . in our love of Nature, there is all the force of individual attachment, combined with the most airy abstraction'. The trouble here is only that the notion of abstraction is so hard to square with that of association. How did his experience under one particular tree take him to that abstract or universal concept which allegedly guides him from then on? But of course no one has to solve that notorious teaser of philosophy, the problem of universals, to find a place for his repose.

Animals, too, can be seen taking shelter under a tree without having been taught philosophy. Hazlitt's requirements were surely somewhat more discriminating. He presumably did not look for shade only, but also for a gently sloping ground, maybe a mossy stone from which he could look out into the landscape, and—an important requirement he forgot to mention—a place without ants or too many other creepy-crawly things. We may assume that here as usual the mind did not go from the particular to the general, but from the general to the particular. But once he had discovered that there are trees which he can love, the experience could again take on a wider emotional meaning. He could have mentioned the imperishable image from the Song of Solomon (II: 3): 'As the apple tree among the trees of the wood, so is my beloved among the sons. I sat down under his shadow with great delight, and his fruit was sweet to my taste.'

What Hazlitt does say is that 'When I imagine these objects, I can easily form a mystic personification of the friendly power that inhabits them, Dryad or Naiad, offering its cool fountain or its tempting shade. Hence, the origin of the Grecian mythology.'

Here speaks once more the son of the Age of Reason whose picture of the alleged origins of mythology and religion is somewhat oversimplified. But we can now safely leave him under his tree unmolested by further quibblings, simply acknowledging that long before nature and art detached themselves as identifiable entities, mythology and religion must have answered the needs of the mind for symbols and metaphors. Not the patchwork mind, if I may so call it, of the associationists which, as you have seen, is composed of single impressions, but a structured mind—using the term without reference to the controversies surrounding a particular school of thought.

4. CULTURE AND THE NATURAL ORDER

If the mind is not a patchwork of individual sensations, neither is nature a chaos of random events. It offers us the experience of a multitude of interacting but ordered regularities which the Greeks called the cosmos, using a term which means both beauty, as in cosmetics, and the universe, as in cosmic radiation. The mythology and rituals of countless religions testify to the embeddedness of culture in the natural order. Without such an order man could not form expectations, could not plan, could not develop science and, maybe, not art either. For the alternations of day and night, birth and death, the round of the seasons in temperate climates, and the rhythms of the tides, are not like the actions of a clockwork; there is constant variety in regularity, which must have impressed itself on the mind since the dawn of consciousness. Like a patient language teacher, nature familiarized the mind of man with recurrent processes in ever changing modifications, establishing a communicable pattern of events which determined survival but always needed fresh attention.

You need not listen to anything more solemn than talk about the weather to know what I mean: 'It's cold, but we must not complain, the winter has not been too bad.' I know that talk about the weather has other functions in English culture than communication, but even this minimal form of social contact illustrates the way nature seeps into our consciousness, however much we try to expel her with pitchforks or air conditioning.

It was during a recent visit to Japan, however, made under very favourable circumstances, that the responsiveness of the mind to the language of nature was brought home to me. No doubt, there is a connection here between the original nature religion of the country and that transition from cult to culture which I observed. The cycle of the seasons is very marked in Japan, and so is their significance in the minds of the Japanese. It is one thing to read of their love of cherry blossoms (Fig. 18), another still to see the festive crowds enjoying this magnificent token of the arrival of spring. The round of the year sets the key for many genres of art. The painter will select the characteristic flowers of each of the seasons to compose a sequence for folding screens or other forms of painting and, unless we are told, we are likely to miss the overtones of mood and response which these images are traditionally meant to evoke. In that popular and highly formalized tradition of the seventeen-syllable 'Haiku', the poetic rules demand an indication of the season which provides the setting of the scene or reflection.[4] It may, we read, be a definite reference such as summer heat or autumn wind, or more likely an allusion to features like snowflakes or plum-blossoms. The degree of refinement and the aesthetic sense of this tradition are equally evident in the art of gardening, where nature and art come together. Let me comment here on an episode in the astounding novel of the eleventh century, *The Tale of Genji*, by Lady Murasaki, which is only accessible to me in translation—and I still use the one by Arthur Waley.[5]

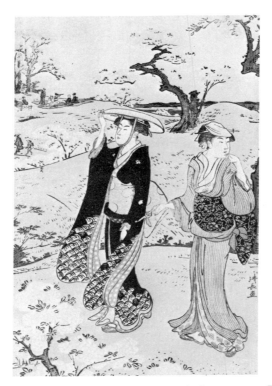

18. Torii Kiyonaga: *Cherry-blossom at Asakayama near Edo.*
c. 1787. London, British Museum

On page 430 of that translation the story of the loves and vicissitudes of the 'shining prince', as he is called, has reached a point when Genji begins to take stock of his amorous life and decides to expand his palace to offer accommodation to four ladies who particularly hold his affection. To provide for each of them what she loved most,

He effected great improvement in the appearance of the grounds by a judicious handling of knoll and lake, for though such features were already there in abundance, he found it necessary here to cut away a slope, there to dam a stream, that each occupant of the various quarters might look out of her windows upon such a prospect as pleased her best.

To the south-east he raised the level of the ground, and on this bank planted a profusion of early flowering trees. At the foot of this slope the lake curved with especial beauty, and in the foregound, just beneath the windows, he planted borders of cinquefoil, of red-plum, cherry, wistaria, kerria, rock-azalea, and other such plants as are at their best in spring-time; for he knew that Murasaki was in especial a lover of the spring; while here and there, in places where they would not obstruct his main plan, autumn beds were cleverly interwoven with the rest.

Akikonomu's garden was full of such trees as in autumn-time turn to the deepest hue. The stream above the waterfall was cleared out and deepened to a considerable distance; and that the noise of the cascade might carry further, he set great boulders in mid-stream, against which the current crashed and broke. It so happened that, the season being far advanced, it was this part of the garden that was now seen at its best; here indeed was such beauty as far eclipsed the autumn splendour even of the forests near Oi, so famous for their autumn tints.

I must not linger over the north-eastern garden designed to offer refuge from the summer heat through a cool spring and tall forest trees 'whose thick leaves roofed airy tunnels of shade'. Let me tell, however, that Lady Akashi's rooms in the north looked out on a close-set wall of pine trees,

planted there on purpose that she might have the pleasure of seeing them when their boughs were laden with snow; and for her delight in the earlier days of the winter there was a great bed of chrysanthemums, which he pictured her enjoying on some morning when all the garden was white with frost. Then there was the mother oak (for was not she a mother?) and, brought hither from wild and inaccessible places, a hundred other bushes and trees, so seldom seen that no one knew what names to call them by.

No doubt the passage, for all its refinement, looks somewhat alien to our Western conventions and traditions; but I singled it out because it illustrates precisely the fusion between the objective orders of nature and the response of sensitive minds. If it were not so chilling I would say that it also illustrates the way the mind can turn the cosmic order into a filing system of its most personal feelings. Murasaki, the young girl Genji had brought up almost like a father, stood in his mind for spring; Lady Akashi, the aloof princess whose favours he had won in exile against all odds and who had borne him a child, stood on the opposite side of his emotional life.

But do we really not know this kind of reaction in our Western tradition?

> No spring, nor summer beauty has such grace
> As I have seen in one autumnal face.

says John Donne in an elegy called 'autumnal', and Shakespeare:

> Shall I compare thee to a summer's day?
> Thou art more lovely and more temperate.

Shakespeare the master of rhetoric was, of course, using here a well-known figure of speech combining metaphor with comparison. For my purpose I might say pedantically that the categories offered by the filing system of Nature will not accommodate such excellence without extension and modification.

Admittedly metaphors can become so conventionalized that they cease to be creative. Those busy filing clerks, the poets and rhymesters of the Western world, have been so used to filing May, birds and love together that we would be startled to see them separated. Not surprisingly, the independent existence of these categories in the poetic genres of idyll or pastoral have irked honest minds who wanted to break through the veil of make-believe towards the social and psychological reality. I am thinking of the words of George Crabbe in his poem 'The Village', written a few years before Hazlitt's essay on the Love of the Country:

> I grant indeed that fields and flocks have charms
> For him that grazes or for him that farms;
> But when amid such pleasing scenes I trace
> The poor laborious natives of the place;
> And see the mid-day sun, with fervid ray,
> On their bare heads and dewy temples play;
> While some, with feebler heads and fainter hearts,
> Deplore their fortune, yet sustain their parts;
> Then shall I dare these real ills to hide
> In tinsel trappings of poetic pride?

But the very years which witnessed Crabbe's protest also saw a more thoroughgoing revolt against the dead wood of poetic metaphor. It was the aim of William Wordsworth's reform to free nature from the network of rhetorical tropes and to confront her face to face, as it were.[6]

> Ye Presences of Nature, in the sky
> And on the earth! Ye Visions of the hills!
> And Souls of lonely places! can I think
> A vulgar hope was yours when Ye employ'd
> Such ministry, when Ye through many a year
> Haunting me thus among my boyish sports,
> On caves and trees, upon the woods and hills,
> Impress'd upon all forms the characters
> Of danger or desire, and thus did make

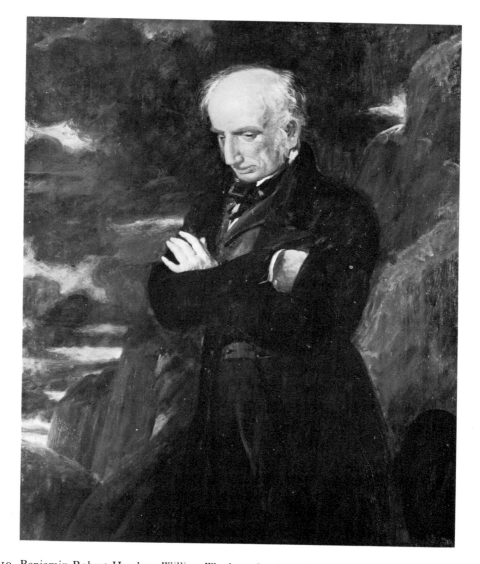

19. Benjamin Robert Haydon: *William Wordsworth*. 1842. London, National Portrait Gallery

> The surface of the universal earth
> With triumph, and delight, and hope, and fear,
> Work like a sea?   *The Prelude*, Book 1 (490–501)

It is easy to say and to see that the communion with Nature which
Wordsworth (Fig. 19) celebrated in *The Prelude* was really a form of
self-communion, a projection of subjective feelings onto the screen of

Romantic scenery. But such a description would be one-sided. No doubt the poet lent Nature his feelings, but he also owed to Nature the capacity to give them a local habitation and a name.

In any case that new striving for freshness and intensity which ushered in the worship of Nature to which I referred in the beginning of this lecture must have been felt to meet a need of the mind which was left untended by the slow decline of religion, which had for so long filled and nourished the inner life. It was in this constellation also, I believe, that the arts began to rival nature as a source of emotional sustenance.

5. SECULARIZED RELIGION

That conviction of Lord Leverhulme's, that 'Art and the beautiful civilize and elevate because they enlighten and ennoble', would have puzzled a Renaissance patron or a Baroque cardinal, however much they liked to surround themselves with works of art. Its beginning may be traced to Lord Shaftesbury in eighteenth-century England, but it did not take full root among the English connoisseurs and collectors of the time so much as in German-speaking countries. It was there that Johann Joachim Winckelmann in his writings on ancient art set the key for a response to classical statuary which bordered on religious rapture, an almost pagan worship of beauty. Thus many generations of art lovers learned through him to find in the sublime serenity of the Greek Olympians and in the untroubled sensuality of satyrs and nymphs metaphors for their own psychological aspirations.

But the true embodiment of the new attitude to nature and to art in German-speaking countries was Johann Wolfgang Goethe, a genius whose vivid response to nature was expressed in his beautiful lyrical poetry no less than in his scientific investigations into geology, anatomy, botany and optics, and whose love of the arts encompassed the antique, northern Gothic, and, of course, the art of Italy, which he had studied and absorbed during a memorable journey.

I know that to many English people Goethe is little more than the name of the author of *Faust*, a play which is neither a play nor a philosophical poem and which anyhow loses its spell in translation. Thus the magic of Goethe's overpowering personality may be even harder to convey to another tradition than that of his contemporary Dr. Johnson, whose authoritarianism he shared to some extent.

Unlike Dr. Johnson, however, Goethe explicitly rejected Christianity. Declaring himself a pagan, he endeavoured all the more to rescue from the ruins of the orthodox faith the spirit of veneration and awe which was consonant with a certain pantheistic attitude towards all manifestations of sublime nature and great art. He once summed up his creed in the simple epigram of his *Zahme Xenien*:

> *Wer Wissenschaft und Kunst besitzt,*
> *Hat auch Religion;*
> *Wer jene beiden nicht besitzt,*
> *Der habe Religion.*

> He who has knowledge of Nature and Art
> Will never lack religion,
> Whoever lacks a knowledge of these
> He must not lack religion.

I would not deny that the opinion here expressed incurs the charge of élitism. After all, it implies that the enlightened do not need formal religion, for they have a valid alternative. It is only those without the blessing of this nourishment of the mind who must not go without some other kind of organized faith.

Élitist or not, Goethe certainly practised his own faith and advocated its devotions. As he makes one of his characters in *Wilhelm Meisters Lehrjahre* (Book V, Chapter 1) say:

> One should not let a day pass without listening at least to one little song, reading a good poem, seeing a fine painting and—if that were possible— saying at least a few sensible words.

That sceptical insertion 'if that were possible' saves the injunction from sententiousness. Goethe and those who took him as their model certainly did not always talk sense, but they looked upon a daily communion with nature and art as the equivalent of daily prayers. And those who followed him certainly included a large proportion of the middle classes in German-speaking countries of the nineteenth and early twentieth centuries. I suppose their eagerness to embrace Goethe's faith of culture, or *Bildung*, was due in no small part to the demise of organized religion. We know today through hindsight that this earnest faith of culture, to which so many of the practitioners owed their self-respect and their mental world, was insufficient to prevent the collapse of civilized values and the perpetration, or at least condoning, of unspeakable crimes against humanity. Alas, there are few religions against which similar charges could not be levelled. And with your permission I should still like to reflect on its assets rather than its unforgivable failures, for—not to beat about the bush—together with many other Central Europeans of my generation I was still brought up in this religion. I am not using the term loosely. It was the rule in my Viennese childhood for my father to take us children on almost every Sunday either to a museum or to the countryside, the famous Vienna woods, and I remember distinctly that he thought more highly of this routine than of the religious observance to which we were urged at school. He never was a friend of high-sounding words, but he gently intimated that this was and should be for us the equivalent of divine worship.

Not all people of our acquaintance responded with equal readiness to all aspects of *Bildung* or culture. For most Viennese it was of course music which meant most; performances of classical masterpieces again bordered in spirit and devotion on religious rituals. I was certainly brought up to regard great music as a revelation of higher values and I do not regret it. For others the beauty of nature offered the most elevating moments; and many reformers set themselves the task of weaning the working classes away from their pubs and skittles and making them responsive to the majesty of Alpine peaks and the joys of climbing and, somewhat later, also skiing. The *Naturfreunde*, the Socialist Society of Friends of Nature, exerted an enormous pull and must have transformed the life-style of many.

But the enjoyment of mountain scenery would not exclude contact with art, visits to old churches, monasteries and ancient cities, and for those more affluent a descent into Italy for a few weeks' sight-seeing in Venice or Florence. School, of which we only had four or five periods in the morning, was felt to be a bothersome interruption in this process of initiation. The teachers of the Gymnasium did their best to teach us Greek and Latin grammar, quadratic equations and the Spanish wars of succession, but the curriculum included neither the history of art and music, nor many other fields of knowledge which belonged to the tradition of *Bildung*.

I make no great claims for the universality of that tradition. Compared to the knowable, its map of knowledge was arbitrary and schematic in the extreme. As is true of all cultures, certain landmarks were supposed to be indispensable for orientation while whole stretches of land remained *terra incognita*, of relevance only to specialists. Shakespeare and Dickens were marked in bold letters in the section on literature, Jane Austen not even in small print. But what I am trying to convey is that at least there was a map.

6. THE LANDSCAPE OF ART

Like the world of nature the universe of culture was felt to be not a chaos but a cosmos; it did not consist of random pieces of information, but of a coherent manifestation of the human mind. Music, literature and art, each had its own landscape, with forbidding peaks, charming valleys, and, to return to Hazlitt's example, shady trees by a brook inviting repose.

As an historian rather than simply a lover of art I have developed reservations against this emotional equation of the works of nature and the works of man. The works of man, after all, were made to be understood, we want to find out what they mean or meant to their makers and to their age—it is a laborious task and there is no short cut to this intellectual goal. The works of nature impose no such demands and no such heart-searchings. We cannot understand a tree as we might understand Michelangelo's Moses. In the first case we must be subjective, in the second we should try to transcend our personal reaction. And yet, I hope, I have never overdrawn this undeniable contrast. We must not repress our humanity when standing before the Moses. We can be impressed by the majestic grandeur of Egyptian sculpture, the poise of Greek statues, the mysterious glow of Byzantine icons, the serenity of Renaissance Madonnas, or the playfulness of Rococo decorations, without falling into the trap which I have described as the 'physiognomic fallacy', the trap of confusing the style with the age or, worse, with the men and women who made up the age.[7] Historical explanation and subjective response can be and must be kept apart. There is a letter by Lord Leverhulme on his views about interior decoration which perfectly illustrates such a personal classification of the changing styles of art.[8] Whether or not you share his reactions, it reflects the kind of differentiation I have in mind:

I feel [he wrote to Thomas H. Mawson in 1910] that in the course of centuries we have gradually gained experience in the type of architecture suitable for each room. For instance, I prefer Georgian dining-rooms as the rooms in which to give large dinners; for small dining-rooms I prefer Tudor. For drawing-rooms I prefer what is called the Adams style; for entrance halls the Georgian. For a large room such as a music-room, I prefer the period which I should call the Inigo Jones type of Renaissance.

I trust you will not take me to be advocating this prescription, though one must be careful here. Since the recent crisis in modern architecture there is a danger of any programme finding adherents. What impresses me is simply the degree to which some seventy years ago styles were still felt to be charged with emotional meaning, and this may, after all, be preferable to an entirely aseptic scholarly approach. Art demands involvement, or else it will turn into artefacts. You may like genre painting or hate it, you may be partial to Van Gogh or find that Poussin speaks more immediately to you. In any case you can always discover new idioms, new masters, new works which offer you new nuances of seeing, of feeling, of human sympathy. The portraits of Rembrandt, the landscapes of Claude, the dreamy whimsicalities of Paul Klee, there is always more for the responsive mind, not only to know, but to absorb and assimilate.

I have called this lecture 'Nature and Art as needs of the mind', not as 'the' needs of the mind. It would be folly to claim that no other set of experiences can perform a similar function. For the vast majority of the people of this globe it must be their religious faith which shapes their inner life. Not wanting to obtrude here, however, I may still ask how the needs I have singled out are faring today.

That nature is now threatened by the inroads of man has become painfully obvious to many, but this very awareness has its positive side. Only recently *The Times* carried a headline: 'Nature in the countryside thrills walkers young and old'.[9] The Royal Society for the Protection of Birds has eighty nature reserves and its membership stood at 34,000 in 1980; there may be more than a million bird watchers in Britain, many of whom surely learn to respond also to the other sights of nature. Nor do I think we need worry about that other means of maintaining contact with nature; I mean the art of gardening, which has always had a special place in the traditions of this country. Granted that the aspirations and the means of Prince Genji have always been outside its reach, it is precisely the strength of that art that it can be appreciated and practised on any scale from the tending of houseplants to the laying out of grounds like The Hill at Hampstead, one of Lord Leverhulme's creations, which sometimes offers me that pleasure of repose which Hazlitt found under his tree.

7. THE DANGERS OF BARBARISM

Turning from nature to the arts, it would be futile and impertinent to pass them all in review, let alone to rank them according to the benefits they can bestow on the mind. What is not futile to ask, I believe, is whether it is possible to justify a ranking order within the arts in the light of my interpretation? Is highbrow art really more valuable than its lowbrow counterpart? Does classical music offer more to the mind than pop, Shakespeare more than thrillers, and Cézanne more than comics? Is it not simply a matter of taste and prejudice?

I have often said that I do not think that the value of any work of art to the mind can be demonstrated, and my deliberations today may go some way in explaining this impossibility. If art, like nature, offers us a range of metaphors, their meaning and import can only come to life in the context of the whole. Once we acknowledge this cohesion in the various languages of art, however, we are entitled to speak of poor and rich vocabularies and resources, possibilities for differentiation and discrimination which cannot remain without effect on the mind. There may be a natural transition from an interest in gossip columns to an enjoyment of trashy novels, but one hopes that the ladder continues to increasing subtlety and richness in the articulation of human problems. Psychoanalysis speaks of sublimation when describing the distance from immediate gratification and the compensatory rewards of increasing mastery.

Believing, as I do, in these rewards, I must ask in conclusion why there are so few takers on the market place? I do not think the answer is as simple as it once was when George Crabbe rightly reminded the poets of his time of the poor laborious natives of the place who have to toil in the sweat of their brow simply to satisfy their bodily needs. Even where these physical needs are happily satisfied, the needs of the mind may still be in danger of atrophy. For frequently, I suggest, their satisfaction is blocked by another overriding need, the social need for companionship, for the approval of one's peers, what are known as the pressures of conformism and the antagonism of rivalling groups. If proof were needed of the strength of these psychological forces it would be found, of course, in the overwhelming attraction of spectator sports, not as sources of interest, but as means of creating and fostering group identities to the point of mutual warfare. But the same need for the security of the group also operates in the field of language and taste. If the idiom of your group is inarticulate, you had better be careful not to be too refined if you do not want to be ridiculed and expelled. If pop and comics are the pabulum of your peers, a preference for Mozart and the Elgin marbles would stamp you as an outsider and a hypocrite to boot, for how can anyone pretend that this stuff really means anything to him? Unfortunately it is a fact of social psychology that such mutual antagonisms are self-reinforcing and tend to escalate. They lead to the mutually exclusive images of the effeminate aesthetes on the one side, whose attitudinizing merely reveals a lack of common humanity, and on the other side the hearty philistines who claim to know what's what and have no use for all this flim-flam. Once the self-respect of groups is involved, they become impervious to persuasion. There is nothing new in this situation; the barbarians have always been at the gate. What is new and disturbing is that today the inarticulate have found highly articulate spokesmen who denounce civilized values as privileges in disguise. The charge of élitism I mentioned at the outset is part of that syndrome. I am afraid it has prevented faint hearts from taking that first step towards the museum or concert hall which is the one which counts.

Thus the complexity of the situation has certainly increased since the days of Lord Leverhulme. While radio and television have enabled countless people to make contact with new ranges of experiences at the pressure of a button, they have also threatened to perpetuate the distinctions of taste through their division into channels of differing sophistication, the public acknowledgement that the arts are a minority interest. Even so, the channels do not run in watertight compartments, and there is no doubt that they have spread a knowledge of the wonders of nature and the masterpieces of literature, music and the arts beyond the privileged few.

But against this very positive achievement we must not deny the dangers they have enhanced. I mean most of all the danger of over-stimulation and under-organization, the two sides of the same coin. The need for novelty, for fresh impressions and fresh sensations may counteract the benefits I have just mentioned. Moreover, there are the understandable pressures of living creators and their friends to gain a hearing, which nobody should deny them. It is only when these social pressures try to mobilize a kind of parochialism masquerading as progressivism that one feels like hoisting a warning signal. I have in mind the call 'What about us? What about our own age, our own art?' which can sometimes be heard when the achievements of the past are presented. Is it not inevitable that the poets, composers, and painters who stood the test of ages may often outshine the unsifted efforts of the hour? It takes time for an artistic creation to fuse with the landscape of art, to turn into a landmark on our mental map. When it comes to safeguarding this landscape against over-hasty developers I am a conservationist.

But in my field, at any rate, over-stimulation also takes another form. I mean the craze for exhibitions, which too often monopolize the time of the genuine art lover. I sometimes quote the remark I heard attributed to a crusty old don: 'Whenever a new book comes out I read an old one.' There is some wisdom in this advice, at least as far as the arts are concerned. The way these exhibitions are often publicized and promoted to bring in the crowds, leads me to another distorting element, one moreover which is much more in evidence in my own field than elsewhere. I mean the emphasis on material value, on possession and all the false sensationalism it generates.

I am frequently tempted to envy the students of literature or music because they are but rarely concerned with these irrelevancies. Autograph collectors may compete for the manuscript of a Beethoven Sonata or of a poem by Wordsworth, but who else minds where it is and what it costs? The sonata, the poem, belongs to all of us. I know I shall be told that painting and sculpture are different, because they elude reproduction and publication. I agree that we have to travel to see the Acropolis as we have to see the Grand Canyon. Some of these treasures like some of the sights of nature may be inaccessible to ordinary mortals. But how much is accessible which nobody ever looks at? Would it not be better to draw the attention of all to the immense riches right under our noses? Granted that their meaning may not be immediately obvious to the casual visitor; need he remain a casual visitor? Could he or she not be made to seek out the real pleasures offered by our permanent collections, if only their displays were more permanent?

8. THE FAILURE OF OUR SCHOOLS

I think that the decline of concern for the needs of the mind is indeed a 'problem of the day affecting the welfare of society'. If we no longer believe in our own civilization the forces of vulgarity and barbarism will surely triumph. I do not see that those who are in charge of education are always aware of their responsibility in this matter. It is a responsibility which has increased immeasurably even within my lifetime. It may have been culpable for our schools to neglect these needs of the mind, but at least they had the excuse that in many cases the deficiency was likely to be made good by the home. In the changed conditions of our age and outlook this excuse is no longer valid, and yet our schools still wash their hands of the problem. It is still possible, indeed likely, for a child to pass through school without ever hearing a piece by Mozart or seeing a work by Rembrandt in the classroom. As you remember, I am not a believer in the teaching of art appreciation. But I believe that much more could be done in 'exposing' the children, as the jargon has it, to great art without appearing to ram it down their throats. I know that individual teachers do so, and often have encouraging success, but such activities are still extracurricular. Alas, there is even a school of thought among educators which strictly condemns such efforts. When I once lectured to a teachers' training class I was firmly told in the discussion that no teacher must ever show what he personally likes since he must not influence the child. I was even told elsewhere that visits to art museums by schoolchildren were frowned upon by teachers, who alleged that the late Sir Herbert Read put freshness and originality above every other concern. But why allow oneself to be influenced by Herbert Read and not by Rembrandt? Why teach the child the words of our language but not the images of our tradition? None of us has discovered Rembrandt unaided; how can any growing mind find a point of entry into the cosmos of art without being given the opportunity? We must not be discouraged if a good many, for social and psychological reasons, remain indifferent. Here one *must* be élitist and say that it is the few who are responsive who matter, and are likely to benefit from such contact for the rest of their lives. We hear a lot about our heritage these days, but is not this spiritual heritage even more vital than its material counterpart?

I know that art history has become a school subject, one of the options now available for 'O' or 'A' level if the right teachers can be found, but I hope I am not speaking against the interests of my colleagues and students if I doubt that this is the answer. Both at school and at the university the cosmos of art is broken up into examinable chunks which you are expected to study in depth. You can take Autumn as your speciality, including fruit marketing and harvest festivals, but then you need not know of the birds that sing in the spring. To survey the round of the year counts as superficial, for there is a widespread prejudice against general surveys. Believing, as I do, that the progress of the mind is more often from the general to the particular, from the approximate to the precise, I think that even a crude map is better than no map. Indeed, having written such a rough survey myself, I have also experienced the surprise to find that the need for it must have been very widely felt. I am humbled by the thought of the multitude of readers who have chosen my *Story of Art*[10] as a guide; humbled, because if I had had the slightest inkling of their numbers I would have weighed every word so carefully that I could never have written the book. What gave me the courage or, if you like, the cheek to write it off the top of my head was, of course, that background in a vanished tradition to which I have alluded. I believe that for all its faults this tradition still has something to offer to growing minds if only the schools could be made to see it.

I am fortified in this belief by an encounter I had in America some years ago with an unusual man, a ranger in the National Park of the Grand Canyon of Colorado, Mr. C. R. Webb. I had the good fortune of meeting him when I was looking for somebody who could drive myself and my wife to Oraibi, a distant settlement of Hopi Indians which Aby Warburg[11] had visited before the turn of the century. In the end we palefaces were not permitted to enter this ancient village, but I have no reason to regret the excursion because I found in Mr. Webb a man whose response to nature and to art struck a familiar chord. I learned that he had been a school teacher, I believe in Kansas City, and had tried with much ingenuity and pedagogic skill to interest his pupils in art and music. The result, alas, was not unexpected: the pupils loved it, but the parents came running to complain that he was wasting their children's time with subjects they did not need for the examinations. In the end he quit and withdrew into the majestic nature of the National Park, of which he has written a guidebook illustrated with his own photographs. He has also sent me typescripts explaining the structure of courses he advocates for the initiation of beginners into the fields of art and music which, next to nature, mean most to him. Living with his wife in a caravan filled with art books and records of classical music, he was, I found, as different from the popular stereotype of an aesthete as anyone could be. I asked him how he had come to develop these enthusiasms? Well, he said, in the war he had been stationed in Alaska and for a time he shared his quarters with a fiddler, a refugee from Vienna who liked to play classical music. It was this encounter which opened up the world of Beethoven to him, and the rest followed. The scattered seed of a submerged tradition had been blown across half the world by the storms of the age and had taken root in a receptive mind. It is this kind of miracle which vindicates the faith in civilization.

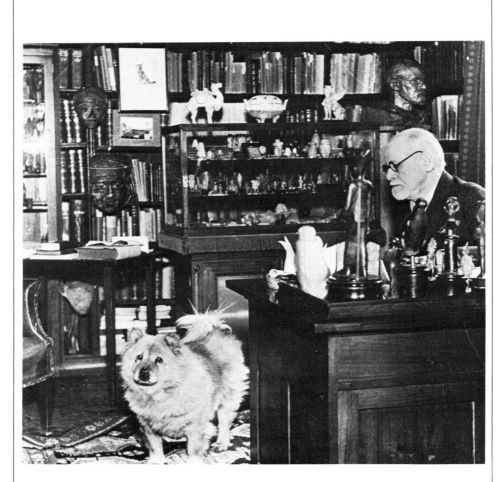

20. Sigmund Freud in his study in Vienna
with his art collection and his chow. *c. 1936*

*Sigmund Freud—Founder of Psycho-analysis, as he is described on the commemorative
plaque of his London house—was born on 6 May 1856 in Freiberg in Moravia, which
was then part of the Austro-Hungarian Empire. In 1860 his father, a wool-merchant,
moved with his family to Vienna where Freud attended school, including a classical
grammar school, before entering Vienna University as a medical student in 1873. He
graduated in 1881. At the time his interest (and publications) centred on neurology and
in 1885 he spent four months in Paris with J. M. Charcot, a leading authority on the
subject. In 1886 he established his private practice in Vienna and in 1895 published,
jointly with Josef Breuer,* Studies in Hysteria, *which laid the foundations of his theory
about the causes of neuroses.* The Interpretation of Dreams *appeared in 1900. The
occupation of Austria in 1938 compelled him as a Jew to leave Vienna and seek refuge
in England. He died in London on 23 September 1939.*

Verbal Wit as a Paradigm of Art

The Aesthetic Theories of Sigmund Freud (1856–1939)

A RECENT display in the exhibition rooms of the British Library assembled in a special showcase the first editions of three books which constitute landmarks in the intellectual history of Europe: Galileo Galilei's *Dialogue concerning the two principal World Systems* of 1632, the book which ultimately secured the victory of the Copernican system against all opponents; Charles Darwin's *The Origin of Species* of 1859, a work which encountered similar resistance in its attempt to define the place of man in the evolution of organic life; and finally *The Interpretation of Dreams* by Sigmund Freud published in the year 1900, the book which ushered in a new epoch in the exploration of the human psyche. This work also met with much hostility and misunderstanding, not only because in it the power of instinct was assigned a greater role than was generally welcomed, but most of all because for the first time the mental life of normal adults was considered in conjunction with the symptoms of neurotics, indeed of psychotics. After all, the dream is here interpreted as a result of mental conflicts which so frequently deny to civilized man the fulfilment of instinctual urges. During that third part of our lifespan in which waking consciousness is out of action, the same forces fight for dominance which can serve also in the explanation of madness and neurosis.

I am not a psychiatrist, but an historian of art, and it would be impertinent of me to attempt in my turn to interpret *The Interpretation of Dreams*. But the art historian can no more ignore its implications than the ethologist can neglect the impact of Darwin's oeuvre. Least of all can he do so if his interests include the theory of art.

I can only attempt to indicate the stage of development in which the work of Sigmund Freud entered the theory of art, and even for this purpose I must

---

Lecture given at Vienna University in May 1981 on the 125th anniversary of the birth of Sigmund Freud.

93

digress a little. To put it briefly, up to the eighteenth century the theory of art in the Western world was dominated by ancient philosophy. It was most of all Plato's metaphysic which, in a number of variations and even distortions, attributed to the artist the capacity of perceiving the divine ideals of beauty beyond the world of the senses and of embodying them in his creations. The rejection of this mystical view of art in the course of the eighteenth century, most of all in England, was bound to make theorists turn to psychology, a new branch of knowledge which had become prominent in the philosophy of John Locke. Foremost among them was Edmund Burke, whose *Philosophical Enquiry into the Origin of our Ideas of the Sublime and Beautiful*, first published in 1756, created a profound impression also in Germany. It was the first time that an author undertook to establish aesthetics on biological foundations, and he thus struck a note which still reverberates in Freud's writings. According to Burke, the human mind is dominated by two basic emotions, the desire for self-preservation and that for the propagation of the species. The latter manifests itself, of course, as the sexual instinct, and Burke explains the sensation of the beautiful as deriving from the attractions of a fine physique. The instinct for self-preservation rests on the striving for safety and on the avoidance of any threat. This avoidance is served by fear, which constitutes as it were a biological warning system. Fear in moderate doses explains the sensation of the sublime which the poets celebrate in storms and tempests.

What separates Burke's approach from the psychoanalytic theory of art, despite a certain rudimentary kinship, is above all the fact that Burke concerns himself not with the artist but with the beholder. As a student of emotional effects he is indebted to the tradition of ancient rhetoric, to which he also owes the concept of the sublime. It centres on the power of the poet, the musician and the painter to arouse or to calm the passions. What psychological dispositions enable the creator to play on the keyboard of the soul is much less at issue. M. H. Abrams in his classic study *The Mirror and the Lamp*[1] has described the decisive reorientation that led from the aesthetics of effects to the aesthetics of self-expression at the time of Romanticism and its aftermath in our age. In Germany it was the movement of 'Storm and Stress' which marked the break, as when a young lover in Goethe's *Götz von Berlichingen* says, 'Thus I feel this moment what makes the poet: a heart wholly overflowing with emotion', or when Goethe later makes Tasso speak the beautiful words, 'Where man falls silent in torment, a god gave me the power to say what I suffer.'

In the late eighteenth and nineteenth centuries, therefore, the theory of art shifts from objective to subjective criteria. In poetry, music and the visual arts, interest centres on the experience of the creator; indeed, in the absence of genuine experience the work of art is considered wholly bogus, a kind of forgery or confidence trick which pretends that the artist had felt something whereas in reality he was only out for effects. Around 1900, the year of Freud's *Interpretation of Dreams*, three names commanded immense respect among critics of art: Nietzsche, who approximated artistic creation to intoxication, Tolstoy, who in his book *What is Art?* equated art with the communication of feeling, and Benedetto Croce, who dismissed all art as mere rhetoric if it failed as genuine lyrical expression.

Small wonder that Freud's book made its greatest impression on artists and critics, who had always inclined to regard the work of art as subjective expression and to consider its affinity with the dream. The kinship of the genius and the madman had in any case been a favourite topic of the *fin de siècle*. Freud also paid tribute to the aesthetics of expression when he tried to interpret a work of art like a dream or a day-dream, above all in his famous study of Leonardo da Vinci.

Freud's characterization of this study in a letter to the painter Hermann Struck[2] deserves to be quoted in full since he always weighed his words very carefully. '*Es ist uebrigens auch halb Romandichtung. Ich moechte nicht, dass Sie die Sicherheit unserer sonstigen Ermittlungen nach diesem Muster beurteilen.*' ('It is, incidentally, also half novelistic fiction. I would not want you to judge the certainty of our other investigations by this example.') A good deal of ink could have been saved if that remark had been known before the publication of Freud's correspondence in 1960. When Freud referred to 'novelistic fiction' (*Romandichtung*) he was obviously thinking of the famous historical novel on Leonardo da Vinci, the second volume of an ambitious trilogy by the Russian author D. S. Merezhkovsky, published in German in 1903, which is mentioned in Freud's study. It must indeed have been an episode in that novel which sparked off Freud's interest in Leonardo's childhood. In chapter nine Leonardo visits his childhood home as a man of fifty, prior to joining Cesare Borgia's army, and reminisces about his past.

> Leonardo remembered his mother as in a dream—especially her smile, tender, imperceptibly flitting, full of mystery, seeming somewhat sly and odd on her simple, sad face of an almost austere beauty . . . The little house where Caterina [his mother] dwelt with her husband was situated not far from the villa of Ser Antonio [his grandfather].

Describing the young Leonardo's secret day-time visits to his mother we are told that 'he would throw himself upon her, and she would cover with her kisses his face, his eyes, his lips, his hair'. But, we read, the boy liked the meetings at night still more. Knowing the times when his stepfather was out young Leonardo would

> with exceeding caution arise from the wide family couch, where he slept beside his grandmother Lucia: half-dressed he would noiselessly open the shutter, crawl out of the window . . . and run to Caterina. Sweet to him were the chill of the dewy grass . . . the fear lest his grandmother, awakening, miss him; and the mystery of the seemingly criminal embraces, when, having gotten into Caterina's bed, in the darkness, under the blanket, he would cling to her with all his body.

The way is not far from this imaginary oedipal scene to Freud's reading of Leonardo's *Virgin and St. Anne* (Fig. 21) as representing his 'two mothers'.

I wish to stress from the outset that Freud's wide culture and his insights saved him here and elsewhere from the mistake of confusing the biography of an artist with the theory of the arts. What he says about this point in his autobiographical account could not possibly be more explicit.

> It must be confessed to the layman, who may possibly expect too much of analysis in this respect, that it does not throw any light on two problems which probably interest him most. Analysis has nothing to contribute to the explanation of an artist's gifts, nor is it competent to lay bare his method, his artistic technique.[3]

With these words Freud decisively indicated the frontiers between his insights and the concerns of the art historian. For if he did not want to enter into a discussion of artistic gifts, he thereby eliminated the problems of value. If, for instance, Leonardo means so much more to us than his pupil Luini, this is ultimately due to their different talents. To renounce discussion of the artist's method or technique affects still wider and more decisive problems. The methods which both the most gifted and the less talented must learn from their masters are, after all, inseparable from that manifestation of art which concerns the art historian most, I am speaking of style. Without the technique of vaulting there would be no Gothic architecture, without the technique of oil painting no Rembrandt, without the art of the fugue no Bach, and without the development of the drama no *Oedipus the King* by Sophocles.

Freud was fully aware of the significance of this renunciation. In his essay on 'Dostojewski and Father-Killing' of 1927 he declares right at the outset that *The Brothers Karamasov* is the greatest novel ever written, and the episode of the Grand Inquisitor one of the high points of world literature. 'Unfortu-

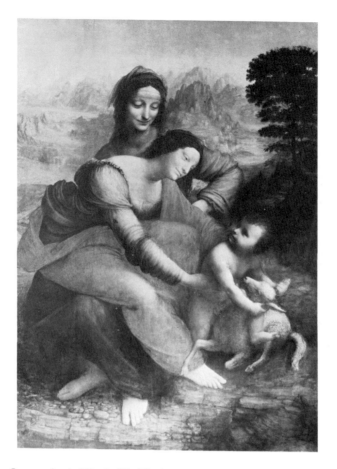

21. Leonardo da Vinci: *The Virgin and Child with St. Anne. c.* 1508.
Paris, Musée du Louvre

nately', he continues, 'analysis must surrender arms when confronted with the problem of the creative writer.'

But though Freud was not afraid here to draw the line, we must not infer that he wished subjectivism in art to be given free rein. On the contrary, throughout his life he energetically opposed the conclusions which some of his contemporaries wanted to draw from psychoanalysis in relation to art. He explicitly condemned both currents of radical subjectivism in the art of the twentieth century, Expressionism and Surrealism, and I must not pass over these remarks, despite the fact that I have commented on them before.[4]

His criticism of Expressionism was stimulated by a little book from the pen of Oskar Pfister, the Zurich parson with whom Freud engaged in a lively exchange of ideas and who, in 1920, sent him his publication on

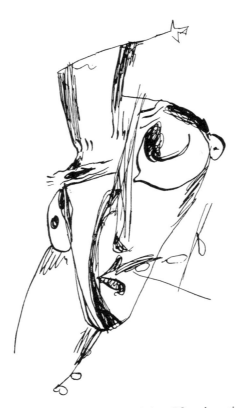

22. *Self-portrait* by one of Oskar Pfister's patients

Der Psychologische und Biologische Hintergrund des Expressionismus (The Psychological and Biological Background of Expressionism). In the introduction Pfister protests against 'the shrieks of horrified maiden aunts' and scolds the philistines who, as he says, 'believe they have done enough when they bandy about words like "disgusting", "barbaric", "daubs", "perverse" and "pathological" to characterize the new movement'. 'To get our bearing in the chaos of these serious problems', he continues, 'we must peer into the secret womb of the unconscious' and use the methods of Sigmund Freud which 'penetrate below the outer crust of the conscious mind'. Pfister wants to define Expressionism as 'any subjective representation which totally or almost totally distorts nature'. But he also includes abstract art, referring explicitly to the Cubists and the Dadaists, wishing, however, to refrain from any aesthetic judgement. For a short time the author had taken an artist of this school into analysis and during the sessions the patient made drawings and offered his free associations for interpretation (Fig. 22). With good reason, therefore, Pfister dealt with these images as he would have dealt with a dream told by his

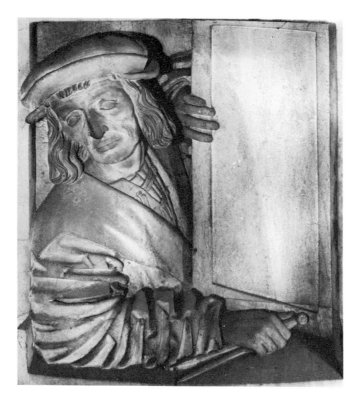

23. *Self-portrait* by Anton Pilgram from the Pulpit in
St. Stephen's Cathedral, Vienna. *c.* 1513

patient. He distinguishes between their manifest and their latent content, and
attempts to probe the private meanings which appear behind the enigmatic
shapes. He is profoundly disquieted by what he found there. He writes:

> After analysis has made us see what a welter of hatred, revenge,
> helplessness, inner conflicts and confusion sometimes lies in these
> images, one becomes doubly disinclined to attribute any human value to
> this autism. What concern to us are those brawls, disappointments,
> miserable childhood incidents which the Expressionist secretly embodies
> in his work?

One can certainly understand Pfister's outburst, and yet I think that it is also
unjust. We must not be surprised if the analysis of an artist produces
associations of this kind since that was part of its purpose. It seems to me
entirely possible that Anton Pilgram, the great master of the pulpit of St.
Stephen's Cathedral in Vienna (Fig. 23), or Ferdinand Waldmüller, the

lovable painter of *Springtime in the Vienna Woods* (Fig. 24), might have produced similar associations on the analyst's couch which also would somehow have been connected with their works. But this speaks neither for nor against these creations. What distinguishes the works of the Expressionists from those of Pilgram's or Waldmüller's time is not so much their origin as their style, the idea the artist wished to realize. The artists whom Pfister had in analysis could not be blamed for the prominence their subjective experience assumed in their creations; the responsibility lies with that theory of arts which, as I hinted, increasingly put the accent on self-expression and demanded nothing but honesty of these intimate exposures.

For the same reason I cannot agree with Pfister who, like so many others, wishes to explain the Expressionist cries of anguish by referring to the distress of the age. No doubt the age was indeed distressing, but then which age is not? Anton Pilgram certainly had reasons to be terrified by the danger threatening Vienna from the Turks, and even beneath the apparent idyll of Waldmüller's art there grumbled the volcano of social and national tensions.

What was at issue in the movement of Expressionism was nothing less than a new conception of art, a new idea of the task and indeed of the duty of the artist, and without taking note of this conception it will never be possible to do justice to these creations. What we call 'art' is among other things a social phenomenon and the artist also identifies with the role which society assigns to him. Thus the psychology of artistic creation is intimately connected with the theory of art which happens to be dominant in a period. In case this formulation sounds puzzling I should like to relate an experience I had in Vienna some fifty years ago: I was approached by a young man of my age in the lecture room of the University who told me that he was an artist and urged me passionately to look at his works. He took me to his rooms and pointed to a covered work. On lifting the dust sheet with great solemnity I saw an almost shapeless lump of clay in which one might possibly, and with much goodwill, find the marks of a human face. On my embarrassed silence he assured me with fanatical intensity: 'It is a work of art, I know it is a work of art because it originated like a work of art.' What he wanted to say was that he had experienced the urge to create and that the product had arisen from the depth of his soul. To cut short any further discussion, he opened a drawer in his desk and took out a sheet of paper covered with neat handwriting. It was a letter addressed to him which was signed 'Michelangelo' and said roughly: 'At last you have achieved what I always tried to do.' I was glad to get safely out of the door, but I have never forgotten the experience because from the point of view of an extreme subjectivism, it would indeed have been impossible to refute the argument of that poor madman. Yet even he sensed somewhere that

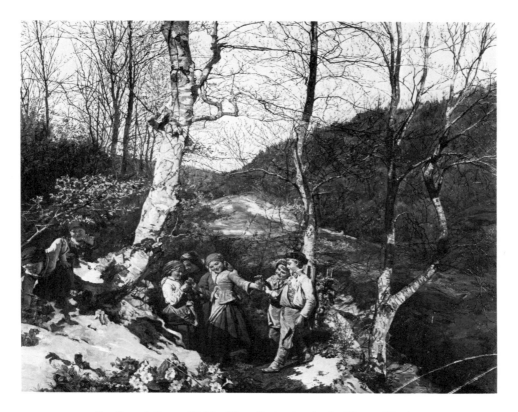

24. Ferdinand Georg Waldmüller: *Springtime in the Vienna Woods*. 1861.
Vienna, Österreichische Galerie

his subjective convictions alone were not enough, for else he would not have produced the fantasy of a testimonial by Michelangelo, whose name stands for such a totally different conception of art. What matters to us in Michelangelo's oeuvre is less how it originated than what he accomplished.

Sigmund Freud, who during his stay in Rome stood every day in front of Michelangelo's statue of *Moses* to probe its meaning, never doubted the importance of the artist's mastery even though he felt unable to discuss it. But like his contemporaries he took it for granted that this mastery had to be placed in the service of a personal artistic concern. His reading of Leonardo's *Virgin and St. Anne*, for instance, rests on the implicit assumption that the urge to create it arose from within the artist and not from without, as was the rule in the Renaissance. For Freud technical skill consisted in the ability of realizing fantasies. But just as in a beautiful letter about ethics[5] he quoted the saying of Friedrich Theodor Vischer: 'Morality must always be taken for granted', so he probably would have said: 'The aesthetic must always be taken for granted.'

Precisely because he found his expectations here disappointed he rejected with the utmost vigour the whole movement of art which Pfister called Expressionism. His letter to Pfister of 21 June 1920 may well alienate readers today, but it cannot be ignored.

Dear Doctor,

I took up your pamphlet about Expressionism with no less eager curiosity than aversion and I read it in one go. In the end I liked it very much, not so much for the purely analytic parts, which can never get over the difficulties of interpretation for non-analysts, but for what you connect with it and make of it. Often I said to myself: 'What a good and charitable person free from all injustice Pfister is, how little you can compare yourself to him and how nice it is that you must come to agree with everything at which he arrives in his own way.' For I must tell you that in private life I have no patience at all with lunatics. I only see the harm they can do and as far as these 'artists' are concerned, I am in fact one of those philistines and stick-in-the-muds whom you pillory in your introduction. But after all, you yourself then say clearly and exhaustively why these people have no claim to the title of artist.

Let me therefore thank you cordially for this new enrichment of my psycho-analytic storehouse.

More formidable even was the thunderbolt hurled by the irate writer at a poor painter who had made a portrait of Karl Abraham in 1922:

Dear Friend,

I received the drawing which allegedly represents your head. It is ghastly. I know what an excellent person you are, I am all the more deeply shocked that such a slight flaw in your character as is your tolerance or sympathy for modern 'art' should have been punished so cruelly. I hear from Lampl that the artist maintained that he saw you in this way. People such as he should be the last to be allowed access to analytic circles, for they are all-too-unwelcome illustrations of Adler's theory that it is precisely people with severe inborn defects of vision who become painters and draughtsmen. Let me forget this portrait in wishing you the very best for 1923.[6]

Who would have expected to encounter here of all places an anticipation of the hatred against an allegedly degenerate art? Maybe Freud wrote with so little restraint because he himself sensed somehow that the younger generation found in psychoanalysis a bridge to that movement of art which he so passionately disliked.

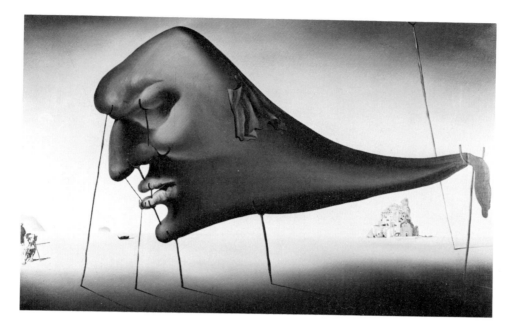

25. Salvador Dali: *Sleep*. 1937. Private Collection

Thus it is wholly understandable that it has meanwhile become usual to explain and if possible to excuse Freud's rejection of modern art by pointing to the prejudices of his generation and of his milieu. But it is always somewhat risky to dispose of the views of a great man which we find uncomfortable. Moreover, I think that in the case of Freud this escape route is barred. If there was ever anyone who proved that the prejudices of his generation had no such power over his thought it was Sigmund Freud. We may be quite sure that he had theoretical reasons for his attitude.

Fortunately opportunity arose for him to explain these reasons in a letter. By a happy coincidence he was prompted to clarify his position towards the most extreme form of artistic subjectivism, the movement of Surrealism, which relied programmatically on the kinship between the dream and the work of art and hence on the automatism of creation: Stefan Zweig had asked Freud to receive Salvador Dali (Fig. 25) in London and Freud, then eighty-two, agreed and wrote on 20 July 1938:

Dear Doctor,

I can really thank you for the introduction which yesterday's visitor brought me. For up to then I was inclined to consider the Surrealists, who appear to have chosen me as their patron saint, pure lunatics or let us say 95 per cent, as with 'pure' alcohol. The young Spaniard with his patently sincere and fanatic eyes and his undeniable technical mastery has suggested to me a different appreciation. It would indeed be very interesting to explore the origins of a painting by him analytically. Yet, as a critic, one might still be entitled to say that the concept of art resists an extension beyond the point where the quantitative proportion between unconscious material and preconscious elaboration is kept within a certain limit. In any case, however, these are serious psychological problems.

I owe it to the guidance of Ernst Kris[7] – who, before his exile, was a Keeper at the Kunsthistorische Museum and a joint editor of the psychoanalytic monthly *Imago*—that I may perhaps venture to interpret Freud's highly complex utterance and thus to elucidate what he here considered to be 'serious psychological problems'. He first remarks that it would be interesting to explore the origins of a painting by Dali analytically, in other words to interpret it through free association and memories like a dream, as Pfister had done in his time. But, Freud continues, as a critic one might still be entitled to say that even so it was not by any means a work of art but precisely something like a dream, because 'the concept of art resists an extension beyond the point where the quantitative proportion between unconscious material and preconscious elaboration is kept within a certain limit'. Too much unconscious material and too little preconscious elaboration does not result in what Freud would acknowledge as a work of art.

The terminology which Freud uses points to one of his works which is of decisive importance for the theory of the arts; I am thinking of his book *The Joke and its relation to the Unconscious* of 1905. This estimation should not come as a surprise. For it was precisely in this context that Freud demonstrated what the comparison with the dream could achieve and where it lets us down. When we speak of good and bad dreams we surely mean something very different from calling a joke good or bad. The problem of value, which no theory of art can ignore, stands in this brief and highly personal book in the centre of attention and I believe that some light is thrown in it even on the problems of technique and of style.

Freud's starting-point is the observation of the frequency with which we can find in dreams witty comparisons, puns and allusions, which must serve the purpose which he attributes to all dreamwork: the purpose of both liberating and disguising wishful fantasies.

What Freud in *The Interpretation of Dreams* describes as the mechanism of the primary process, that is condensation, displacement and the transformation into an image, can also be found in the joke. It was particularly the pun in which the double meaning of a word makes us laugh that interested Freud.

Puns, of course, resist translation, but even before illustrating the kind of verbal joke which Freud enjoyed it may be worth pointing out that contrary to the popular stereotype of his bias his book on the Joke by no means concentrates on sexual innuendos. On the contrary, he singles out for quotation the witticisms of 'one of the leading figures of Austria who after a brilliant career in science and in the civil service now occupies an exalted post in the State'. The joker had made fun of an historian who happened to have red hair, calling him something like 'that ginger bore who bores his way through the history of Napoleon's family'. Admittedly the pun is a little wittier in German;[8] but even if these witticisms were translatable they would hardly make us laugh today since we no longer know their butts. However, what Freud wished to bring out was that an educated man would hardly have allowed himself to express his distaste of tedious writings, let alone of red hair, except in a malicious quip. We feel free to laugh because the derogatory remark does not appear as naked aggression, but as a play with language which, as it were, seduces us to share in the speaker's sentiment.

It is precisely this possibility of sharing which represents the decisive difference between the joke and the dream. 'The dream', as Freud writes,

> is a wholly asocial psychic product: it has nothing to say to anyone else. Having originated within a person as a compromise between contending psychic forces, it remains unintelligible even to that person and is wholly uninteresting to others. Not only can the dream dispense with intelligibility, it must even beware of being intelligible, for else it would be destroyed; it can only exist in disguise. Hence it can make full use of those mechanisms which dominate our unconscious thoughts, distorting them beyond any possibility of retrieval. The joke on the other hand is the most social of all psychic achievements aiming at pleasure . . . thus it is bound by conditions of intelligibility.[9]

This intelligibility—if I may pursue this thought—rests of course on the common store of culture, most of all on the common possession of language. Freud regarded the pleasure in wordplay as a continuation of the childish pleasure in experimenting with speech sounds, experiments which gradually lead to the mastery of language. The pleasure in free permutations and twistings of words manifests itself in verbal tomfoolery as well as in witticisms; it is part of that regression to earlier psychic states to which Freud's theory assigns such an essential role. What ultimately matters is that in Freud's theory play and regression are simply the means of which we make use when cracking a tendentious joke, regardless of whether we proceed consciously or the joke comes to us as a fully fledged idea. To quote Freud's own formulation again:

> The work on the joke manifests itself . . . in the choice of such verbal material and such imaginary situations which make it possible for the old game with words and ideas to withstand the test of criticism, and for this purpose all peculiarities of the vocabulary and all constellations of associated connections must be most skilfully exploited.[10]

'The most skilful exploitation of all the peculiarities of the vocabulary', that is the demand we make on the joke. The wittiest writers, whether Karl Kraus, whose jokes about psychoanalysis Freud understandably failed to relish, or Lichtenberg, whom he highly esteemed, were all masters of language. To put it in a nutshell, a good joke is not an invention but a discovery. The identity or similarity of speech sounds on which the pun rests did not have to be invented: it had merely to be discovered, though one might quarrel over the word 'merely'. In a letter to Jung[11] Freud speaks in this connection of language meeting us half-way, just as he also acknowledges coincidences meeting us half-way. But both the coincidence and language only meet those half-way who are already on the road.

I can illustrate the situation by means of a *mot* attributed to Erwin Panofsky, who warned his students to be aware of the 'boa constructor', a danger he knew he had courted himself. We might imagine the discovery of the verbal similarity between constrictor and constructor by picturing two libraries, one neatly arranged according to subject-matter where no doubt the giant snake would be found under Herpetology, while construction might be treated in the section on Engineering. There would be no way from the one to the other. But according to Freud's model of the psyche the library of our waking consciousness is supplemented by one deposited in a dark basement where books and loose pages are piled up in wild confusion. Here the word 'constructor' might accidentally adjoin 'constrictor', for instead of well-trained librarians imps are having their fun down there, assembling texts or words according to their own whim, for instance according to sounds, images or emotional associations. The result will certainly lack rational meaning, and without further interpretation it might look like mere verbiage. But anyone who, like Panofsky, enjoys dressing a thought in a surprising garment has more chance of making a useful discovery down there than in the well-ordered library upstairs.

The successful joke, therefore, demands a brief descent into the cellars of the unconscious, but also an elaboration by the preconscious of the finds made down there. In contrast to mere punning the successful witticism must satisfy at least two standards, that of meaning and that of form, and in the choice of both there lies an element of style. In Anglo-Saxon circles the pun is much less highly esteemed than in Freud's Austria or Panofsky's Germany. Punning is considered the lowest form of humour because traditionally it is confined to a juggling with sounds rather than with meanings.

But naturally the verbal pun is far from being the only form in which the surprising arrangements of the unconscious come into their own. We need only think of that humble device, the rhyme. Anyone who has ever tried to compose a few lines of doggerel knows that he must surrender to the life of language to find the desired meeting of sounds which may at least mildly please or evoke a smile. The experienced word-smith knows the territory and will avoid the tritest of rhymes because he is sure of making more inspired discoveries. The real poet, of course, is endowed with genuine mastery, and you will not suspect me of confusing rhyming with poetry.

It will be seen how effortlessly Freud's approach in his book on the Joke permits a transition to those areas which he considered outside the competence of psychoanalysis, that is the areas of artistic gifts and of artistic techniques. And yet we may also divine the reasons which deterred Freud from proceeding further along that road: any attempt to translate a verbal joke is doomed to failure. To use traditional terminology, the joke simply does not permit us to separate form from content. However, this was precisely what Freud aimed at in his clinical work. He regarded himself as a translator who was able to interpret for his patients the latent contents of their dreams and their symptoms. To 'interpret them' could only mean to put them into words. But what the theory of art, to which Freud approximated the theory of the joke, teaches us is precisely that this kind of interpretation will never be possible; one can never put into words what a work of art 'says'.

Freud realized that this impossibility troubled him. Thus he prefaced his interpretation of Michelangelo's *Moses* with a telling remark which should by no means be taken to be a mere *captatio benevolentiae*:

> I must begin with the declaration that I am not an expert on art but a layman. I have often noticed that the content of a work of art attracts me more than do its formal and technical qualities, which the artist values most of all. I lack the proper understanding of many media and several effects of art.[12]

I believe Freud to have been too modest in this declaration. He exaggerated his difficulties because he identified understanding with the capacity to comprehend the means and effects of art in terms of a content which could be translated into words, as he was trying to do with the posture and gesture of the statue of *Moses*. It was probably on this occasion, when he first attempted to reconstruct the various stages of the hypothetical movement of the Prophet in a series of drawings, that he arrived at the conviction to which he gave expression much later in a letter to Lou Andreas-Salomé: 'But despite the compliments they pay me I am not an artist, I could never have rendered the effects of light and colour and could only have drawn hard contours.'[13]

We must not doubt his words, and yet—would he not have despaired of achieving the effects of light and of colour if he had not understood their subtleties?

How indeed could Freud have so enjoyed collecting art and visiting art centres if he had lacked a natural response to the works of the masters or to the splendours of the Acropolis? But what in this letter he described as 'hard contours' may perhaps be compared with his insistence on literal understanding, which also explains how he could tell Romain Rolland that music was a closed book to him.[14] Music eludes verbal interpretation but not understanding, and it almost looks as if Freud had debarred himself from this natural access in a posture of defiance.

In a cheerful letter which he wrote to his family from Rome in 1907 he describes a performance of Bizet's *Carmen* and mentions quite naturally that he had stayed until the Third Act despite the endless intervals, because he so loved the music of the fortune-telling episode. Nor does he refrain from criticizing the performance: 'The wonderful tunes came well into their own, but everything was somewhat coarsened and too noisy.'[15] No one who quite lacks an ear for music could have made these remarks.

It would scarcely be just, however, to blame Freud's one-sided approach to art simply on his personal bias. The responsibility lies again with the theory of art which was dominant at that time, the theory which identified art with expression or even with communication. The most profound criticism of the theory is contained in an epigram by Friedrich Schiller headed 'Language': 'Why is the life of the spirit for ever concealed from the spirit? When you hear the soul *speak*, know that here speaks not the *soul*.'[16] Immediate contact between soul and soul, in other words, is an unrealizable dream. If that were not the case, we may add to Schiller's words, we would not stand in need of psychoanalysis.

I do not want to be misunderstood. In questioning the proposition that artistic creation can be identified with communication, I do not want to deny that the artist is concerned with the effect of his work on others. But this effect results from the manipulation of his medium, the lines, colours or tones through which he can move the human heart. Such an aesthetics of effects rests on the empirical observation that we all react to sense impressions,

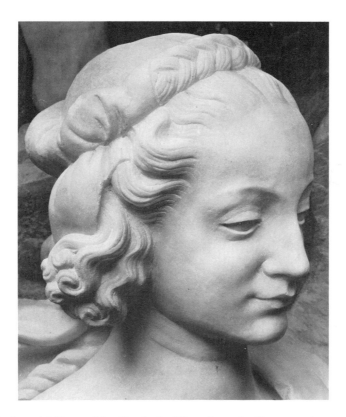

26. Andrea del Verrocchio: Head of a *Virtue* from the Forteguerri monument.
Completed in 1489. Pistoia Cathedral

whether we experience them in nature or in front of works of art. It matters little whether we can regard such effects as constant or whether they are conditioned by culture. There certainly exist elementary reactions which are almost or wholly universal, for instance the impression made by light, by bright or shining surfaces, by the disgusting and by the erotically arousing. What concerns me is only that all arts make systematic use of such effects and that the artist therefore builds on observations he has made on himself and on others. That is why I like to insist on the formulation that the artist must be a discoverer. Just as the verbal joke is discovered in the language, so the masters of other artistic media find their effects prefigured in the language of style which—to return to Freud's words—'meets us half-way'. Even if Freud was right in accepting Merezhkovsky's intuition that Leonardo had developed his ideal of womanhood out of memories of his childhood[17]—something that can neither be proven nor refuted—the artist must in any case have discovered it among the female types of his master Verrocchio (Fig. 26), which he varied

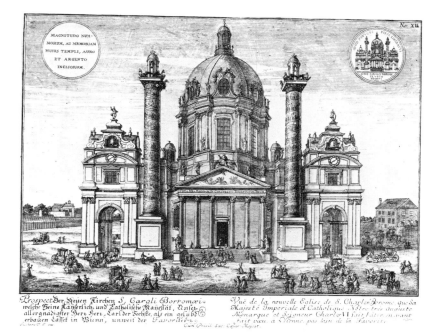

27. H. Sperling after S. Kleiner: *Karlskirche, Vienna*, built by Fischer von Erlach. *c.* 1725

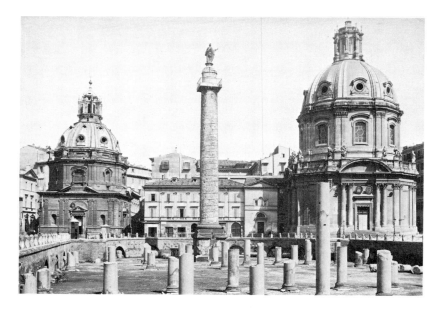

28. *View of Trajan's Forum* with the 16th-century church of S. Maria di Loreto on the right, Trajan's Column (dedicated in A.D. 114) in the centre, and the church of SS Nome di Maria (completed in 1738) on the right

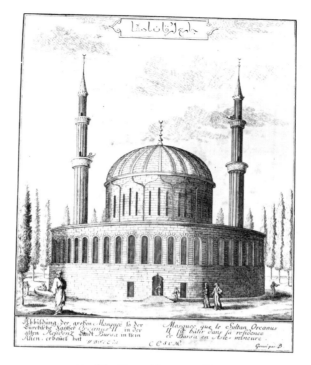

29. *The Great Mosque at Bursa.*
Illustration from Fischer von Erlach, *Entwurf einer historischen Architektur*, Vienna, 1721

and refined. Without the mason's lodge and pattern books Anton Pilgram could not have designed his beautiful pulpit in St. Stephen's Cathedral, and without the achievements of Romantic landscape painting Ferdinand Waldmüller would not have been able to conjure up for us his *Springtime in the Vienna Woods*. Even Cubism has been observed to rest on certain faceting effects in the late paintings of Cézanne where, of course, they served a different artistic purpose.

As for architecture: however original Fischer von Erlach's Karlskirche in Vienna (Fig. 27) may be, he too discovered rather than invented its forms and even their combinations; far from creating them out of nothing he merely modified and re-interpreted what he found in tradition. Even so the church is not a mere pastiche, but a masterpiece because the architect knew how to render the individual set pieces pliable as it were and to fuse them together: the memory of the domed churches, temple fronts and triumphal columns of Rome (Fig. 28) is combined with an allusion to the scheme of the mosque with flanking minarets (Fig. 29), to mention only some of the elements.

Music I need hardly talk about, since the whole structure of the tonal system of Western music can be described as a series of discoveries which enabled the composers to create their towering works. Naturally this could never have happened if there had not been musicians who responded to tones and harmonies which meant something to them; in fact they meant everything to them, but not as translatable symbols, at the most as metaphors which only have meaning within the context of the language itself. I know of a musician who had the feeling as she was lying in bed half awake, during an illness, that if she could only find the position in F sharp minor she would be able to sleep. To the analyst such emotional relationships must be familiar, but what matters to me is the fact that even feelings of this kind presuppose an existing tonal language which meets the fevering patient half-way. An out-and-out atonal composer or possibly a conservative Indian could never have sensed this equivalence. Naturally, also, nobody would expect such a private meaning to be communicated in performance. What asks for interpretation is the increasing refinement, I would almost say physiognomization, of the language of tones through which the sound poem can ultimately make us respond, whatever private associations it may evoke in us.

What the study of effects suggests is that we are in need of a special branch of psychology which might be called 'metaphorics'. It can be exemplified from a section in Goethe's *Theory of Colour* to which he gave the fitting heading: 'The sensually-moral effect of colours' (*die sinnlich-sittliche Wirkung der Farben*). A few extracts must suffice:

> The pleasantly cheerful feeling which reddish-yellow gives us is changed into the sensation of intolerable violence when it is heightened into intense yellowish-red. The active aspect manifests itself here in its extreme energy, and so we need not be surprised that energetic, healthy, rude people evince a particular pleasure in this colour. This preference has been universally noticed amongst savages. And when children who are left to themselves begin to paint they will not spare vermilion and red lead.

To illustrate these 'moral' effects Goethe mentions a highly intelligent and observant Frenchman of whom it was told that 'he had noticed that the tone of his conversation with Madame had changed after she had changed the upholstery of the furniture from blue into crimson.' We do not hear in what direction the tone of the conversation had altered, but Goethe tells us later that the French obviously hate crimson (*cramoisi*) since the expressions '*sot et cramoisi*' or '*méchant et cramoisi*' signify the extreme of tastelessness and evil. Poor Madame probably had to suffer for her lapse in taste.

Possibly Goethe's anecdote sounds a little like Andersen's famous tale of the

'Real Princess'. To find out whether she was indeed genuine the Prince's mother placed a tiny pea on the bedstead and piled upon it twenty mattresses and twenty feather beds for her to sleep on. When she complained next morning that she hardly slept a wink because something in the bed had badly disturbed her she had passed the test triumphantly. What makes a real artist is precisely such a heightened sensitivity, responding to the slightest differences in shade imperceptible to a less delicate sensorium.

Goethe, of course, was a poet, not a painter, or at the most a failed painter, if we remember his own confession in the 'Venetian Epigrams':

Much have I tried in my life, to sketch and make copper engravings,
Painting pictures in oil, modelling figures in clay;
Lacking persistence, however, I learned and produced next to nothing,
Only through one of my gifts came I to mastery close:
That of writing in German, and thus, I unfortunate poet
In the meanest of means squandered my life and my art.

We must not hold this spell of ill-humour against the great man. I only quote these lines to bring out the contrast between his sensitive response to all the shades of colour and his self-confessed inability to master colour as he mastered language. So much has to come together to transform artistic sensibility into artistic creativity. In this context, of course, the historical situation must not be left out of account. The son of a Frankfurt middle-class family who had taken drawing lessons in Leipzig with Oeser, Goethe was much too old for a change of careers at the time of his Italian journey when he first fully discovered the greatness of the masters. But who would apportion the respective shares to luck and to merit in the life of such a man?

Would Freud have felt equally honoured, on receiving the Goethe Prize, if Goethe had ended up a painter rather than a poet? He himself, after all, was a master of language, a wizard with words, who in his turn embarked on voyages of discovery in Goethe's work and who on any occasion could produce an uncannily fitting quotation from Goethe's *Faust*. It cannot be denied that his attitude to painters was much more reserved. He had much less understanding of their world. After having spent an evening with painters he wrote a letter in English to Ernest Jones which speaks of his impatient reaction: 'Meaning is but little to these men all they care for is line, shape, agreement of contours. They are given up to *"Lustprinzip"* [pleasure principle].'[18] He must have forgotten at that moment that these men could never have become artists if line, forms and contours had meant nothing to them. And while he approached poets and writers with real humility he seems to have derived his image of the artist from the novels of the turn of the century which wallowed in the depiction of the *vie de Bohème*; witness a letter he wrote in November 1914 to Hermann Struck, who had painted his portrait and to whom he sent his article on the *Moses* of Michelangelo: 'I must hurry to say that I am well aware of the basic weakness of my work. It lies in my effort to see the artist rationally like a scientist or engineer while he is after all a very special kind of being, aloof, self-centred, unprincipled, occasionally rather unintelligible.'[19]

We will not enquire whether Struck liked to hear that he belonged to such an 'unprincipled' ilk. But in Freud's repeated insistence that artists remained rather unintelligible to him, we also sense his desire to distance himself as a scientist from their alleged irrationality.

It is only in a work of Freud's old age, *Civilization and its Discontents*, that a different attitude towards the artist comes to the fore. He there discusses the burden civilization imposes on us by barring the satisfaction of our drives; he mentions the Eastern and Western ideals of their control and continues:

> Another technique of defence against suffering makes use of that shifting of libido which our psychic apparatus permits and through which its function gains so much in flexibility. It must solve the problem of how to shift the aims of the drives in such a way that they cannot be affected by the denials imposed on us by the environment. Here the sublimation of drives will help. The optimum is achieved when one knows how sufficiently to increase the pleasure gained from the exercise of mental and intellectual faculties. In that case fate will have lost much of its power over us. Satisfactions of this kind, such as the pleasure of the artist in creating, in embodying the visions of his imagination, that of the scientist in the solution of problems and the discovery of truth, have a special quality which we certainly will be able one day to characterize metapsychologically.[20]

Here the achievement of the artist is accorded the same rank as that of the scientist searching for truth, and Freud expresses his confidence that it would be possible one day to discover the psychic sources of this mental attitude. But even here his confidence concerns a future psychology of the artist rather than a psychology of the arts. He never denied the limits of his methods, and even less did he hide them behind a fog of impressive words as has so often happened and still is happening in the theory of art.

The more one concerns oneself with Sigmund Freud's life-work, the more impressed must one be by his personality, his human dignity. We have seen him strictly observe the moral imperative of the scientist never to say more than he thought he could answer for. Even the most daring flights of his intellect do not tell us more of his greatness than does this noble reserve. He certainly was no friend of flag-waving and so it seems to me that on this day we cannot honour him better than by refusing to make these matters look simpler than they happen to be.

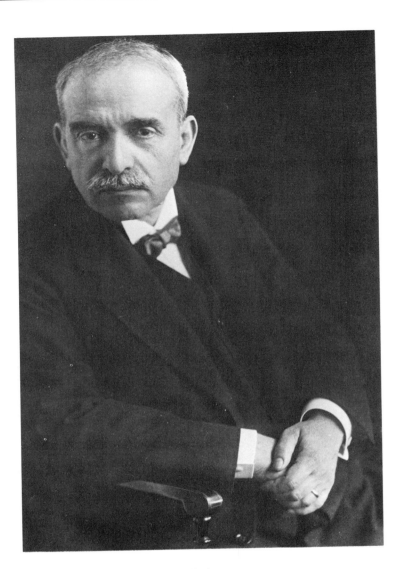

30. Aby Warburg. *1925*

Aby Warburg, art historian and founder of the Institute which bears his name, was born in Hamburg on 13 June 1866, the eldest son of a banker. He entered the University of Bonn in 1886, taking courses in art history and classical archaeology. A term spent in Florence in 1888 was decisive for the choice of his dissertation on Botticelli, which he completed at Strasbourg. In 1895 he visited New Mexico, then in 1897 settled in Florence. Returning to Hamburg in 1904, he devoted himself to the building of his library while elaborating his ideas on the art and mentality of the Italian Renaissance and the transformation of mythological and astrological imagery. The collapse of Germany after the war led to his mental breakdown, from which he recovered in 1924. He spent the last five years working on a synthesis of his theoretical ideas. He died a highly respected scholar on 26 October 1929. His foundation, Die Kulturwissenschaft-liche Bibliothek Warburg, had to move to England in 1933 and was incorporated in the University of London in 1944 as the Warburg Institute.

The Ambivalence of the Classical Tradition

The Cultural Psychology of Aby Warburg (1866–1929)

I AM very conscious of the honour of having been asked to give this address today, all the more as I cannot claim any personal acquaintance with the great scholar. I never met Aby Warburg. Others are able, and indeed entitled, to tell of the impression made by his personality, of his wit, his histrionic talents, his gifts as a raconteur, but also of the uncompromising demands he made on himself and on those around him. Of all this I could only talk from hearsay. And yet it may not be inappropriate, after all, that on the hundredth anniversary of the birth of this scholar you should be addressed by someone for whom Aby Warburg already is part of history. First of all, of course, he is part of the history of the Institute to which my fate took me more than thirty years ago and for the direction of which I am now responsible to the University of London and to the republic of learning. There may be no other public research institute which carries the name of its founder with the same justification as does the Warburg Institute. For what he left us were not funds but instruments and problems of research. The library which he built up, and which we attempt to continue building as far as the means of the University of London permit, still carries the stamp of the working library of a scholar. The fields of his interest, the questions he asked, his preferences and his projects are still reflected in the library and in our photographic collection, in their arrangement, in their richness, and even in their *lacunae*. Though I came to that library six years after the death of its founder and two years after its emigration, I had the opportunity to get to know the guardians of his heritage during the hardest time of its crisis and to witness how Fritz Saxl, the Director of the exiled library, and Gertrud Bing, his faithful helpmate, remained determined to accomplish the founder's mission regard-

Address given at Hamburg University on 13 June 1966 on the centenary of Aby Warburg's birth.

117

less of what might happen to their personal lives. For Fritz Saxl and Gertrud Bing, Warburg was in no way part of history, he was their mentor, their colleague, the exacting and caring head of a private institute of research to whom they had surrendered body and soul. It was above all Gertrud Bing, the dedicated assistant of the scholar throughout the last few years of his life, who introduced me at that time to Warburg's thoughts and ideas. She nourished the hope of utilizing Warburg's literary remains for the completion of his oeuvre, which should explain and sum up his life-work.

It hardly belongs within the framework of a festive address to talk of the problems which prevented and still prevent such a publication. The private jottings of a scholar, who liked to elaborate his formulations on paper in ever fresh permutations and who, moreover, operated with words and symbols of his own coinage which would be unintelligible without a lengthy commentary, present the pious editor with unsurmountable problems. Warburg himself would surely have been the last one to offer these slips of paper for publication. We know from his published writings how ceaselessly he strove to let his person disappear behind his theme and let the past speak by itself through the image, the word or the symbol.

True, as source for the historian these papers offer an inexhaustible mine. Like other born collectors, Warburg never threw anything away. The records of more than forty-five years are here preserved, his letters from the time of his military service, the notes he made of the lectures he heard at Bonn and Strasbourg, the drafts for his dissertation and for all later works, both those he published and those he left incomplete, private diaries and the records of the Library which he also used in his last few years for brief allusions to his working projects, all this together with an infinite mass of correspondence and bibliographical notes has been stored in this archive.

It is an irretrievable loss that it was not granted to Gertrud Bing to evaluate these treasures, which she alone knew completely, for a biography of Aby Warburg. In attempting to say something about it today I am sadly conscious of the fact that she and not I should stand here. But somehow the content of these literary remains must be made known if his personality and his role is to become intelligible. For however weighty his published contributions to the art and the cultural history of the Renaissance may be, only the most attentive of readers can find through them access to the philosophy of culture, indeed to the psychological system underlying this philosophy, at which Warburg was aiming from the very beginning.

I say the very beginning, because the fundamental frame of reference with which Warburg operated reaches back to his formative years—as is so often the case with scientists and scholars. In his case its foundations were laid long before the nineteenth century had run its course. This applies above all to the notion of a science of culture (*Kulturwissenschaft*), that is, to the hope of basing a scientific explanation of cultural progress on the well-proven results of psychological research. After all, Warburg's university years coincide with that heroic age which still believed in the possibility of such a synthesis. True, the romantic system of Hegel's philosophy of history looked by then somewhat outdated, but in its place the theory of evolution, which had triumphed in science through Darwin, offered an even more tempting prospect of a general explanatory law. Herbart's psychological doctrines had been fortified experimentally and so the time appeared to be ripe for the description and explanation of the phenomenon of cultural evolution in all its manifestations. Perhaps I may here remind you of that optimist Wilhelm Wundt, the author of the *Völkerpsychologie*, who was born thirty-four years before Warburg and devoted his long life to such a synthesis. Warburg never heard Wundt lecture but he attended Karl Lamprecht's courses in history at the University of Bonn. Lamprecht more than any other German historian of his time nourished the ambition to interpret the states of cultural evolution psychologically and to explain them on the basis of Herbart's theories as the result of the increasing mass of associations within the consciousness of an age. Equally decisive for Warburg was the personality of Hermann Usener, who in his lectures on classical mythology investigated the origins of mythological thinking by searching for the 'elementary and unconscious mental processes' which could serve as explanation for such psychological tendencies as the animation of nature and the personification of natural forces.

Stimulated by Usener, the young Warburg also read the book of an Italian pioneer of comparative psychology, Tito Vignoli's *Myth and Science*, which decisively influenced his ideas. Following Darwin, Vignoli takes as his starting-point the reaction of animals to external stimuli and concludes that the fear with which animals respond to unexpected movements must be due to an instinctive disposition to regard everything that moves as a potential threat. Only man has learned to dominate this fear by searching for the cause of the movement. First the human mind postulated the existence of mythical beings like the Gods of wind or thunder, but in the end logical thought offered salvation from this phobic reaction by revealing the true structure of the world through the investigation of causal connections. Even in his very last years Warburg was deeply impressed when Eckener's Zeppelin crossed the Atlantic, and he noted in one of those aphoristic jottings of which I have spoken: 'The mercury column as a weapon against Satan Phobos'; the barometer, which allows the meteorologist causally to explain and therefore to evade storms, liberates man from the fear of the unknown.

You do not have to be a psychologist to sense why it was above all this idea of a primeval fear which impressed Warburg so lastingly. He had to fight all his life against inexplicable and unexplained states of anxiety which threatened his mental balance. The doctrine which sees the evolution of culture in terms of the conquest of fear not only offered insights into the psychological roots of science, but also appeared to be applicable to art. As a motto for 'fragments towards a psychological theory of art' Warburg wrote down the sentence: 'You are alive but you do not harm me'; the image is alive and yet banished into its own sphere; the artist creates distance.

Warburg increasingly liked to describe this distance as the 'space for reflective thought' (*Denkraum der Besonnenheit*), because reflective thought, *Sophrosyne*, alone can save us from unconsidered fears and restrain our instinctual reactions. Not only anxiety threatens this space for reflective thought; every passion, every instinctual impulse leads to immediate discharge in movement. Greed leads to grasping, fear to flight. Only reflection creates that interval between stimulus and action which distinguishes civilized man from creatures of instinct.

For Warburg these considerations were logically linked with Darwin's findings, whose work on the expression of emotions in animals and man he described in a note as 'At last a book which helps me'. Darwin, too, searched for the roots of human expression in those motoric reactions of animals which assisted survival. Originally the clenched fist prepared the blow, the bared teeth the bite. It is precisely the weakening of the reaction which distances the emotion and distinguishes man from the animal. It is the same type of sublimation which in one of Warburg's favourite formulas led from the grasping hand to the mental grasp, that is to conceptual thought.

We cannot tell where these trends of thought might have taken Warburg if he had carried out his intention of switching to medicine. But this tendency was counteracted by the influence of his teacher in the history of art in Bonn, Carl Justi. As an historian Justi was a thorough individualist. Unlike Lamprecht he did not aim at vast historical perspectives, but at the illumination of an individual life or an historical situation; he was the master of monographic studies and his books on Winckelmann, Michelangelo and Velazquez are still unforgotten. They are all masterpieces of cultural history, but Justi saw culture quite concretely as the interaction of individual people in individual circles. This approach exerted its spell on Warburg. A considerable part of his career was devoted to the exploration of one particular circle, that of Lorenzo the Magnificent and his Florentine contemporaries. It was this tension between his theoretical interests and an historical method that aimed at the concrete detail which dominated Warburg's scholarly life.

In the year 1888 he had gone to Florence to work there for a term under the direction of August Schmarsow, an art historian whose writings testify to his interest in psychology, and it was there that Warburg conceived the plan for a doctoral thesis on the handling by Quattrocento painters of the movement of drapery. Justi considered the subject too theoretical, which prompted Warburg to go to Janitschek at Strasbourg. His choice was certainly not fortuitous. Janitschek, still known as the first editor of Alberti's *della Pittura*, was also the author of a book about Art and Society in Renaissance Italy. He there celebrated the achievements of Renaissance art as a victory of reflection over passion, in other words he regarded the art of the High Renaissance as a moral triumph. There can hardly be an element in the web of Warburg's ideas more alien to our age than this equation of aesthetic and moral achievement. And yet no one should hope to understand Warburg who fails to respond to this attitude. Naturally the intimate link between art and ethics had been a familiar thought since the writings of Winckelmann, whose ideal of 'noble simplicity' reflects a moral condition. But towards the end of the nineteenth century the problem had again become topical in a very different context. This was the period of the battle for modern art, a battle which was conceived by the young as a fight against philistine obscurantism. They saw it as a struggle for emancipation, for freedom, air and light. At that time the art of Arnold Böcklin (Fig. 31) was also seen as a symbol of a new frank sensuality as was the *plein-air* painting of the Swede Anders Zorn (Fig. 32). They were appreciated for the contrast they represented to the official style of the Salon with its tedious concentration on detail and its pedantic insistence on authentic historical costume.

There are distant echoes of these issues in Warburg's conception of Quattrocento art. We known from his drafts that what interested him in Botticelli first of all was to observe how far the artist departed from down-to-earth realism. How could one explain a stylistic tendency that appeared to contradict Vasari's vision of history, according to which Italian art learned slowly but surely to achieve fidelity to nature? It was thus that Warburg arrived at his hypothesis that Botticelli's unrealistic style of drapery (Fig. 33) must be laid at the door of the learned Humanists, who told the painter that in representing classical figures such as Venus and the Graces he should adopt the style of Neo-Attic sculpture (Fig. 34). Here, as in the poetry of the ancient world, the graceful movement of a dancing nymph or maenad with fluttering garments and hair blowing in the wind was considered the hallmark of beauty and charm. The originality of this hypothesis lies in the fact that Warburg here boldly followed Lamprecht's lead of exploring the mental images peculiar to a culture. Thus Botticelli's

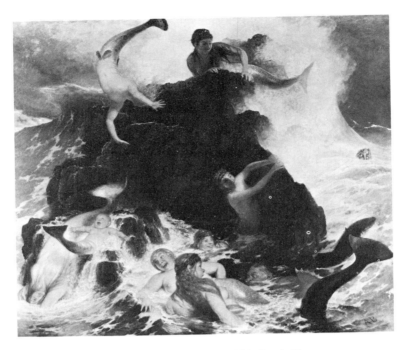

31. Arnold Böcklin: *Naiads at Play*. 1886. Basel, Kunstmuseum

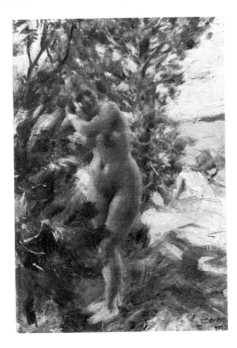

32. Anders Zorn: *After the Bath*. 1895. Stockholm, Nationalmuseum

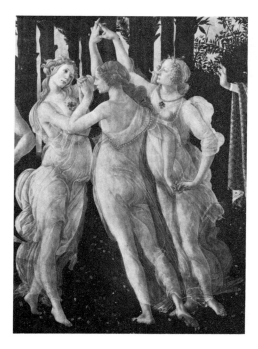 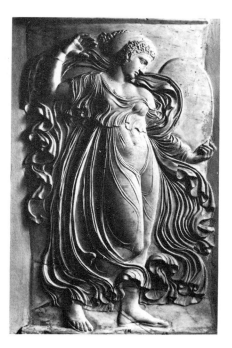

33. Sandro Botticelli: *The Three Graces*
(detail of Fig. 40)

34. *Dancing maenad.* Neo-Attic relief, 1st
century B.C. Madrid, Museu del Prado

style is not simply seen as the expression of a nebulous Hegelian spirit of the age, it is the result of the concrete collaboration between the painter and his Humanist adviser Poliziano, whose mental images of classical antiquity are transmitted from poet to painter, from painter to poet. The history of art should not concern itself with stylistic evolution in the abstract, but with real human beings who, having to make decisions, seek guidance both from the present and from the past.

It is to this conviction we owe the Warburg Library. For Warburg came to recognize that the normal working library of the art historian with its reference books and monographs was wholly insufficient for the realization of such a programme of research. His motto was to be: 'The word to the image' (*Das Wort zum Bild*). You cannot work on Botticelli without having the text of Poliziano next to you and without finding out how his patrons lived. Since the turn of the century Warburg systematically collected books from all fields which might throw light on these problems: general books on psychology, anthropology, art history, the philosophy of language and of myth, and specialized literature about the Renaissance and its sources in antiquity, in philosophy, literature, art and the crafts. In short he collected everything that

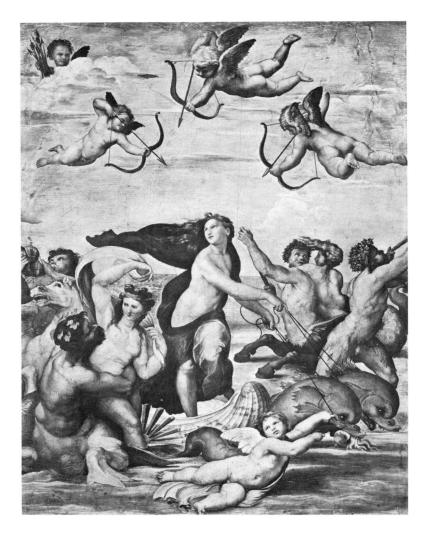

35. Raphael: *Galatea. c.* 1514. Rome, Villa Farnesina

could contribute to the reconstruction and the explanation of the milieu,
including the history of religion and economic history, which were at that time
still very much neglected; add to this the history of libraries, of costume and
of folklore, for these are further aspects of daily life which historians so often
fail to consider.

The mental images shared by a group of people might be reflected in
pageants no less than in the decoration of *cassoni* or in wall-hangings. They all
can become reflective mirrors—as Warburg put it—which allow the historian
to explore a symptomatic idea. Thus Warburg was bound to abhor the cult of

the specialists and what he called the frontier guards. An art history that is only concerned with painting will never be able to solve the riddle of the formation and the change of styles. For the historian everything can become evidence, everything a clue, and so Warburg purchased all that his means and those of his generous brothers allowed.

After a journey to America in 1896, which took the thirty-year-old scholar to the Pueblo Indians of New Mexico, Warburg settled in Florence, for it was only here that he could hope to find the answers to the questions which haunted him—what caused that momentous change that led to the High Renaissance? Where can we look for the true roots of the heroic art of a Michelangelo or of a Raphael (Fig. 35)? Did not Michelangelo himself emerge from the milieu of Lorenzo the Magnificent, was he not the pupil of Ghirlandaio, who had decorated the family chapels of the partners of the Medici Bank, the Sassetti and the Tornabuoni? In his archival researches for the exploration of this milieu Warburg again did not confine himself to looking for documents about artists. He concerned himself with the patrons and endeavoured to visualize their real mode of life, till he had completely immersed himself in the culture of the Medici circle and had, as it were, learned to speak with their accent.

In pursuing this work Warburg regarded himself at first as a follower of the greatest historian of culture, whose name I have not yet mentioned, Jacob Burckhardt. He had sent the great man his dissertation on Botticelli and had received an encouraging letter. Throughout his life Warburg never wavered in his admiration for Burckhardt. And yet the immediate contact with documents made him cautiously question some of the generalizations which can be found in Burckhardt's book, *The Civilization of the Renaissance in Italy*. The human beings whom he conjured up in his mind through his readings differed from those free and unfettered individuals that Burckhardt's masterpiece had led him to expect. He was forced to agree with Hippolyte Taine that they were still much closer, in their feudal and devout mentality, to the Middle Ages. Most of all they were much less harmonious, much less free of contradictions than the aesthetes of his time liked to imagine Renaissance man.

Many remarks in Warburg's drafts indicate how lonely he felt among the art historians in pursuing this path of an historical psychology and how reluctant the educated public at the turn of the century was to follow him when he undertook to interpret the art of Ghirlandaio as a 'reflecting mirror' of a divided mentality. Michelangelo's master, after all, was the representative of a rather down-to-earth realism, but this did not prevent him from enlivening his altar painting for Sassetti (Fig. 37) with a motif taken from the devout art of Flanders (the Portinari altar by Hugo van der Goes, Fig. 38) just as he did not scruple to incorporate in his fresco cycle pagan-classical motifs, which

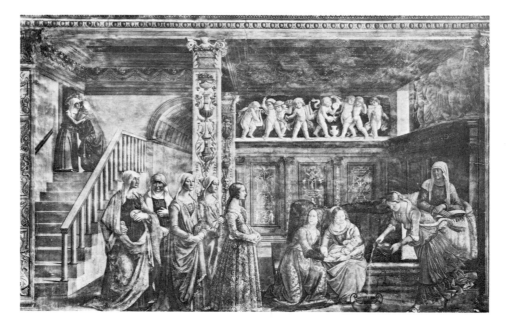

36. Domenico Ghirlandaio: *The Birth of the Virgin*. Completed 1491.
Florence, S. Maria Novella

sometimes penetrate even the style of the narrative itself (Fig. 36). In contrast
to the academic restraint of his published papers, Warburg in his drafts often
gave free rein to his irony. You actually hear him speak:

> Ghirlandajo is not a kind of rural bubbling brook for the refreshment of
> Pre-Raphaelites, nor is he a romantic waterfall which inspires that other
> type of tourist, the superman on Easter holiday with Zarathustra in the
> pocket of his tweed cape, seeking fresh courage from its mad cascadings
> for his struggle for life, even against political authority . . .

What attracted Warburg to this period of transition was precisely its
divided self, which was anything but naïve. He regarded the predilection of
the Medici circle for Flemish realism, the way its patrons and artists delighted
in sumptuous costumes, in brocade and in ladies laden with jewellery, as the
stylistic and psychological obstacle which had to be overcome, if the ideals of
Michelangelo and Raphael with their classical nudity were to triumph.
Psychologically he saw in this pleasure in earthly possessions a loss of that
'space for reflection', an inability to achieve distance, and in his description of
this mentality he again drew on topical and personal motifs, remembering his
own opposition to the milieu of a banker's family and his struggle for the
ideal—as he was later to jot down in looking back on this conflict: 'The

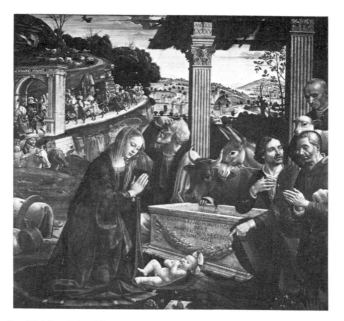

37. Domenico Ghirlandaio: *The Adoration of the Shepherds* (Sassetti Altarpiece). *c.* 1485.
Florence, S. Trinita

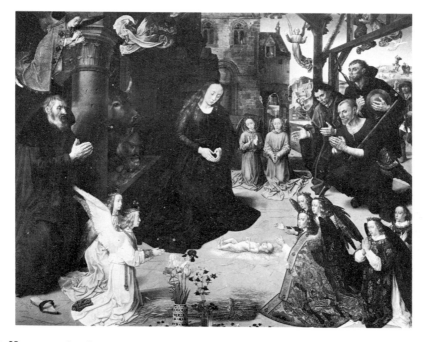

38. Hugo van der Goes: *The Adoration of the Shepherds* (Portinari Altarpiece). *c.* 1475.
Florence, Galleria degli Uffizi

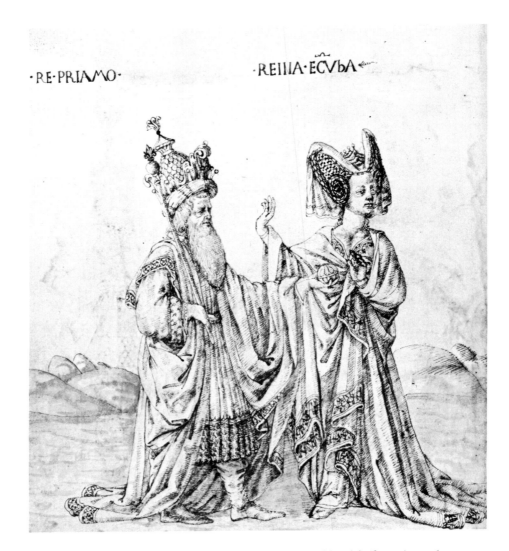

·RE·PRIAMO·   REIIIA·ECVbA

39. *Priam and Hecuba* from the *Florentine Picture Chronicle* (f. 34v.) *c.* 1465.
London, British Museum

opposition against property and against Frenchified elegance, the shores of the Alster'. But behind this act of identification which facilitated empathy we also discern the psychological interests of his early years in the problem of expressive movement. The heavily attired fashionable figures *alla franzese* (Fig. 39) will be too inhibited in their freedom of movement, their peacock-like vanity has stifled the free expression of passion and only the countervailing force of the uninhibited instincts of antiquity can here lead to liberation. Thus pagan sculpture in its rendering of Dionysiac frenzy and unbridled

aggressiveness now appears as a guide to free expression; Böcklin versus
Anton von Werner.[1] For Warburg the casting off of the restricting fashionable
finery in favour of the free-flowing drapery of the classical costume, which
gives full scope to the movements of the body, became a symbol of that
liberation through art, which on the other hand also harboured danger.

However profoundly Warburg valued the triumph of the idealizing classical
style of Raphael and Michelangelo, he remained convinced that such a
passionately agitated formal idiom only deserved our respect as long as it was
not devalued by inflated use or reduced to an empty flourish. In a well-known
article on Dürer and Italian antiquity written in the year 1905 he argued that
the Northern artist owed the true language of passion, the 'pathos formula', to
pagan antiquity. But this pathos can only have a liberating effect when it is
balanced by opposing forces. In this respect Warburg was entirely a child of
his time: he regarded the styles of Mannerism and Baroque as wholly
decadent, a 'muscle rhetoric', as he called it, which no longer reflected a
genuine pathos. These generations had called in the ancients to support the
fight against the uninspiring realism of Flemish fashions, but now they were
unable to lay the ghosts they had conjured up.

Thus if Warburg insistently posed the question to which he was to dedicate
his library, the question of what the classical legacy meant for Western man,
he never intended to express a bias for the influence of the classical tradition.

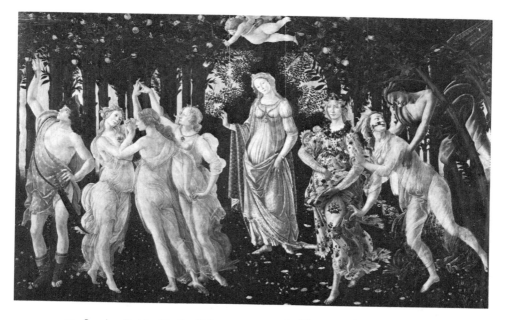

40. Sandro Botticelli: *La Primavera. c.* 1478. Florence, Galleria degli Uffizi

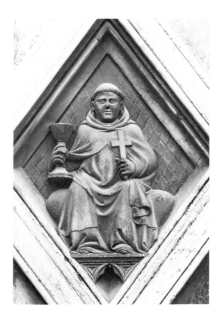

41. School of Andrea Pisano:
The Planet Jupiter. Mid 14th century.
Florence, Museo dell' Opera del Duomo

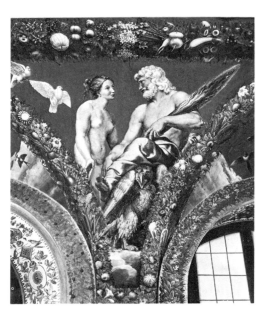

42. Raphael: *Venus and Jupiter.* 1517.
Rome, Villa Farnesina

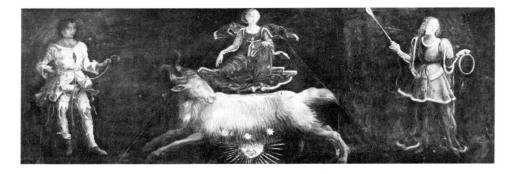

43. Francesco del Cossa and Cosimo Tura: *The Month of March* (detail). *c.* 1480.
Ferrara, Palazzo Schifanoia

That influence can either lead to the conquest of a 'space for reflection' or to its loss, a duality that can manifest itself both in art and in man's effort at orientation. Here it was the astrological imagery of the early Renaissance which held Warburg enthralled after his return to Hamburg from Florence. The transition to this topic came naturally to an historian who aimed at interpreting the symptomatic significance of the appearance of classical figures in art. Lady Venus in Botticelli's *Primavera* (Fig. 40) is just as unclassical in her attire as are the figures of the planets in other creations of the early Renaissance. But while the dress of Botticelli's goddess is only faintly medieval, the attire and the type of some of the planet divinities (Fig. 41) manifest the influence of much older and more surprising sources. It is the Oriental–Arabic tradition of astrological texts which makes itself felt in these images. Their dress and attributes derive in part from instructions for the designing of amulets.

It was with the help of such texts that Warburg succeeded in explaining the enigmatic cycle of frescoes from the fifteenth century in the Palazzo Schifanoia in Ferrara in which the figures of Oriental-Egyptian 'decans' are associated with the signs of the Zodiac (Fig. 43). But in certain respects Warburg's triumphal demonstration of these connections at the Art Historical Congress in Rome of 1912 has actually obscured his principal concerns. He was now considered the learned iconographer, the polymath who had succeeded in discovering an out-of-the-way source. His explicit assurance that he was not out to solve a pictographic riddle was probably not wholly understood. And yet he meant what he said. What fascinated him was the analogy with the triumph of the idealizing style. Here too the ancient gods had to be stripped of their disguise. Indeed the moral and symbolic significance of such a liberation was here even more manifest than it was in the struggle against the modish costumes of the realistic style. For the degrading transformation of the ancient Olympian gods was closely connected with their misuse as demonic oracles. That loss of the 'space for reflection' which superstitiously regards the constellations on the firmament not as aids to orientation but as hieroglyphs for prediction served Warburg as a perfect example of the dangers which always threaten civilization. It was only the art of Raphael which cleansed these magic runes of their poison and elevated them again into the sphere of art—in the frescoes of the Farnesina (Fig. 42), where the gods are at last assembled again on Olympus in their pristine shapes.

Warburg's astrological studies thus led him back to the basic questions which had formed his starting-point. In its perception of the constellations the ordering spirit of man is at work creating images out of the scattered points of light in the night sky. But this ordering activity is menaced by what Warburg called the 'slither logic' of astrology, which regards, say, the constellation of Aries (the Ram) as the cause of a combative disposition and which finally even uses the image as an amulet for its alleged power. The study of astrology reinforced a conviction in Warburg which is already adumbrated in his analysis of the change of style in Florence—a conviction which increasingly alienated him from the optimistic conceptions of history purporting to explain psychologically how mankind had progressed so wonderfully far beyond the animal and beyond primitive man. That primitive mentality, that loss of the 'space for reflection', the urge to grasp physically rather than mentally, all that did not represent a very long-past phase of development, it was a permanent menace, against which human rationality must be on constant guard.

I have alluded before to the profound psychological dangers which threatened Warburg's own mental balance. There is no reason to gloss over this fact, particularly as Warburg himself in the last years of his life often talked about his struggle against insanity. In 1920 the collapse of Germany, which seemed to surpass his worst nightmares, shattered his hard-won poise. Anxieties and delusions led to his confinement in the mental home at Kreuzlingen. It must be left to the biographer of Warburg to describe the moving spectacle of his resuming work, partly with the self-sacrificing help of Fritz Saxl, and the way this work in turn strengthened his own insights into the nature of his illness. Maybe it was precisely his theories about the overcoming of fear and about the control of passion in art and in thought which helped him in his struggle to gain distance. In 1923 he offered to give a lecture to his fellow patients about his theories and experiences, and this time he went straight to the point and spoke of his contact with primitive mentality during a brief visit to the Pueblo Indians of New Mexico, whose snake dances he had studied intensely, though he had not witnessed them himself.

I cannot refrain from quoting the wonderful words which Warburg wrote on the manuscript of that lecture:

> I do not want even the slightest trace of blasphemous science-mongering to be found in this comparative search for the eternally unchanging Red Indian in the helpless human soul. The images and words are intended as a help for those who come after me, in their attempt to achieve clarity and thus to overcome the tragic tension between instinctive magic and discursive logic. They are the confessions of a schizoid, deposited in the archives of mental healers.

These words are not only profoundly moving. They also indicate a decisive change in Warburg's solitary life as a scholar, 'the images and words are intended as a help', he wrote, 'for those who come after me' in the struggle for clarity. His awareness of the severe danger in which he had found himself could help other endangered fellow humans. And was not human civilization always endangered? Was the scholar who had perceived these connections in his own self entitled to withhold such insights from others?

Warburg's correspondence testifies to his generosity towards colleagues in imparting his own discoveries and giving access to his books. But now there matured the plan, conceived and supported by Saxl, to open the library to the public in the absence of its founder. The actual foundation of the 'Warburg library on the Science of Culture' as a research institute, with its series of public lectures and studies, is the work of Fritz Saxl, whom Aby Warburg's brothers provided with funds. During that period of post-war inflation American assistance for the purchase of books was particularly welcome and also particularly generous. Thus when Warburg had recovered, he found himself in a wholly changed environment. The solitary thinker who had avoided all academic ties throughout his life and had even declined invitations to important chairs was now the admired creator of a respected research institute, which bore his name. Soon he also gave courses as a titular professor at the new-founded University of Hamburg, where he encountered admiring colleagues of the rank of Ernst Cassirer and Erwin Panofsky.

Add to this the fact that in the intellectual climate of post-war Germany Warburg's fields of research had suddenly moved from the periphery to the centre. The World War had dealt a severe blow to the optimistic faith in progress. The mythical, the irrational, the night-side of life, had—if I may so put it—become the height of fashion. A library concerned with the history of astrology and magic and with the psychology of primitive man, a trend of research which emphasized these frequently neglected aspects also in the civilization of the Renaissance, could be certain of a wide response. It is all the more important to emphasize that Warburg never condoned this modish trend. He was and remained a champion of the enlightenment. In a beautiful essay on the position of Freud in recent intellectual history Thomas Mann defines his position regarding those currents of irrationalism which had also exerted their spell on himself.[2] He argues that Freud's psychoanalysis is the only manifestation of modern irrationalism which resists any attempt to misuse it for reactionary purposes. He was right that Freud's message, 'Where there is id, ego must be—it is work in the service of civilization like the draining of the Zuider Zee',[3] constitutes an appeal to human reason, but when Thomas Mann represented Freud as wholly isolated he clearly overlooked Warburg.

The very organization of the library in its individual sections shows that Warburg created it as an instrument for 'orientation', as he called it. The way leads from astrology to astronomy, from alchemy to chemistry, from number magic to mathematics, from liver auguries to anatomy. The new arrangement of the library in a purpose-built house in the Heilwigstrasse offered him the opportunity further to elaborate his philosophy of symbolism, which is based on a progression from ritual action to mental orientation, linguistic expression and visual images leading back to the origins of human culture.

In these new surroundings Warburg began to sum up the results of his researches and to test his cultural philosophy by means of new examples. Two motifs merely hinted at in his earlier notes now stood in the foreground of his thoughts: the motifs of polarity and of *mneme*, memory.

The idea of polarity became familiar to Warburg mainly through the doctrine of astrology according to which an individual planet, such as Mercury, is neither good nor bad in itself but owes its contrasting characteristics to its position within the horoscope. Had he not also observed something like that with the legacy of antiquity? The coinages of pagan sculpture with their excited gestures had proved salutary in the struggle against the modish costumes of petty realism. They became noxious in the 'muscle rhetoric' of the Baroque. These contrasting effects therefore could not be attributed to the coinages themselves but to the role which was assigned to them on their re-emergence.

It was this re-emergence which Warburg wished to characterize with the metaphor of 'mneme'. He saw the pagan imagery of ancient sarcophagi (Fig. 44) as the expression of those instinctual energies in Dionysiac frenzy and murderous rage which have left their trace in the human soul. A book by Richard Semon on memory[4] provided Warburg with the expression of the 'mnemic engram', and those 'primeval coinages of the expressions of the gesture language' as he called them, which had gained shape in classical sculpture, were seen by him as 'mnemic engrams' or 'dynamograms' which exert their spell on later artists precisely because they stand for those primitive urges from which Darwin had once derived the development of expressive movement. He who can dominate and distance their inherent energies is helped by them to achieve the 'space for reflection', he who allows them to dominate him will lapse into empty rhetoric.

This was to be the main theme of the *magnum opus* in which Warburg hoped to sum up his life-work. It was conceived as a picture atlas in which the coinages of the ancient world and their positive and negative effects on certain periods of culture were to be illustrated, with the history of astrology and astronomy forming a kind of counterpoint. Two of the titles which Warburg noted for this project may thus become intelligible: 'Mnemosyne; the awakening of the pagan gods in the age of the European Renaissance as the transformation of energy into expressive values' and 'The creation of the "space for reflection" as a function of culture. An essay in the Psychology of Human Orientation based on the universal history of images'.

The titles I have quoted clearly indicate the esoteric character of this project. In the course of his long research certain works of art, certain images and motifs had turned for Warburg into symbols which evoked in him whole

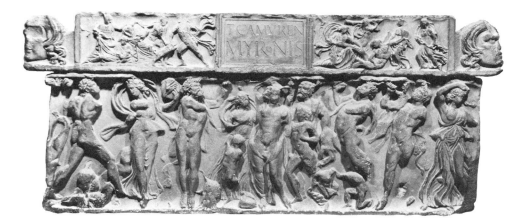

44. *Bacchic scenes*. Roman sarcophagus. 2nd century A.D.
Pisa, Campo Santo

clusters of emotion. The Atlas would have become such a web of symbols, a kind of symphony of images, part interpretation of history, part autobiographic meditation. Warburg sensed himself that this interpretation of history was somehow rooted in his personal experience. 'Sometimes it looks to me', he wrote in the diary of the library, 'as if, in my role as psycho-historian, I tried to diagnose the schizophrenia of Western civilization from its images in an autobiographical reflex. The ecstatic "Nympha" (manic) on the one side and the mourning river-god (depressive) on the other . . .'

It goes without saying that this share of personal meanings does not deprive the factual results of Warburg's research of their value. He was neither the first, nor, let us hope, the last student of human culture to be prompted by personal motivations to dare the descent into the darkest shafts of the past. The finds which he brought to the surface remain valid whatever had tempted him into the depths.

Warburg's finds and the questions he asks developed into a method of research which testifies to the solidity of his factual results even where revisions in detail have proved necessary. This movement has carried Warburg's name round the world and has even given rise to the adjective 'Warburgian' for an approach which pays particular attention to the symbolic aspects of works of art.

Even so, Warburg should not be counted among the scholars whose personality can and must disappear behind their achievement. Like Winckelmann in the eighteenth century and Ruskin in the nineteenth he impressed his contemporaries not only as a scholar but above all as a prophetic figure. Like these two other great visionaries Warburg was in the last analysis a poet whose prose could rise to dithyrambic rhythms when his deeper concerns began to surface:

> In the work of humble masons bequeathed to us by the grandiloquent boastfulness or the tragic despair of the pagan world, the hard stone rejoices and laments as a living dance of death; the passion of man here continues to live among the dead in such lasting immortality, in the form of a frantic desire to grasp or a frantic desire to be seized by passion, that anyone late-born endowed with a feeling heart and responsive eye must inevitably speak in the same style whenever he is shaken by the deathless compulsion to give vent to his feelings.

It was not for nothing that Gertrud Bing in her last years conceived of the plan to gain access to Warburg's true greatness through an investigation of his language and style. Even the few examples which I have translated suggest how idiosyncratic this language was, how weighty and how portentous, as if it told of those abysses into which he had peered. Naturally this style resists translation and one may even wonder whether his utterances were always understood in his own formulation, but who could possibly remain unimpressed when this ailing scholar with his melancholy eyes and his sparkling eloquence concluded his seminar of the year 1928 by addressing its participants as follows:

> It has been granted to us to linger for a moment in the uncanny vaults where we found the transformers which transmute the innermost stirrings of the human soul into lasting forms—we could not hope to find there the solution of the enigma of the human mind; only a new formulation of the eternal question as to why fate consigns any creative mind to the realm of perpetual unrest where it is left to him to choose whether to form his personality in the Inferno, Purgatorio or Paradiso.

Centenary celebrations share with other traditional rites what Warburg said of the 'pathos formula': they can tempt us into empty rhetoric or inspire us to genuine sympathy. What compels such sympathy in the case of Warburg is the passionate intensity of his search for truth, a search completely devoid of narrow specialism and academic arrogance. He always knew how to make his listeners and readers feel *tua res agitur*, it concerns all of us. It was this gift which made him a true teacher. His call for the exploration of the night-side of culture linked with his faith in the liberating power of knowledge should set an example also to further centuries. But what concerns us most today on his hundredth birthday and what should cause us most to reflect is that aspect of his life-work which is least in tune with our times and which may strike us as most outmoded, I mean his ruthless readiness to pass judgements also on historical events. As historians of culture we are now courting the danger of lapsing into the relativism of a purely descriptive neutrality in order to emulate the natural sciences. Warburg had the courage to stand in his work for those moral values on which human civilization rests. His pupils were grateful to him for this and so should we be.

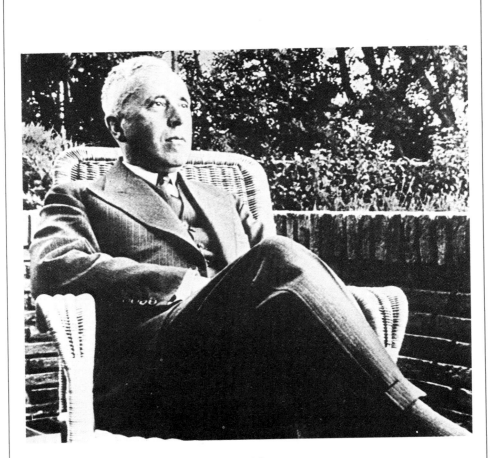

45. John Huizinga. *1937*
From Huizinga, *Martinus Nijhoff, The Hague, 1973*

Johan Huizinga, Dutch cultural historian, was born in Groningen, Holland, on 7 December 1872. A gifted linguist, he acquired Arabic while still at the classical grammar school. Entering Groningen University in 1891, he turned to the study of literature and to Sanskrit, graduating with a thesis on ancient Indian drama. In 1905 he obtained the Chair in History at Groningen and in 1915 that at Leiden. In an essay, 'My Path to History', he has sketched his intellectual development, his youthful enthusiasm for heraldry and numismatics, his disappointment with Eastern studies, and the conception of the book that established his international fame, The Waning of the Middle Ages *(1919). The rise of totalitarian ideologies spurred him to defend Western culture in his book* In the Shadow of Tomorrow *(1935), and in* Homo ludens *(1938) he asserted his faith in transcendental values. He was interned as a hostage and subsequently confined to a village by the German occupying power in 1942. He died, unbroken in spirit, on 1 February 1945, shortly before the liberation of his country.*

The High Seriousness of Play

Reflections on *Homo ludens* by J. Huizinga (1872–1945)

WHEN I was honoured by the invitation to share in this tribute to a great and noble historian of culture I had no doubt in my mind as to the aspect of his rich and varied oeuvre I most wanted to examine and discuss. Like all of us who are interested in cultural history I have had frequent occasion to remember that inspired coinage of Huizinga's which matched the idea of *homo faber* with that of *homo ludens*. Long ago I wrote a little essay entitled 'Meditations on a Hobby Horse or the Roots of Artistic Form' which developed into a book entitled *Art and Illusion*,[1] largely concerned with that most elusive of mental states, that of fiction. Later, when I studied the idea of personification of such entities as Fama and Fortuna,[2] I remembered the pregnant pages Huizinga devoted to this strange twilight of ideas between mythology and abstraction in his study of Alanus de Insulis and again in *Homo ludens*. Now I am once more in the orbit of his problems in a study that is to deal with decoration, ornament and the grotesque.[3]

But I had an even more personal reason for my choice. The only time I was privileged to see and hear Johan Huizinga was in February 1937, when he came to England to present his ideas on culture and play in a public lecture at the Warburg Institute, which had recently arrived in London. When, in the autumn of 1933, Huizinga had reviewed the edition of Aby Warburg's *Gesammelte Schriften* with much sympathy and understanding, he had also paid tribute to Warburg's foundation and expressed the hope 'that this beautiful plant should not perish in the storms of our harsh times' (IV, 560). What was more natural than that Fritz Saxl, Warburg's successor, who had

---

Address given at Groningen University in December 1972 in honour of the centenary of Huizinga's birth.

139

piloted the Institute through the storm from Hamburg to the provisional haven of a London office block, had not delayed long till he invited the greatest living representative of *Kulturwissenschaft* to give a lecture.

Like Huizinga, Warburg had been entranced by the complex tensions between the culture of Burgundy in the fifteenth century and the dawning Italian Renaissance, and Saxl hoped that the author of *The Waning of the Middle Ages* would lecture on a subject of this kind. Huizinga replied on 15 November 1935 that he could not do this. 'Unfortunately I have felt so remote from Burgundian subjects for some years that I could hardly find a topic in this field that I could deal with without a great expenditure of work.' Naturally Saxl replied that he left the choice to Huizinga, who still expressed doubts whether his theme would fit into the programme of the Warburg Institute: 'I do not believe that I could offer you a subject that would fit exactly in your programme. What I like best is to talk about the play element of culture.' Saxl of course not only accepted the choice, he and his colleagues built the entire programme of lectures for the term around this important topic, and we all were looking forward with tremendous anticipation to the great occasion when the admired historian would speak to us about what he insisted on calling 'the play element of culture' rather than 'in culture' as had been originally announced. I was at the time a very junior research fellow at the Warburg Institute and I do not think that I was introduced to the distinguished visitor. What has remained in my mind of this occasion is the elusive image of a gesture, the way he acknowledged a greeting or perhaps applause with that mixture of shyness and aloofness we once associated with the old-fashioned eminent professor.

Maybe this impression remained in my mind because, if the truth is to be told, it was also my reaction at that time to the lecture itself. I very much admired Huizinga's art of evoking the images of the past and I had evidently hoped and expected that the theme of human play and human culture would offer him scope to display this mastery. Instead, as those will realize who know the book that grew out of this lecture, or the text of the Leiden address of 1933 (V, 3-25) on which it was based, we were to be plunged into philological investigations into the various words for play in many languages, the elusiveness of the concept of play and of our customary distinction between *spel* and *ernst*, playfulness and seriousness. There was an overwhelming range of examples culled from anthropology, literature and history, and an almost defiant refusal to accept the aid of psychology in coming to terms with this category of behaviour. Quite obviously Huizinga's confession that he had moved far away from the *matière de Bourgogne* had not been a polite excuse for choosing a different topic; it was a different Huizinga we met on that occasion,

not the author of an historical bestseller, but the deeply troubled critic of
civilization who felt the urge to return to fundamentals and to draw his
personal conclusions from a lifetime of study.

The book *Homo ludens*, which came out in 1938, confirms this impression.[4]
I think it is fair to say that for every ten readers who have been captivated by
The Waning of the Middle Ages there may be only one who has really read
through *Homo ludens*. True, its title is widely known. We all know from
introspection and from observation that this designation illuminates an
important aspect of life and culture, we do play and we do play-act, we
indulge in tomfoolery and we step into roles, we wait for the sports results and
we attend conferences. Like Huizinga himself, we often want to be sure
whether we are serious or merely playing a game.

Light is indeed thrown on these questions by the book, but it is mostly
indirect light reflected from that extraordinary array of variegated facts
Huizinga had assembled in years of reading and through his many academic
contacts. They are spread out for our inspection in chapters headed Play and
Law, Play and War, Wisdom, Poetry, Philosophy, and Art; and in more
general reflections on the play function, on philology, myth, and on the
role of play in the history of Western civilization. Vedic riddles and Eskimo
drumming contests, potlatch feasts and initiation rites, university examinations and the swagger towers of Florence are all adduced as instances, but only
rarely does Huizinga permit himself to slacken the pace and to dwell on an
aspect of his material with all that immediacy and vividness that marked his
earlier masterpieces. The pages he devotes to the history of the wig in the
seventeenth and eighteenth centuries (V, 215-17) are such a gem and deserve a
place in an anthology of cultural history. Even so, I hope I shall not cause offence
in advising those who wish to come to terms with this strange book to start
with the last chapter and work their way backward. It is in the last chapter
that Huizinga reveals what his problem really is and why he undertook the
labour of surveying so large and diverse a field for manifestations of play. He
sees human culture against the awe-inspiring backdrop of a metaphysical
problem; deeply religious as he had become,[5] he was concerned with the
ultimate questions of the justification of culture in the eyes of God. 'The
human mind', we read, 'can only disengage itself from the magic circle of play
by turning towards the ultimate' (p. 212; 'het allerhoogste': V, 245). It is in
this thought that Huizinga's questioning comes to rest. He told in his lecture
how he had explained his ideas about *Homo ludens* to a colleague who bluntly
asked him whether he thought of his own work as a noble game? 'The
question shook me. I replied with a half-hearted "Yes", but inside me there
was a shout of "No"' (V, 24). This agonized shout reveals the heart of

Huizinga's conflict that is finally laid bare in the last paragraphs of *Homo ludens:*

> Whenever the perpetual transformations of the concepts of play and of seriousness send our minds into a dizzy spin, we find that fixed point that logic denied us in ethics . . . As soon as our decisions for action are influenced by the feelings for truth and justice, compassion and forgiveness, the question loses all meaning. A single drop of pity suffices to lift our actions beyond the distinctions of the thinking intellect. For any moral consciousness that rests on an understanding of justice and of grace, that whole question of play and of seriousness that had appeared to be insoluble is silenced for ever. (V, 246) (My translation)

I have placed this noble conclusion so near the beginning of this enquiry because I think it offers a key not only to this difficult book, but to a much wider range of Huizinga's thoughts and convictions. For though I have stressed the apparent contrast between *Homo ludens* and Huizinga's more popular books, notably *The Waning of the Middle Ages* and his *Erasmus*, I should still like to demonstrate the impressive unity of Huizinga's oeuvre as an historian and cultural critic. The approach he had chosen and the books he had written led him inexorably to the asking of the questions we find in *Homo ludens.*

Huizinga himself remarked in the Preface to his book that traces of its thesis could be found in his writings ever since 1903. He was probably referring to his inaugural lecture on Buddhist studies (I, 148–72), which already testifies to his interest in riddles and other contests in knowledge and power. Had he written about another historian he would certainly have checked his facts more thoroughly. As it is, he gives us the pleasure of saying like the proverbial German pedant, 'Hier irrt Goethe'. For it is six years earlier, in his doctoral thesis of 1897 dealing with a comic figure in Indian drama, that we read the following anticipation of his lifelong problem:

> It is a delicate task when confronted with an ancient and remote literature to say where the frontier lies between seriousness and non-seriousness. It is even frequently pointless and wrong to insist with an arrogant zeal on a conscious distinction between the two spheres of expression so as to force ideas so remote from us into the orbit of our own preconceptions. For it is precisely where these two states are kept together and are fused even unconsciously that the most moving expression of the innermost thoughts becomes possible to those individuals whose life exhibits a

balance between action and thought in the full flower of a cultured age.[6] (I, 126)

Here we find it all, very compressed and encapsuled, hard to understand in all its implications. There is another piece of evidence, less theoretical and more vivid, that takes us back beyond this formulation of the twenty-five-year-old student. Other contributors have referred to the episode to which Huizinga himself assigned such a crucial importance in his beautiful essay 'My Path to History' (I, 11–42). What he calls his 'first contact with history' happened when he was a boy of six. He was impressed by a pageant representing the entry of Count Edzard into Groningen in 1506, a procession that lingered in his mind as the most beautiful thing he had ever seen up to that time (I, 11), with the Count in shining armour and the flags waving in the wind. It was history in a pageant and as a pageant, and it was also a game of make-believe. Indeed we hear that when it was over, the small boys also wanted to dress up and march through the streets, but here for the first time little Johan encountered the figure who was to turn up again in *Homo ludens*—the spoilsport. The Mayor of Groningen apparently considered it a breach of decorum for little folk to parade through the town in fancy dress and so their show had to be held indoors in the local theatre. Who knows whether this rebuff may not also have led him to reflect on that clash between the world of hard reality and the attractions of a world of fancy? Huizinga himself has characterized the spell that history continued to exert on him less as an intellectual interest than 'a kind of *hantise*, an obsession, a dream as it had been since the days of my boyhood' (I, 29).

He also tells us that he succumbed to the romantic attraction of heraldry and genealogy and confesses that it made him a little susceptible to the glamour of noble birth (I, 13). How easily these leanings might have turned him into a typical romantic, writing nostalgic history or even novels and plays full of pageantry and dreams. But if that had been the whole of his mental make-up we would scarcely have come from all parts of the world to pay tribute to his memory. What made him great was an element of conflict, an awareness of values that transcend romanticism. Truth must not be tampered with, and the greater the nostalgia, the more is the scholar in honour bound to remain critical, to probe, to find out, to consult the sources and to respect the evidence (VII, 26).[7] Far from succumbing to romanticism he turned his own leanings into a problem with which he wrestled. Maybe it was this distrust of his own inclinations that made him first seek the sterner discipline of comparative philology.

Yet it must have been during this period of his self-denying ordinance (around 1897) that he liked to amuse himself composing humorous evocations of episodes in Dutch history, to which he gave the mock-solemn title 'A Selection of Memorable Pictures of Patriotic History' (Fig. 46). The series reveals his ambivalence towards the kind of patriotic history celebrated in the art of the Salons.

But though he had decided to devote himself to linguistics we learn from his autobiographical sketch that his philological interests led him to a preponderantly psychological problem he proposed to tackle, it was the problem of synaesthesia, the tendency of all languages to mix up the sense modalities so that sounds can be described as bright, or light as soft (I, 27). He himself was no doubt a very strong visualizer and the connection of this topic with the main preoccupation of his life is easy to understand. The way the word is wedded to the image (*verbeelding*) intrigued him all the more as he valued the capacity of the historian to see the past with the eyes of his mind.[8] But as we know, he also realized the dangers of such automatic associations. How seriously should we take them? If there is one aspect of linguistic study which raises this question of playfulness—as Huizinga was to acknowledge in *Homo ludens* (V, 166)—it is surely the problem of metaphor. Not surprisingly perhaps, the young student was disappointed in the guidance he had expected from psychologists and linguists and so he abandoned the topic.

It was in the lecture of 1903 on Buddhism (I, 148–172), which I have mentioned before, that he turned to the problematical nature of visualizing in the context of cultural history. He suspected that the appeal which Buddhism exercised on the West around the turn of the century was aesthetic rather than intellectual. The visual image of the mysterious East had more to do with its hold on the fashionable world than the mixture of asceticism and magic he had found in the authentic texts (I, 157). And so the stern scholar reveals himself for the first time also as the anti-romantic critic of his age.

There is another ingredient here in Huizinga's intellectual formation to which he has also drawn our attention. He was captivated by E. B. Tylor's *Primitive Culture* (1871), the first book, I believe, which formulates the demand for a science of culture (I, 17).[9] The vistas which this book opened to him, we read, remained for ever the germs of his scientific ideas. Now what Tylor had in common with other early students of the subject is a tendency to speak of 'primitive culture' or of the 'primitive mind' as a distinct well-defined entity. For Huizinga the interest of Buddhism lay partly in the fact that it was much closer to the primitive mind than its modern admirers realized (I, 169). Even its images of bliss with their emphasis on sensuous pleasure belied the ascetic impulse and revealed that same primitive mentality (I, 171) that expressed itself in the enjoyment of riddles.

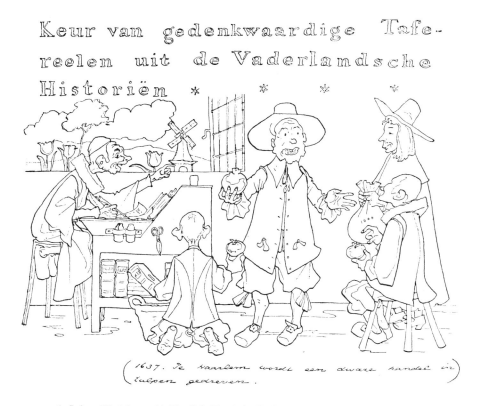

46. Johan Huizinga: 'A Foolish Trade in Tulips goes on in Haarlem' from his
Selection of Memorable Pictures of Patriotic History, 1950

But though he was attracted by the vivid picture Tylor had drawn of primitive mentality he was unwilling to accept the more ambitious claims of the rising discipline of social psychology. He must have frequently heard these claims debated in Leipzig, where he studied in 1895 and where he consulted Wilhelm Wundt, then at work on his *Völkerpsychologie*; for there the most combative champion of this movement, Karl Lamprecht, also held a chair from 1891.[10]

When accident and inclination had finally turned him into an historian Huizinga decided to respond to this challenge in his Inaugural Lecture on 'The Aesthetic Components of our Historical Ideas' (VII, 3–28). What had repelled Huizinga was the arrogance with which Karl Lamprecht claimed to make history 'scientific' by operating with psychological laws of evolution. Granted that some of Lamprecht's observations about the mentality of the German Middle Ages, his concepts of *'Typismus'* and *'Konventionalismus'*, were not uninstructive, how scientific were they really? He did not object to their having been established *a priori*. 'Which categories of this kind had ever been found by induction?' The danger lay in the fact that such auxiliary constructs, which the historian should be able to use and to discard at will, were presented as ultimate realities (VII, 8). Huizinga's intervention in this famous debate is memorable less for the use he made of the methodological theories of Windelband, Rickert, Spranger and Simmel than for the way he attempted once more to formulate his personal problem as one of historical method—the need to see the past in terms of vivid images, and the duty to search for the truth, even if this meant correcting or discarding the original vision.

I do not think it is claiming too much to suggest that Huizinga's masterpiece is constructed around the tensions created by these opposing tendencies. What could be more characteristic here than the passage in the opening paragraph of the third chapter of *The Waning of the Middle Ages*, the chapter that deals with the hierarchical conception of society. 'Romanticism', he says, 'was inclined to identify the Middle Ages with the age of chivalry. It saw there mostly helmets with nodding plumes (*'wuivende Vederbossen'*). And however paradoxical this may sound today, to a certain extent it was right in doing so.' (III, 66)[11]

It was right, we may continue, not because all was chivalry in the Middle Ages, but because chivalry was an expression of the aspirations of the age. However much we may know of the realities of the period, its greed, its squalor, its cruelty and its coarseness, the historian of culture is not only concerned with these realities, he is concerned with collective dreams, with the fiction that is inseparable from civilization, in other words with chivalry not as an institution but as a game which nobility played and the others watched. There are many passages in which Huizinga recurs to this image of a game that was played in war, in diplomacy, in courtly love and in the whole fabric of life. But at that time he had not rejected psychology as an aid to the understanding of this phenomenon. I am referring to the second chapter of the book, which follows his famous dramatic picture of the harsh realities of life in the period. These realities aroused a longing for a more beautiful life and such longing, we read, will at all times find three possible paths towards fulfilment (III, 40).

The first leads out of the world through a denial of all earthly pleasures for the sake of heaven, the way of asceticism, Buddhist or Christian; the second leads to an improvement of this world, it is the way of reform and progress that was chosen by the modern age. Maybe it was precisely because this way was unknown to the Middle Ages that the third was of such importance, the way, in Huizinga's words, into a dreamland, the way of illusion. Granted that this way was fundamentally un-Christian, it was the way chosen by the majority of the élite.

> The whole aristocratic life of the late Middle Ages . . . is an attempt to play a dream, always the same dream of ancient heroes and sages, of the knight and the maiden, of simple and contented shepherds.

True, Huizinga concedes in a significant aside,

> I know that all this is not specifically medieval, the seeds are found in primitive phases of culture, we may also call it Chinoiserie or Byzantinism, and it does not die out with the Middle Ages, as the *roi soleil* testifies. (III, 46)

There is little in the book itself that explains how Huizinga sees the distinction between the game played in the late Middle Ages and that of other civilizations, but I think what struck him was the accentuation of the game, its exaggerations, which so blatantly contrasted with the unseemly realities of life. 'Everywhere', he writes in a pregnant phrase, 'did the lie peep out of the holes of the ceremonial garb of chivalry' (III, 123).

There is more than one hint here that the dream is always more conservative than reality. What may have begun as a serious institution became a pretence, a mere game. E. B. Tylor had included in his book on Primitive Culture a most interesting discussion of games, games of grown-ups and nursery rhymes, pages which one might not have expected to find in a Victorian classic. Tylor looks at the game in the context of his theory of survival. There is an inertia in human civilization that secures the survival of beliefs and rituals into periods in which their meaning is long forgotten. Superstitions have always been recognized as such survivals, as the word indicates. Many games are of a similar character. They reflect old rituals and beliefs which have vanished from serious life and only live on as pastimes. If I am right that this interpretation of games influenced Huizinga this would help to explain his whole reading of the Middle Ages. This reading, as we know from the title of the book, postulates that the period can only be understood as an end, an autumn, not as the birth of something new. Elsewhere[12] I have criticized this emphasis on the autumnal character of the period, and I now know that Huizinga himself came to regret the title he had chosen as too metaphorical (IV, 450). In his last book, *Geschonden Wereld*, he even explicitly rejected the metaphor of rising and declining civilizations (VII, 511). But if at the time when he worked on his masterpiece he saw games largely as survivals, he was bound to emphasize the lateness of a period in which people appeared so eager to play roles or to play at roles which no longer had a serious function in a changed reality.

This interpretation of certain playful forms of life as survivals of earlier phases which is so characteristic of Tylor's approach comes to the fore, for instance, in Huizinga's reflections on what he calls the epithalamic style, the bawdiness and coarseness in erotic matters that he observed in medieval marriage customs.

> These matters become intelligible if they are seen against their ethnological background, as . . . weakened survivals of the phallic symbolism of primitive culture. Here the dividing line between play and earnestness had not yet been drawn across culture and the holiness of ritual was linked with the unbridled enjoyment of life . . . (III, 132)

But Huizinga would not have been the deeply conscientious scholar he was if he had been satisfied with pat solutions. Once in a while the assured narrator gives way to the baffled historian. Discussing the *Mirror of Marriage* by Deschamps the author interrupts himself to ask:

> Did the poet mean all this seriously? One might also ask whether Jean Petit and his Burgundian protectors really believed in all the atrocities with which they defiled the memory of Orleans or whether the princes and nobles really took seriously all the bizarre fantasies and the play-acting with which they embroidered their plans of campaign and their vows. It is extremely difficult within the realm of medieval thought to arrive at a neat distinction between what is play and what is earnest, between honest conviction and that attitude of mind which the English call pretending, the attitude of a playing child which also occupies an important place in primitive culture. (III, 296–7)

Here, of course, is one of the roots of *Homo ludens*. But only one, I believe. We know that for Huizinga the problem became urgent only when it became a moral problem.

I should like here to offer a very tentative hypothesis about the way this moral question increasingly obtruded itself, tentative all the more as Huizinga's autobiographical essay offers no hint in this respect. I refer to Huizinga's unexpected interest in American civilization. He must have worked concurrently on the completion of *The Waning of the Middle Ages* and on his four essays on *Man and Mass in the United States* (V, 247–417), which were published before the other book saw the light in 1919. At that time Huizinga had never been to the States, but he was rightly convinced that

Europeans knew far too little about that new civilization across the Atlantic. He was attracted by the challenge of describing a culture which, he said, could not be encompassed in one of the few traditional forms that offered themselves to the historian as a framework of description (V, 251ff). Even that convenient formula of a conflict between the old and the new nearly broke down there, because in America the old lacked the strength it always had in European history. The real conflict in America was between man and nature; in other words, here was the model of a civilization that exemplified man's desire to improve this world rather than concern himself with hopes of the beyond or with the re-enactment of past glories.

If I am right in my surmise that Huizinga planned at the time to exemplify his conception of the three possibilities open to man in his reaction to the sufferings of life, we might expect him also to have planned a study of a strictly religious civilization. Buddhism had failed to hold him and he seems to have settled on a study of what he calls the pre-Gothic twelfth century. According to P. Geyl it was to be called 'The Spring of the Middle Ages' and to form a counterpart to *Herfsttij*.[13] The project was only partly realized in the form of essays and lectures on Alanus de Insulis, John of Salisbury and Abelard (IV, 1-122), which clearly show how much Huizinga was attracted by the age. It fits my interpretation of this abortive project that Huizinga treated John of Salisbury's book *De Nugis Curialium* as an early attack on that courtly culture that flourished so exuberantly in the late Middle Ages (IV, 102ff). The trifles of the courtiers, the *nugae curialium*, are precisely the games courtiers play instead of concerning themselves with their salvation.

Not that these three figures represent the extreme of Christian asceticism. In the concluding words of the last of these lectures, Huizinga points to the hatred Abelard aroused in men such as Bernard of Clairvaux. He speaks of the contrast that pervades the history of Christian thought, between those who, like Abelard, appealed to the cultural ideal of St. Jerome who, for all his asceticism, was open to cultural values, and those who followed St. Augustine, 'the man with the flaming heart'. 'Whenever a great crisis of faith occurred', he writes, 'the words of St. Augustine weighed more heavily in the scales of the ages than those of St. Jerome' (IV, 122). Is it not likely that Huizinga had once planned also to portray for us this great current of culture? However much he owed to the tradition of St. Jerome, he clearly felt the attraction of the opposite camp.

Nothing would be more misleading than to represent Huizinga's rich and varied life-work as the arid illustration of one particular thesis, but nobody who submits to the spell of this great man can miss the note of personal concern in nearly everything he wrote. The concern became more urgent when he actually visited America in 1926 and found it impossible to reconcile himself to what he saw there. In the 'Random Jottings', *Losse Opmerkingen* (V, 418–89), he published in the subsequent year his personal reaction breaks through the detachment of the observer and tells us of his growing estrangement from the course of Western civilization.

What appears to have hurt him quite particularly was the way in which the various dominant schools of American psychology and sociology interpreted all art and all religion as forms of escapism, 'evasive satisfactions, compensatory fabrications' (V, 481). Maybe this attitude disturbed him all the more profoundly as it bore more than a superficial resemblance to his own metaphor of the three paths out of the misery of this world. Not that Huizinga was inconsistent in his rejection of what we now call reductionism. For him man's urge to transcend reality was always creative. Far from being a sign of weakness, it was a sign of strength. He tells of a conversation he had with a young sociologist who was ready to admit that our present civilization was no longer capable of creating great art. Great art after all arose precisely as an escape from this world, it was no more than a morbid symptom. Huizinga countered by telling the story of the Friesian King Radbod, who was about to be baptized and asked the Bishop where his ancestors were. When he was told that they were in hell he got out of the font and declared that he preferred the abode of his ancestors to the new paradise (V, 482). He, Huizinga, preferred to dwell among the terrors and delusions of an ancient civilization rather than in the promised land of social perfection. He knew it was an inadequate answer. He knew that the sociologist could have replied: 'Take care what you say, you cannot have your cake and eat it.' But he confesses that he was confused and depressed by these encounters. He tells us of a visit to Cologne when he felt annoyed by the way the city had been spoilt and trivialized. By accident almost he had found his way into the ancient church of St. Maria im Kapitol when offices were being read. Suddenly he seemed to grasp the meaning which a true ritual had for a community, quite apart from its religious significance. I sensed 'the tremendous seriousness of an age in which these things were what mattered to everyone. I had the feeling as if nine-tenths of our present culture were strictly irrelevant' (V, 480).

Here, I believe, is the new element, the experience that turned Huizinga from a calm historian of culture into a passionate critic of his own times and, if the truth must be told, into a *laudator temporis acti*. That romantic aestheticism he had always tried to keep under strict control offered itself as the only refuge from the modern world, from which he felt increasingly alienated. Harsh words have been said about Huizinga by such penetrating critics as Pieter Geyl[14] and Rosalie Colie[15] because of his refusal to come to terms with the realities of his time. I feel it would be almost an impertinence even to try to defend him, because if he had been more realistic he would also have been less interesting. I have found[16] that it is from those who react to the problems of their time in an intensely personal way that we can generally learn much more than we do from the well adjusted. I venture to think that none of Huizinga's critics I have read has quite confronted the agony of his position. What had sustained him throughout his life, indeed what had prompted him to reject romantic aestheticism in favour of an uncompromising search for truth, was a faith in absolute values, the values of Christianity and the values of rationality. What so deeply upset him was the spectacle of reason undermining rationality. His stand was to be against relativism in all forms. Whatever we think of individual arguments he employed, it was a noble stand in an important cause.

The two books which were the most immediate expression of his position are *In the Shadow of Tomorrow*[17] and *Homo ludens*. It has rightly been said by Gustaaf Renier[18] that they belong together, indeed neither can quite be understood in isolation. The more topical book explains the author's deep anxieties about the future of Western culture, the other tries to reinforce the argument by explaining what we have lost since the eighteenth century.

The central tenet that holds the wings of the diptych together is Huizinga's conviction that 'Culture must have its ultimate aim in the metaphysical, or it will cease to be culture' (VII, 333).

> By opposing metaphysics the modern spirit has abolished culture. It has done so precisely because it tries to explain away such essentials of culture as morality, law or piety as just so many taboos. (VII, 331)

Several of Huizinga's critics have expressed surprise that his book on play does not even so much as refer to Freud; the question misses the point that Freud's attitude—or what Huizinga took it to be—was precisely one of the main targets of the twin books. Freudianism, as he calls is, had familiarized whole generations with the notion of sublimation, an attempt, in other words, to explain the origins of culture and of art through the transformation of 'infantile appetites'. Huizinga calls it 'essentially even more anti-Christian in its implications than the ethical theory of Marxism' (VII, 374). For his most vehement pronouncement on the latter we must turn to a passage in *Homo ludens* which sums up the other book in a few hard-hitting lines against the nineteenth-century belief in technical progress.

> As a result of this luxation of our intellects the shameful misconception of Marxism could be put about and even believed: that economic forces and

material interests determine the course of the world. This grotesque over-estimation of the economic factor was conditioned by our worship of technological progress, which was itself the fruit of rationalism and utilitarianism after they had killed the mysteries and acquitted man of guilt and sin. But they had forgotten to free him of folly and myopia, and he seemed only fit to mould the world after the pattern of his own banality.[19] (V, 223)

This tone of contempt for the present age owed something to the book by Ortega y Gasset, *The Revolt of the Masses*, in which a warning is sounded against the 'primitives' within the gates of Western civilization.[20] Huizinga alludes to this book in his open letter to Julien Benda of December 1933, in which he diagnoses three failings of our time: puerility, superstition and insincerity (VII, 271). Among the symptoms of the first he cites the antics of mass movements with their uniforms, their marches and their chantings. In his original Leiden lecture on play in February 1933 he still thought that playfulness might be cited here as an extenuating circumstance (V, 24), but in the course of that fateful year he changed his mind. This was not real play. It was what he called puerilism. Did he perhaps remember his own boyish desire to march through the streets of Groningen in fancy dress and had he come to side with authority, as we so often do when we grow older? Be that as it may, he minced no words about onlookers who are impressed by such spectacles, 'This seems greatness, power. It is childishness . . . those who can still think know that all this has no value whatever' (VII, 394).

Those who can still think. For what disturbed Huizinga at least as much as the efforts to explain too much was the trend of irrationalism, the worship of life and of 'thinking with the blood' that was the other side of the medal. Once more Huizinga has been criticized for not attacking National Socialist and Fascist ideologies for what they were, political movements, and rather treating them as symptoms of the sickness of our culture. But this is how they appeared to him, he was less interested in the causes of these movements than in the response they met with, and his strictures were all the more effective at the time because they were not uttered in a political context. Those of us who still remember the nightmare of those years will also recall how grateful one was for this stern voice of reason. For Huizinga felt committed to reason, but it had become a difficult commitment.

These are strange times. Reason, which once combated faith and seemed to have conquered it, now has to look to faith to save it from dissolution. For it is only on the unshaken and unyielding foundation of a living

metaphysical belief that the concept of absolute truth with its consequence of absolute validity of ethical norms can withstand the growing
pressure of the instinctive will to live. (p. 92) (VII, 364)

But why and how, we may ask, did this insistence on faith lead Huizinga
back to his lifelong interest in what he called the play element of culture? I
hope my answer will not be found shocking, it is not intended to be. Playing a
game implies unquestioning acceptance of rules. If you do not, you are the
spoilsport, that figure of whom Huizinga has so perceptively harsh things to
say. The spoilsport, we remember, 'shatters the play-world itself. By with-
drawing from the game he reveals the relativity and fragility of the play-world
in which he had temporarily shut himself with others. He robs the play of its
illusion' and must be cast out as a threat to the play community (V, 39). The
more one reads Huizinga the more one comes to see that it was this character
of common consent, the agreement to refrain from certain questions, that
constituted for him an important condition of civilization. 'Civilization', he
says towards the end of his book, 'will in a sense always be played according to
certain rules, and true civilization will always demand fair play. Fair play is
nothing less than good faith expressed in play terms' (V, 244).

The context in which these words stand leaves no doubt about their
significance. Huizinga was appalled by the book of a National Socialist, Carl
Schmitt, *Der Begriff des Politischen*, which he summed up in the formula that
pacta non sunt servanda (V, 243). He fastened on the German euphemism for
war, *'Eintreten des Ernstfalls'* (the advent of a serious contingency), to remind
his readers that the serious business of mankind is peace. Such peace demands
the recognition of rules, of common ground. It almost looks like an oversight
that he omits to mention the most palpable link between games and peace
recorded in history, the traditional truce between the warring Greek states at
the time of the Olympic games.

In a sense Schmitt's cynical reasoning appeared to Huizinga merely as an
extreme example of the dangers inherent in any type of argumentation that
ignores the existence of values embodied in rules. His reading of the crisis of
our time suggested to him that an unquestioning acceptance of such rules is of
the essence of the game we call civilization. No wonder he looked with a
certain nostalgia back to a time where such questionings lay outside the range
of possibilities, simply because the distinction between playfulness and
seriousness had not obtruded itself on the language and the mental horizon of
the civilizations concerned.

Within the continuity of Huizinga's interest in the subject there is thus a
distinct shift of emphasis between *The Waning of the Middle Ages* and *Homo*

ludens. What had intrigued him in his earlier work was the phenomenon of 'pretending', the flight into a world of fantasy that had much in common with the attitudes of a child at play. There is little of this element in the initial definition of the phenomenon which he proposes in *Homo ludens*. 'Play is a voluntary activity or occupation executed within certain fixed limits of time and place, according to rules freely accepted but absolutely binding . . .' (V, 56).

It is (in English terms) a shift from 'play' to 'games'. This change of accent, which accorded so well with Huizinga's moral preoccupation, was certainly also facilitated by the conception of culture he found in the posthumous work of his great predecessor Jacob Burckhardt, *Griechische Kulturgeschichte*.[21] In his famous characterization of the flowering of Greek culture of the fifth century Burckhardt had coined the word *agonal*, agonistic, and had shown how this ideal had penetrated the whole of life (Figs. 47 and 48). Not only athletics and the arts were conceived as contests, even lawsuits and philosophical dialogues partook of the character and concept of the *agon*. Burckhardt contrasts this striving for fame with our modern striving for gain, but as always he retains his critical detachment. The cult of the *agon* was to him something peculiarly Greek, based as it was on the importance the Greeks attached to the opinion of others. This trait was clearly rooted in the social situation of the *polis*. In the East the institution of castes and the weight of despotism would have stifled such a love of free contests between equals.

It is natural that Huizinga could not accept this interpretation. Burckhardt, he reminds us, had composed his work in the 1880s 'before any general sociology existed to digest all the ethnological and anthropological data, most of which . . . were only then coming to light' (V, 100). It was this limitation that accounts for Burckhardt's picture of Greek culture developing in

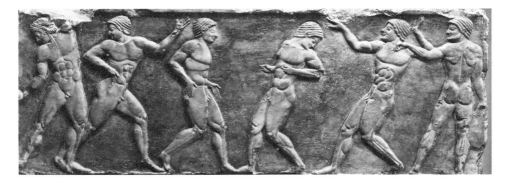

47. *Ball game*. Relief from the base of a statue. Late 6th century B.C.
Athens, National Archaeological Museum

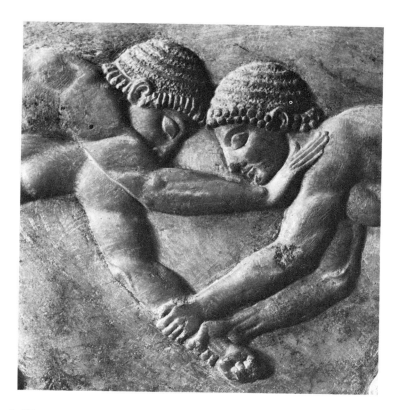

48. *Wrestlers*. Detail of a relief from the base of a statue. Late 6th century B.C.
Athens, National Archaeological Museum

comparative isolation from the phase he called 'heroic' to that he called 'agonistic'. But there was no such excuse, in Huizinga's view, for a classical scholar to repeat this theory in 1935 and to present the transition from the heroic to the agonistic, from battle to play, as a form of decadence (V, 103). For in this respect, too, Huizinga's standpoint had somewhat shifted. He appears to have no longer endorsed Tylor's conviction that certain forms of play had evolved from activities once meant in earnest. Neither in Greece nor anywhere else, Huizinga stresses, was there such a transition from battle to play or from play to battle. 'The play element' was present from the beginning.

Our point of departure must be the conception of an almost childlike play-sense, expressing itself in various play-forms, some serious, some playful, but all rooted in ritual and productive culture by allowing the innate human need of rhythm, harmony, change, alternation, contrast and climax, etc. to unfold in full richness. Coupled with this play-sense is a spirit that strives for honour, dignity, superiority and beauty. Magic and mystery, heroic longings, the foreshadowings of music, sculpture and logic all seek form and expression in noble play. A later generation will call the age that knew such aspirations heroic.[22] (V, 103)

It is a beautiful passage and a beautiful vision, but one that does not disguise its romantic origin. Was there ever such a Golden Age? For once in this book Huizinga ignores the insistent question of the relation between dream and reality. The horrors, brutalities and insanities of past cultures are hidden in the golden mist of that idyllic dream which Huizinga himself had once analysed as a projection of desires.

Remember Huizinga's story of the Friesian King Radbod, who chose hell rather than paradise out of loyalty to his ancestors. What is troubling in Huizinga's later books is his refusal to acknowledge the reality of that hell. True, he might have countered this criticism by the reminder that he was speaking of aspirations rather than of realities. What he emphasized in both books was what he called 'a harmonious balance of material and spiritual values and a more or less homogeneous ideal in whose pursuit the community's various activities converge' (VII, 332). But it is far from easy to make this idea of balance that had already occurred in 1897 fully intelligible in concrete terms. It is clear from *Homo ludens* that, humanist as he was, Huizinga primarily thought of classical Greece and perhaps twelfth-century France. In ancient Rome that balance was already gravely upset. He finds suspicious emphasis in the grandeur of Roman art and in the meretricious glitter of Roman decoration.

> The whole betrays the would-be playfulness of an unquiet mind troubled by the dangers of a menacing reality but seeking refuge in the idyllic. The play element is very prominent here, but it has no organic connection with the structure of society and is no longer fecund of true culture. (V, 208)

It is a charge which is often levelled at the culture and art of the Rococo, but Huizinga loved the eighteenth century and commended it precisely for its playfulness. It is hard to deny the elements of an almost defiant subjectivity in Huizinga's evaluations of cultural elements past and present. Sometimes, indeed, he comes close to the stereotype of the old man out of tune with youth. Having rightly exalted the dance as an expression of culture, he hurries to say that not every form of dancing shows this play quality to the full. 'This

supersession of the round dance, choral, and figure dances by dancing *à deux*
. . . or the slitherings or slidings . . . of contemporary dancing is probably to
be regarded as a symptom of declining culture' (V, 196. The Dutch is less
emphatic than the English version). More surprising still, we read that
'realism, naturalism, impressionism and the rest of that dull catalogue of
literary and pictorial coteries were all emptier of the play spirit than any of the
earlier styles had ever been' (V, 224, as above). Is Renoir really less playful
than Pontormo?

What is surprising is not that Huizinga, like all of us, had his prejudices and
pet aversions. What calls for comment is rather a shift in his philosophical
attitude towards the use of concepts. He repeatedly denied that he had
philosophical gifts or interests, and here, as always, we must believe him; but
this did not prevent him in his earlier years from taking a determined stand
against the attitude of mind that we now call 'essentialism'.[23] It may be
remembered that he had criticized Lamprecht for believing in the reality of
his concepts rather than regarding them as auxiliary constructs. Later, in his
beautiful essay on the task of Cultural History he had devoted a whole section
to this issue when he came to discuss the vexed problem of periodization.

> The only deliverance from the dilemma of an exact division by periods
> lies in the considered abandonment of every requirement of exactitude.
> The terms should be used, in moderation and modesty, as historical
> custom provides them. One should use them lightly, and not build
> structures on them that they cannot support. Care should be taken not to
> squeeze them dry . . . One should always be aware that every term
> pretending to express the essence or the nature of a period is prejudicial
> by that very fact . . . One should constantly be prepared to abandon a
> term . . . (VII, 92–3)[24]

To those of us who share this anti-essentialist approach, which is certainly also
the approach of the natural sciences, it comes as a surprise to find the
Huizinga of *Homo ludens* firmly entrenched in the essentialist camp. It is
obvious that he knew what he was doing.

> From a nominalist point of view we might deny the validity of a general
> concept of play and say that for every human group the concept 'play'
> contains what is expressed in the word—or rather words. (V, 56)

But now the whole structure of the book is designed to exclude this argument.
Like a Scholastic 'realist' or any Aristotelian, Huizinga starts with a definition
designed to capture the 'essence' of the play concept and only then scrutinizes
the words used in various languages to express this essence. The burden of his

second chapter is that some languages 'have succeeded better than others in getting the various aspects of play into one word' (V, 56–7). It is obvious that the failure of Greek to do precisely this in using different terms for contests and for childish play (V, 57–8) disturbed him no less than the tendency of so many languages to speak of love-play in erotic contexts (V, 71–2). This, he felt, must be a mere metaphor, for it fell outside his definition. What he was concerned with was 'play as a primary datum of experience' (V, 234) and it is also clear why he took this line. He had found in this somewhat authoritarian approach a defence against those dangers of 'reductionism' which had come to preoccupy him. Play could not be explained. He speaks of 'that irreducible quality of pure playfulness which is not . . . amenable to further analysis' (V, 34), of the 'absolute independence of the play concept' (V, 34).[25] In other words, play has become for him what Goethe would have called an *Urphäno-men*. Goethe had used this strategy to preserve his notion of colour from the analysis of Newtonian optics. Huizinga withdrew into a similar fortress to ward off the onslaught of psychology and the study of animal behaviour.

It is for this reason, I believe, that *Homo ludens* raises so many questions and offers so few answers. The notion of play as an irreducible fact could not but rule out any attempts at explanation. I hope to have shown that Huizinga was consistent in adopting this attitude, and it can certainly not be the purpose of this paper to enter into the vast range of problems he so deliberately excluded. But enough must be said to indicate why I do not believe that his strategy was either successful or necessary. As far as the concept of play is concerned the anti-essentialist case has meanwhile been put in a famous section of Wittgenstein's *Philosophische Untersuchungen*,[26] in which it is argued that the various meanings of a term need not all have something in common; sometimes their likeness, like family likeness, may only link neighbouring applications without extending over the whole of the field. I am not sure that Wittgenstein's example was happily chosen, precisely because '*Spiel*' (he was writing in German) can always be opposed to '*Ernst*' like 'disease' to 'health'. What has to be demonstrated (and curiously enough has been demonstrated by none other than Huizinga) is that the distinction itself is fluid and, up to a point, a matter of convention. Naturally this does not mean that we are debarred from adopting such a convention when discussing behaviour, we only must not attach more weight to the words we use here than in the case of historical periods. Least of all must we allow an *a priori* definition to block further analysis. Some of the problems that interested Huizinga have indeed acquired a different look since 1938, when *Homo ludens* was published. One such example must here suffice. In the first paragraph of the book he invites us to watch young dogs, to see that all the essentials of human play are present in their merry gambols. They invite one another to play by a certain ceremoniousness in attitude and gesture. They keep to the rule that you shall not bite, or not bite hard, your brother's ear. (V, 28)

The observation is correct, but nobody who has read the writings of Konrad Lorenz[27] or of Huizinga's compatriot Niko Tinbergen[28] will be content any longer with describing such behaviour as an *Urphänomen*. The science of ethology has introduced us to the development of what is called ritualization[29] and to the importance of the achievement of dominance, of ranking, indeed since Huizinga the term 'pecking order' has become part of common parlance.[30] We can guess at the importance of these mechanisms in the animal world. After a brief trial of strength every animal in the flock or the herd has learnt to know its place and does not expend energy in fighting a stronger member of its group. Only at certain moments of crisis, as the strength of the dominant animal fails, will there be contests for a place at the top of the ladder and these contests will end as soon as victory is conceded. Lorenz has shown that the same is true of the fights for territory or for mates. As a rule animals of the same species do not kill each other. Once the outcome is clear and dominance established, the contest is over. The defeated submits and slinks away. Even in the animal world there is no absolute distinction between the sham fight and the real contest. Both are rule-governed. Once we grant that these restraints are of the utmost importance for the survival of the species we are surely entitled to ask about the fate of these tendencies in human communities. In one sense man is less lucky than animals. Endowed as he is with what we call reason he has invented tools and weapons, ruses, stratagems and traps. A human contest is no longer a simple trial of physical strength and the loser, instead of acknowledging defeat, may poison a well or dig a ditch to catch his stronger opponent unawares. There are two ways out of this new situation. Either the victor can kill his adversary to remain in safe possession of his rank or territory, or the group can impose explicit rules for the contest which disallow hitting below the belt, poisoning wells or digging ditches. We are on the way to the rules of contests that interested Huizinga. He knew, of course, that there was a link between the craving for dominance and the role of contests.

The urge to be first has as many forms of expression as society offers opportunity to it. The ways in which man competes for superiority are as various as the prizes at stake. Decision may be left to chance, physical strength, dexterity, or bloody combats. Or there may be competitions in courage or endurance, skilfulness, knowledge, boasting and cunning. A trial of strength may be demanded, or a specimen of art; a sword has to be forged or ingenious rhymes made. (V, 134)

What these and the countless other examples we find in *Homo ludens* suggest is precisely that a competition or contest must be in something, in a definable achievement which allows of an unambiguous decision, like climbing up a greasy pole or putting a man on the moon. Granted that Huizinga is right and that even a learned symposium partakes of the character of play, it would become a game only if we introduced some arbitrary criterion of what constitutes winning. A contest might be arranged as to who can place most quotations from Huizinga's *Collected Works*, a contest which I would certainly lose. The point is always to define beforehand precisely what it is that is to be tested. The need to do so is perfectly rational if you are aiming at a ranking order. What is irrational is the implicit assumption that victory in one type of contest betokens superiority in other fields. The fact that the boat of the Cambridge crew arrives at the winning post before that of Oxford is taken to mean that Cambridge is the better University. I confess I suffer from a rare disability in this respect. I find it hard to understand the feeling that 'we have won' merely because someone has won. Huizinga would of course have dismissed this vulgar reaction as part of the puerilism he did not want to be confused with 'noble play'. It is certainly understandable that he tried to isolate his idea, which he saw as a vital constituent of all culture, from anything he disliked, but in a sense the creation of this negative category of puerilism only serves to cut play loose from that anchorage in the emotional life he had once acknowledged and described. 'Pretending' is surely deeply rooted in our need to find an outlet for our emotions. To learn to play is to learn that such outlets can be constructed in safety.[31] I know of a little girl who plagued her mother every night with fearful howls when she made any attempt to leave the room. But one night the little horror commanded: 'Mummy, go away, I want to cry for mummy'—a textbook example of the pleasures of domination in more than one sense of the term. Watch any baby playing peep-a-bo. It will expect the grown-up to ask loudly, 'Where is baby? I can't find baby', and to burst into delighted cries when baby is 'found'. Surely the moment soon comes when the child knows very well that we are pretending, but only a spoilsport would then say, 'I have seen you all along'.

Huizinga had the right instinct in focusing attention on the spoilsport as a key to our understanding of what play is about. But here as elsewhere his wish to isolate play from the study of the human mind deprived him of some of the fruits of his insight. Remember Albee's play *Who's afraid of Virginia*

Woolf, where the husband takes his revenge by 'killing' the son who never was.

Is there really no transition from such abnormal states to some of the phenomena of culture that interested Huizinga? Need we be afraid of investigating these pressures, for fear of debunking man's stature? Does the fact that cathedrals were built to proclaim not only the glory of God but also the power of the Bishop make them less beautiful? Are they not in any case astounding structures which we can admire for their own sake? I believe with K. R. Popper that what is called 'reductionism' need not make us retreat into a refusal to consider questions of origins.[32] The scientist must indeed frame hypotheses concerning the physical and psychological causation of phenomena, but that need not commit him to denying their autonomy in what Popper likes to call World Three, the world of problem solutions which is also the world of culture and of art.

An illustration is close at hand: I have tried myself to explain some of Huizinga's preoccupations in terms of his psychological development from the time he first experienced the thrill of history in the form of a playful pageant. But I would never claim that I could reduce his oeuvre to mere epiphenomena of such psychological pressures. His books stand up, as do the cathedrals, as beautiful structures, they have solved certain problems and posed many new ones which demand solutions. And though I cannot accept the method adopted by Huizinga in *Homo ludens*, I am sure we have not yet absorbed enough of what the book can teach us.

In my own field, the history of art, we have become intolerably earnest. A false prestige has come to be attached to the postulation of profound meanings or ulterior motives. The idea of fun is perhaps even more unpopular among us than is the notion of beauty. Huizinga's analysis of culture as a game, moreover, exposes the fatal weakness of that cult of change and of dynamism that has taken hold of our world in the wake of the triumphs of science.[33] Marking examination papers in the history of art I have often been struck by the frequency with which the term 'revolutionary' is employed simply as a term of praise for an artist or a stylistic change. Whether a master invents perspective or discards it, whether he paints meadows green or red, if only his art can be seen in terms of a break with conventions it is revolutionary and therefore good. If *Homo ludens* had done nothing but remind us of the fact that conventions belong to culture and to art as much as rules belong to games, the book would have done a service to this hectic age of ours. It was precisely this hectic character of our civilization that Huizinga deplored. He wanted to persuade his contemporaries to exercise restraint, to practise austerity and to seek the simple life. Nothing appeared to them more unrealistic than this plea for renunciation. Unrealistic it may still be, but by now the call has been taken up by the young, who are more critical of the pursuit of profit and power than he could ever have hoped. What attracted him in the model of the game was precisely this element of self-imposed discipline. But he also knew that human life is not a game. There can be no room in a game for pity. Imagine a goalkeeper letting the ball through because he is sorry for the other side. In life pity must be allowed to break all the rules, for without charity all culture is nothing but sounding brass or a tinkling cymbal. Huizinga did not quote the Epistle to the Corinthians, but it cannot have been far from his mind when he wrote the last pages of *Homo ludens*. As the book grew under his hands it changed from a book about man and play to a meditation about man and God.

I have mentioned a game that might be arranged, a competition in spotting quotations. Here is a description of a hunting ritual:

> Only a gentleman has the right to carve wild game. Bare-headed, on bended knee, with a special sword for the purpose (it would be sacrilege to use any other), with ritual gesture, in a ritual order, he cuts the ritual number in due solemnity, while the crowd stands around in silence.

Where does it come from? Not from *Homo ludens*, nor indeed from *The Waning of the Middle Ages*. It is to be found in *The Praise of Folly* by Erasmus.

Naturally Erasmus here ridicules the folly of man's propensity to indulge in this kind of game, he goes through the various aspects of life to make fun of the irrational things done by lawyers, teachers, theologians and philosophers, while *Homo ludens* describes similar specimens of human behaviour as evidence of the link between culture and the play instinct. But when in his original lecture Huizinga spoke of the danger of looking at civilization *sub specie ludi* he warned his audience that 'play is a category that devours everything, just as folly, once it had taken hold of the mind of Erasmus, had to become the Queen of the whole world' (V, 23). To quote Huizinga's words from his essay about *The Praise of Folly*:

> He [Erasmus] had measured all the values of the world against the length of his fool's bauble, and everything of that world was found to be folly by that measuring rod. Wisdom was folly, folly was life. But when in the end he finally also used this measuring rod to gauge the things of heaven everything once more turned round. The figures on the scale of the rod now read in the other direction. Folly became wisdom. Here he had stepped one further step beyond himself. The word had passed from the humanist wit with his wealth of erudition and his noble social sense to the inner man, and he pointed beyond the consequences of an anti-

intellectualism that remained within this world to a sphere in which the contrast between intellectualism and its opposite is dissolved. (VI, 234)

It is impossible to miss the resemblance between this reading of *The Praise of Folly* and the concluding page of *Homo ludens*, which I quoted at the outset of this enquiry (page 142). I believe that the parallel extends much further. To appreciate Erasmus' idea of Folly we do not turn to the debates of modern psychiatrists about the nature of mental illness. In the last analysis the discussion by modern psychologists and anthropologists about the nature and the definition of play[34] are no more relevant to Huizinga's real concern.

I know that Huizinga was sometimes nettled when it was assumed that he identified with Erasmus (I, 41). Somehow the great humanist aroused in him all the ambivalent feelings that sprang from a lifelong fight against the temptations of cultured aestheticism. We are reminded of the distinction Huizinga drew between St. Jerome's and St. Augustine's style of religiosity. He returned to this theme in his centenary address on Erasmus delivered in the Minster at Basle.

These are neither the accents of Luther nor those of Calvin and St. Theresa. The religious sentiments of Erasmus appear to us frequently removed into the middle sphere of poetic erudition instead of calling to heaven from the depths. (VI, 207)

Reading *Homo ludens* with sympathy and understanding even those of us who cannot share Huizinga's philosophy can hear that voice *de profundis*.

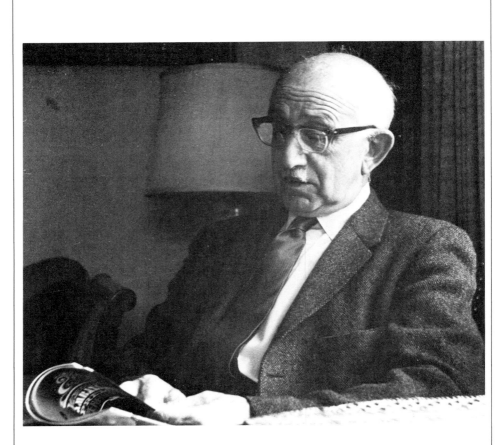

49. George Boas.
1968. Photograph by the author

George Boas, philosopher and founder, with A. O. Lovejoy, of the history of ideas, was born in Providence, Rhode Island, on 28 August 1891. He died in Baltimore on 17 March 1980. After attending classical high school in Providence he went to the Rhode Island School of Design and then to Brown University to read English. From 1913 to 1914 he was at Harvard, reading philosophy, and in 1915 obtained a post at the University of California in Berkeley. After serving in the First World War he stayed in Paris studying Greek philosophy at the Sorbonne. In 1921 he went to Johns Hopkins University in Baltimore where he taught until his retirement in 1957. He subsequently accepted a number of guest professorships.

The History of Ideas

A Personal Tribute to George Boas (1891–1980)

IT IS for me a great honour and also a great sadness to be asked to speak about a dear friend who has passed away in his eighty-ninth year. It is a sadness not only because of our continued grief, but also because I am much aware of my inadequacy to do what is called justice to this extraordinary man. He was a philosopher and I am not, and so my tribute can only be a personal, subjective one. But what else could it possibly be? If George Boas had any one overriding philosophical conviction, it was the one expressed in the old scholastic adage of which he and Lovejoy tried in vain to find the source—the adage that *individuum est ineffabile*. The individual is beyond the reach of speech because language in making use of universals imposes a network of general concepts on the multifarious and teeming world of particulars and in so doing falsifies it. To quote two of his own formulations: 'Reason stops short when confronted with individuals; the most it can do is to invent a proper name for them';[1] and again: 'Since we express our findings in common nouns and adjectives, in prepositions and verbs, in other words in universals, the choice is between applying general terms to particular things and events and saying nothing.'[2]

I have been asked to say something about a great and unique individual, and so I shall begin by reminding you of the many general categories under which he could be pigeonholed, hearing George's sceptical laughter in the background as I proceed. He was a philosopher, an historian of ideas, a critic, an aesthetician, a classical scholar, a linguist equally at home in English, French, Greek and Latin, and well versed in Italian and German. He was a dedicated teacher and, what may be less well known, also a novelist and writer

Memorial lecture given at Johns Hopkins University, Baltimore, on 20 October 1980.

of short stories, a poet who characteristically published his slim volume of verse in only twenty-five copies; he was a trained artist, a museum administrator, a music lover, a farmer. He was a lover of justice and a fighter against intolerance and bigotry, a loving husband, father and grandfather, and an incomparable friend. It is his genius for friendship which encourages me to bring myself into the picture.

I first met him thirty-one years ago, in 1949 in Oberlin when I was in this country on a Rockefeller Fellowship and attended the Annual Meeting of the American Society for Aesthetics, of which he was President at the time. I confess that I had always been a bit suspicious of aesthetics and only went to read a paper there because my sponsors had urged me to do so; to my delight I found in George Boas a student of aesthetics who did not talk in vapid generalities but whose wit and lucidity cut through all such verbiage like a sharp knife. He was interested in my paper but not uncritical of its conclusions, and I felt it was no mere gesture when he urged me to visit him on his farm near Baltimore whenever the occasion arose. When my book *The Story of Art*[3] was published a few months later, I sent him a copy and he responded most generously, repeating his invitation, and so in September 1951, I went to Baltimore to meet him, as was arranged, in his office here at Johns Hopkins. I found him reading a Latin medieval manuscript of the fourteenth century, the codex *De Macrocosmo*, of which he later published an account in the Proceedings of the American Philosophical Society.[4] Immediately he involved me in conversation about the problems he had just encountered: Surely the Magister Petrus here mentioned must be Petrus Comestor? The aesthetician I had met in Oberlin was obviously a specialist in medieval thought and palaeography. I never was, but my years at the Warburg Institute had habituated me to the shop talk of scholars and I immediately felt at home.

Here was an *anima naturaliter Warburgiana*, a born encyclopedist who could play on the instruments of scholarly information with the same ease I had encountered among some of the greatest European humanists. We got into his car and he drove me out to Cherry Farm, where I first met Simone, and also his daughter Sylvia; the talk was about everything, but I particularly remember his suggestion that he might play me a record of Haydn's Nelson Mass, one of his favourites, which I had never yet heard. I enjoyed and admired this great work as much as he did, and have been a devotee of Haydn's Masses ever since; I rarely listen to one of these creations without remembering with gratitude that it was George who introduced me to these marvels. I also remember that George knew how to change the mood, playing me one of the records of Anna Russell poking devastating fun at Wagner's

Ring. How he could laugh at her sallies! Having taken me to Baltimore the next morning, he was kind enough to introduce me also to his sister Belle Boas, with whom we had lunch and talked, if I remember rightly, about the art classes for children given at the Baltimore Museum—or was it the Walters?—with George, of course, being as well informed about art education as he was about Haydn and fourteenth-century cosmology.

It was but the first of very many happy meetings both here in the States and also, of course, in London, where George became a welcome visitor at the Warburg Institute and formed friendships with many members of its staff, most of all with Frances Yates and D. P. Walker. Each of these encounters, which were spread out over nearly three decades, was equally enriching and exhilarating; and in the intervals we exchanged many letters, for George was a wonderfully prompt and informative correspondent. He never indulged in academic gossip, and he rarely talked about himself. But in the course of the years he occasionally relaxed and reminisced a little, and treasuring these fragments of information about one I admired so much I often went to my room and jotted down what I had heard. It is through these jottings, supplemented by facts kindly supplied by his niece, the historian of science Marie Boas Hall, and the references encountered in his writings that I can attempt here to give a few facts of his life.

George was born in Providence, Rhode Island, in 1891, on 28 August, sharing his birthday with St. Augustine and Goethe, two great men he professed to dislike. He was the fifth of seven children in a middle-class family; his father died at the age of forty-two. The first poem in George's brief volume of poetry,[5] entitled 'Laius', is a sonnet assessing this trauma in his life in words I should like to read to you, as it shows how George confronted facts without illusions or self-pity:

> My father died when I was six years old.
> I barely knew him, cannot recall his face
> Nor hear his voice, nor have I any trace
> Of what he loved or hated. No one told
> Me then that death is like a mold
> Hardening souls in everlasting forms,
> Turning them into statues, rigid, cold,
> Which no lament nor weeping ever warms.
> I thought that he was gone, but he has stood
> Beside me while I slept, has walked behind
> Me like my shadow, silent when I would
> Some warning voice might speak. He is not kind,

No, nor unkind, simply a presence standing
Congealed, unspeaking, dead—and yet demanding.

One of George's elder brothers, Ralph, became a well-known scholar and teacher of English Literature, his sister Belle was the art teacher I have mentioned.

There is a moving snatch of childhood recollection in one of his philosophical books[6] where he illustrates the emotional character of memories by recalling his first school day which, as he says,

> involved fright, fear of the unknown, a severance of family relations, hostile and suspicious eyes, the warm smile of the teacher against the mocking leer of the older boys, the smell of unwashed children, blackboards grey with chalkdust, in short a great mishmash of what I projected into the scene and what was impressed upon me by it. Not all boys are terrified by their first day at school; not all children smell; not all teachers smile. . . . If I can even now toward the end of my life recall that scene with revulsion, I can only conclude that I must have been unusually timid, cowardly, shy, or otherwise incapable of facing novelty.

In an astringent address on what he called 'Superstitions in Education',[7] George confesses that he found life in the primary and secondary schools an uninterrupted torture. Attending Classical High School as he tells elsewhere,[8] he studied Latin for eight years and Greek for six, but with the exception of one teacher these two languages were developed exclusively for the use of grammarians and philologists without any reference to the contents of the texts: 'With a memory which in those days could retain anything printed, I could reel off rules by the dozen,' he remembers, 'and thus get excellent marks in the classics, but I could hardly have said what any of these men wrote about.' Being George, however, he soon discovered that one need not take courses in order to learn things, and so he began to read the classics for himself. He must have read them for some seventy-five years. On leaving school, however, he did not opt for the classics but for art. He went to the Rhode Island School of Design under Henry Hunt Clark, whose influence he appreciated. But he also had some wry comment to make both in conversation and in print: he did not think much of the method of Denman Ross he was apparently asked to follow: 'Plugging away at painting', at which he had great ambition, he disliked being told that what he was really doing was not learning to paint pictures but to 'express himself' in colour and form. Here was another superstition, for he says, 'I had no self of much account to express, but what there was of it was doing pretty well in conversation.'[9] At the end of the second year George's widowed mother, who cannot have found it too easy to make ends meet, got worried about the high fees and small prospects and suggested he should ask whether he was talented. He was confident the answer would be yes, but cruelly it was 'no'; it was probably not his lack of talent but his lack of reverence which cast doubts on his vocation. There seem to have been no such doubts when he transferred to Brown University to read English. He won all the prizes except in Mathematics, but he hated it. Though he finished in three years, he was not allowed to leave, and used the fourth for postgraduate work. At the age of nineteen he wanted to see the world and secured a passage to Europe on a cattle-steamer bound for Liverpool; he recalled how the cattle were given salt to make them thirsty, for having drunk a lot they would weigh more. From Liverpool he made his way to Ely and Cambridge and then to London, seeking work as a bookbinder, but only obtaining a post as a paying apprentice. He was invited by his brother to Paris but felt he was not welcome. That year, 1911, was marked by a stevedore strike which blocked his return. He had to pawn his gold watch, but in the end the Consulate lent him passage money. In 1913 he took his MA from Brown and then had a happier time at Harvard, where in 1913–14 he frequented the course in metaphysics given by Josiah Royce, which made a deep impression.[10] He also heard the lectures of Bertrand Russell, but got little out of his course except the association with 'a mind as sharp as a needle'.[11]

After a further year at Columbia he obtained in 1915 a post at the Law School of the University of California to teach Forensic Logic, that is, argument in public speaking. It was at Berkeley, where he continued his philosophical studies, that he frequented a seminar on the Self—a memorable event, for there he met the young artist Simone Brangier, a daughter of a remarkable French family, who took him out of his self. He also formed a lifelong friendship with Jacob Loewenberg, a philosophy professor at Berkeley, who persuaded him to write a PhD thesis. It is entitled *An Analysis of Certain Theories of Truth* (1921)[12] and was written in a few weeks in Carmel, the 103 footnotes being added afterwards to conform with academic usage. The Preface, dated April 1917, is the first of many which are so revealing of the writer's attitudes and outlooks that they almost ask to be quoted. I shall not resist this temptation as much as if I were giving a purely academic lecture, for whenever possible I would like to let George speak with his own voice.

The man who would make a study of any philosophical problem encounters at the outset of his work difficulties which seem almost insuperable. He finds that his problem, far from being the simply definable discipline which first appealed to him, is the generation of a series of other problems almost without limit. He finds, too, that those ideas whose novelty was so thoroughly satisfying are, after all, neither his own nor the better exposition of another's.

'Besides these difficulties, inherent in philosophical research,' he continues, 'there are scruples of taste to hamper one's expression. One hesitates, for instance, to chime in with the facile lyricism that is so prominent a part of our contemporary literature.' He is equally disapproving of belligerence and confesses that his essay is written with a full, perhaps an exaggerated, consciousness of these difficulties. This is a self-portrait of George at the age of twenty-six, and the lineaments remained the same throughout his life.

About the content of his first work I do not feel competent to speak. Least of all could I say where and how far it approximates Tarski's epoch-making work in this field. There is a full awareness of the propositional nature of all knowledge: only sentences can be true or false. 'Epistemology', he argues, 'excludes all talk of sensation . . . the mere sense data are purely subcognitive; they belong to psychology.' But 'the philosopher's knowledge is no more or less certain than that of the physicist or astronomer . . . if it be certain, it will be for exactly the same reason, namely that it has stood every test he can devise to try it by. . . . At any moment . . . it may have to be rejected in favor of a more sturdy one.' What has struck some observers as George's scepticism is thus rooted in his profound awareness of the fallibility of man.

But the year was 1917, and the war in Europe was raging. George volunteered for the army, obtained the rank of Lieutenant, and was sent to France, where Simone was doing relief work behind the lines. He told me that he only saw action in the last battle because his knowledge of French had led to his being appointed *aide de camp* of General Charles Kilburn, whom he much respected. He recalled with some amazement that he had actually served as *Ortskommandant* of a little German place, I think in the Rhineland, after the occupation, duties in which he was reluctantly involved in court-martials.

Here, I think, it is legitimate to fill in the factual and psychological background from his one published novel, *Never Go Back*,[13] that came out in 1928. Not that it can be entirely autobiographical. The first part, the story of life in a lotus-eating academic community, may contain echoes of California, but the hero, Harper, is certainly unlike George, despite the fact that at a certain moment in the story we read that 'Harper began to feel like a character in a popular novel, which, God knows, was the last thing he really was like'. As neatly turned a paradox as I know in fiction. In any case, there can be little doubt that from the moment Harper is sent to France the novel becomes autobiographical and all the more moving for that. Though he longs to be sent to the trenches, he is asked to stay further back as a kind of quartermaster and interpreter, witnessing the hardships which the American army imposed on the French population and learning 'a truth which proved to be his greatest sorrow in later years, the relativity of human values and impossibility of compromising when two antagonistic interests were involved.' 'That some events must result in tragedy', he says, 'is a conclusion which most people are unwilling to accept.' The reward for these painful experiences and the horrors of a few days in the trenches was the continued contact with Simone.

He eagerly seized the opportunity of staying in Paris after demobilization, and it was at the Sorbonne that he laid the foundations of his unique mastery of the Greek language and philosophy. He read Plotinus and Porphyry with the great French scholar François Picavet, and the difficult texts of these difficult authors remained familar to him throughout his life. He later made an index to Ficino's translations of Plotinus, which he generously gave to the Warburg Institute shortly before he died.

Maybe it was significant for the future also that among Picavet's publications there was a study of the French ideologues subtitled 'Essai sur l'histoire des idées . . .', for it was the history of ideas which now engaged George's attention. His book on *French Philosophies of the Romantic Period* (1925) was begun in 1921 and no doubt largely written in France. The Preface adds some invaluable touches to any portrait of George. His intention, he claims, was to describe the rise and decline of certain ideas, not to judge them; 'only', he confesses, 'when the pompousness or insolence of the author grew intolerable I yielded to the temptation of suggesting how little ground there was for his self-appraisal.' He continued occasionally to yield to this kind of temptation, not always the best way of making friends and influencing people. He was equally uncompromising in his first historical work about the social utility of scholarship: 'Historical curiosity is useless; its satisfaction serves no ulterior end. No one was ever the wiser in a practical way for knowing history; no one was ever the more intelligent for ignoring it. History is simply another means of sophistication and as such invaluable. It should be the mother of tolerance and the scourge of fanaticism. But unhappily, it seldom is either, for'—and here he gives the thought an unexpected turn and punch—'it can be known only through bad translations.' I wish his remark were taken to heart by the many who advocate the teaching of everything through the muddied medium of translations. This was not George's way.

He was by then bilingual in French and English and, of course, read the Greek and Roman classics without the aid of a crib. Maybe it was this extraordinary combination of linguistic ability and erudition that led to the main turning-point in his academic career. He was invited in 1921 by Arthur O. Lovejoy to join Johns Hopkins University as an historian of Philosophy. Lovejoy was eighteen years his senior and, though the two collaborated for many decades, their relationship remained formal. The older scholar always addressed George as Mr. Boas.

George served at this University for thirty-six years until his retirement in 1957. His beginnings cannot have been easy: he received $3000 a year and had to eke out his earnings by editorial jobs and by writing short stories which, as he said, he continued to do till he became embarrassed. But intellectually he was as active in the first ten years of his stay here as he remained. There are what one might call technical articles on strictly philosophical problems, connected with the idea of the *datum* in recent epistemology,[14] there is a *Critical Analysis of the Philosophy of Emile Meyerson* (1930), and a translation (1929) of Maine de Biran's study of the *Influence of Habit on the Faculty of Thinking*, with an introduction; but most of all there are two complementary volumes of major scope, the one a sweeping survey of *The Major Traditions of European Philosophy* (1929), the second a topical treatise entitled *Our New Ways of Thinking* (1930), a work which seems to me to differ from all his other writings by its intellectual optimism and its involvement in the latest currents of scientific thought. He felt that a new dawn was coming because the traditional instruments of thought were at last being discarded. Remember how deeply he felt about the gulf that separated the concrete world of particulars from the network of classes and concepts imposed on it by every philosophical system of the traditional cast. Such a system could only be static; it could not accommodate the Heraclitean insight that everything is in flux, for what is in flux must first be arrested before it can be talked about. Writing in 1930, he felt that here a breakthrough had at last been achieved by the recognition that time cannot be left out of the account and that genuine novelty must be acknowledged. The theme of his book, in his own words, is 'how growth has superseded mechanical impact as the basis of change and is remaking the classic conception of the Universe'. He finds evidence of this in 'the substitution of statistics for Aristotelian logic which may loosely be called a shift from absolute, final "truth" to changing and growing "probability" . . . and the substitution of what is called the will for the reason as the source of human acts'. Modern physics, Bergson and Nietzsche are all seen pointing in this direction. As we read in the companion volume, 'Nietzsche, for all his nonsense (and there is plenty of nonsense in him), was the great liberator of modern thought,' a liberator whose impact the author also sees at work in art 'through the influence of Isadora Duncan, who proclaimed herself his disciple'.[15] It is a hint which still demands to be followed.

It would be an impertinence to speculate why this sense of buoyancy gave way to one of detachment or even scepticism. What we know is only that George increasingly turned from these topical issues to the history of ideas. No doubt the influence of Lovejoy played a part in this development. Together with George and Gilbert Chinard, he had founded the History of Ideas Club in 1923, which met every month to hammer out the new discipline which has become all but identified with the name of George Boas.

In the year of the foundation of the club Lovejoy had published his famous essay on the 'supposed primitivism' of Rousseau's *Discourse on Inequality*, which opened up many questions. Primitivism was thus a tempting choice for an exercise in the history of ideas. The only fruit of their intimate collaboration, however, was the monumental work *Primitivism and Related Ideas in Antiquity*, subtitled 'A documentary history of primitivism and related ideas', Volume I (1935). The book is, of course, a classic both in form and in method. There is no need here to fear wrong translations, for all the texts are given in the original Greek and Latin as well as in English, while the *Prolegomena* introduce the student to the reading of these texts and alert him to the change in the meaning of terms.

The semantic approach was Lovejoy's, but it cannot but have appealed to his partner, who had become so wary of the belief in rigid concepts. Indeed, it may perhaps be surmised that Lovejoy's method offered an escape from that logical dilemma which George had always felt so keenly, the tension between the richness of life and the poverty of abstract notions. He had little patience with the traditional approach to the history of philosophy, for as he once wrote: 'Such a subject as the history of philosophy as a whole, or the history of science, or the history of art, is an impossibility. Names like "philosophy", "science", "art" are names given to sheaves of problems and to the answers which men have given to them.'[16] He thought much the same of those ages or periods of which historians like to make so much: 'Ages, *Zeitgeister*, national and racial minds seem to me to have outlived their usefulness, if they ever had any.'[17] 'There has never been an age when everyone was in harmony with everyone else. . . . The reason why our own age seems more confused than the past is that we know more about it.'[18]

Now in the history of ideas as practised by Lovejoy, George found a method of dissecting rather than masking these confusions, for here it was the notion, the idea, which became the subject of study, not in an abstract void but in its actual role in life, ever changing, ever new. Every user meant something

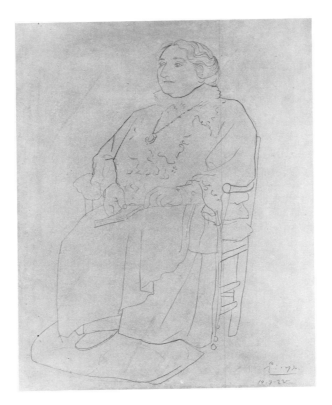

50. Pablo Picasso: *Claribel Cone*. 1922.
The Baltimore Museum of Art

different when talking about the primitive, but the word itself, like other terms, had acquired what Lovejoy liked to call a 'metaphysical pathos'; it had become a word of power which offered itself to thinking men as a basic metaphor which no one wished to question. The documentary history remained a fragment: it got stuck in Volume I, but George picked up many of the related themes and problems in book after book. Even before the joint opus was out he had published a delightful study of such a subsidiary theme in his book *The Happy Beast in French Thought of the Seventeenth Century* (1933), an account of theriophily, the exaltation of animals as happier and wiser than *homo sapiens*, testifying to the author's mastery of a wide field and his utter lack of pedantry.

A life as rich, as varied, and as active cannot of course be related along one dimension only. Even looking at the list of George's publications one becomes aware of the polyphony of his interests and activities. Thus, in the later 1930s, the history of ideas had to share attention with his commitment to the cause of contemporary art. Simone, of course, was a distinguished sculptress, a

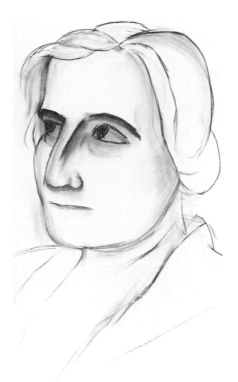

51. Henri Matisse: *Etta Cone*. 1934.
The Baltimore Museum of Art

student of Bourdelle, and Baltimore has been fortunate in having among its citizens the sisters Cone, those enlightened collectors whose donation we can all admire at the Museum of Art. In a moving tribute (1955)[19] George has described how on arriving at Johns Hopkins in 1921 he was warned that of course he could visit the Cone collection if he wished, but that its owners were beyond doubt mental cases. 'What a struggle we faced in those days,' he writes,

> had one tried to grow flowers in concrete, one could not have met with greater difficulties. It was in vain that one pointed out the futility of living in the past; people were doing it only too successfully. . . . Try as one will to avoid oversimplification, one is forced to admit that the gap between those of us who had gone through the First World War . . . and those who had not, was too great to be bridged.

His concern with art criticism no doubt stemmed from this conflict, and he was happy to have the Miss Cones (Figs. 50 and 51) in the audience of his courses on Aesthetics. Their first fruit was *A Primer for Critics* (1937), in which he tried to wean his readers from a reliance on high-sounding words, though he never expected much success in this enterprise. One of the scholarly by-products of his interest is a masterly article which, characteristically, questions the central dogma of modernism; it is entitled 'Il faut être de son temps' (1941) and traces the history of this idea or ideal in French Romanticism. Progressivism was another side of the coin of primitivism.

Meanwhile, the plan of continuing the documentary study of primitivism in three further volumes on a scale like the first had run into difficulties. The material available from the Byzantine and Latin Middle Ages proved too vast, and even a projected volume confined to the Patristic period, for which the texts had been collected, never came out because the outbreak of the Second World War diverted the energies of both authors.

George volunteered for active service and found himself rejected by the army because there was a black point in the records which turned out to concern an unknown namesake. He was then sent to a crash course in Japanese, which he hugely enjoyed, but ultimately he was enlisted in the Navy and was sent first to England and then to Brussels. Promoted to full commander he became the ranking naval officer at Eisenhower's headquarters, in which capacity he was happy to suggest to the chief that the Ghent Altarpiece by the Van Eycks, which had been discovered in an Austrian salt mine, should be returned to the Belgians. Not surprisingly, he had to write down the name for the military to remember. Let us recall that he was fifty-four at the time.

On his return he settled down at Cherry Farm, which he had bought before the war and where, with Simone and his two daughters, he led an active existence as farmer and horse breeder while never for a moment abandoning his reading and scholarship. Unlike Lovejoy, he continued to nurse their original project, publishing his volume of *Essays in Primitivism and Related Ideas in the Middle Ages* (1948), which is brimful of stupendous erudition. And yet it was no accident that the medieval volume appeared in this fragmentary form. His heart was not in it. For all his distrust of abstractions and systems George was a dedicated believer in reason. 'The rationalistic method' (as he was to write in his book on *Rationalism in Greek Philosophy*, 1961)

is the only one which is self-correcting. By accepting as a rule of thought the Law of Contradiction there is no escaping its power. Philosophy began to totter as soon as someone gave it a moral rather than intellectual purpose. For when one engages in an intellectual enterprise for peace of mind, the good of the state, or the greater glory of God, one tends to lose sight of one's error and easily lapses into dream. This is amply illustrated in the rise of philosophic sects, the acceptance of authority, the justification of sacred texts.

And George knew what he was talking about. He once told me: 'You know, I was of course brought up on the idea that the Middle Ages had been much maligned. I would not claim that I have read through the whole of the *Patrologia Latina* for our projected volume, but I think I turned every page'—something only George could mention so casually—'but I found', he continued, 'that medieval texts were as repetitive, superstitious, and bigoted as they had always been said to be.' Not that George shunned the irrationalist tradition. His edition of the *Hieroglyphics of Horapollo*,[20] a prime source of esoteric trends, is a model of its kind.

But meanwhile, irrationalism had reared its head nearer home in the form of McCarthyism and other pressures of conformity and regimentation. Here George gave no quarter. In a noble paper on 'The Humanities and Defense', subtitled 'The Importance of the Dissenter',[21] which should be required reading, he warned of the dangers to civilization from the petrification and ritualization of teaching.

We, who have the good fortune to work in smaller universities, unencumbered by platoons of deans, super-deans and infra-deans, committees on curriculum, accreditation boards, and the need of giving our students 120 points credit, or whatever the fashionable number now is, are at least given the opportunity to nurture those individuals who can thrive on freedom.

He entered the fray with zest, fighting for those of his colleagues who had been victimized for refusing to swear the oath of allegiance in California, notably Ludwig Edelstein. The persecution of Owen Lattimore touched him deeply and he organized his defence.

Intolerance of any kind was and remained anathema to him. He once told me that he had been very friendly with T. S. Eliot, whom he had known at Harvard and who used to be a house guest of the Boases in Baltimore, until the moment when he made a slighting remark in a lecture about not wanting free-thinking Jews in his ideal community. 'I can at least rid you of the company of one', wrote George to him, and never received a reply.

But his involvement with public issues obviously did not divert him from his study as has happened to so many others. How much he must have read and absorbed became clear on his retirement in 1957 when he had the leisure to gather in the harvest. During the following five years, book after important book and study after profound study came out, covering every one of the fields that had engaged his attention in the past and, no doubt, had also formed the subject matter of his courses in this University, of which unfortunately I know too little. The first of these books, a volume of 660 pages,[22] takes up the theme of the historical surveys written thirty years earlier. To quote again from the Preface:

> In the old days the title page of this volume would have read as follows, with appropriate spacing and changes of the type face: Dominant Themes of Modern Philosophy, being a Selection of Those Philosophic Ideas which the Author believes to have recurred since the Fifteenth Century in Occidental Thought, as well as some which have established new Traditions, no attempt being made to include all philosophers usually mentioned, if only briefly, in such works and little regard having been paid to traditional prejudices, the whole based upon a re-reading of Original Sources and the Whims of the Author.

Here you have a self-portrait of George at the time of his retirement. He wanted to dissociate himself from the dull routine of academic orthodoxy and could afford to shock his colleagues by his disdain of secondary sources and of the apparatus of redundant footnotes, for unlike most he formed his opinion by reading the texts.

Shortly after his retirement he sold Cherry Farm, and before moving to their lovely house in Ruxton, where he spent the last twenty years of his life, the Boases went on a leisurely tour around the world, together with Jacob Loewenberg, mainly to see Angkor Wat under the guidance of Alex Griswold. Of course, he also accepted guest professorships, notably at Pittsburgh and at Wesleyan Universities, while working all the time on his further projects. We must be particularly grateful for the opportunity he was given to expound his epistemological views when he was invited to give the Carus Lectures, which he entitled *The Inquiring Mind* (1959). 'I have always had a sceptical turn of mind,' he says, 'which my colleagues have found distressing. But I think my argument will show on what my scepticism rests.'

The Inquiring Mind, for all its touches of wit, is not an easy book to read and certainly not a book that can or should be summarized. George told me that it received not a single review, and it is clear even to a non-philosopher like myself why it was found to be quite out of tune with current fashions of academic philosophy, the positivists basing their theories of knowledge on an analysis of primary sense-data, and the language philosophers being concerned with the meaning of words. The brief answer is stated in the very title of the book. The mind does not simply register stimuli from outside; perception itself is always an answer to a problem, and a problem arises when one becomes aware of a deviation from the rule. The rules we expect to work are really habits of mind, which may or may not correspond to the facts. We have a tendency to cling to those habits as long as we can, and, as he says, 'the compulsion to see the world as regular may drown out the irregularities.' Admittedly, 'it would be impossible for men to establish habits unless there were some regularity in the world'; but 'one can find only that order one is looking for, and one never knows in advance what order will be sought.' Thus, it is not the observations or so-called facts which are the primary constituents of knowledge but the problems which arise in our encounter with the world. 'Even looking and seeing are tests,' he insists, 'using organic instruments of detection instead of manufactured tools'; and further on, 'I want to be able to admit the possibility of error as well as truth. . . . such a modification permits constant amendment of our beliefs, constant correction in the direction of greater precision.' Since I had imbibed a similar account of perception from Karl Popper and applied it in my book on *Art and Illusion*,[23] it will be seen that our friendship was cemented by a close intellectual accord.

But for George these insights presented only one aspect of the larger problem of how the mind arrived at answers to the ultimate questions which confront it in real life. Given the gulf on which he had always insisted, between the world of universals built up by logic and the world of individual things and events, he remained especially interested in the role of basic metaphors which are used by the mind to establish some semblance of intelligibility in an unpredictable universe.

To test his conviction George had carried out one of his incredible feats of persistence and hard work. He had read through the whole Greek corpus of Aristotle to extract some of the assumptions which formed the foundations of the philosopher's reasoning, publishing his searching enquiry in the *Transactions of the American Philosophical Society* of 1959. Three further books continue this line of thought, every time with a different slant. I refer to his book on *Rationalism in Greek Philosophy* (1961), which I have already quoted and which, in his own words, became a story of degeneration. It may sound surprising at first to see this book accompanied by one entitled *The Limits of Reason* (1961), but of course there is no contradiction. Far from gloating over these limits, the book points to the need for resignation and to the dangers of dogmatism. 'Reason,' he writes, 'is not religious, but the aspirations of the religious man impel the scientist towards his truth.' He finds it unlikely that the sphere of reason will ever embrace all that is now included under the arts and religion. In his John Danz Lectures on *The Challenge of*

Science (1965) he further elaborated on human emotional needs and the claims of science, dealing in turn with the arts, philosophy, and religion. 'I have no claim to be a religious leader,' he concluded, 'much less a prophet. But I might venture the opinion that if we ever reach a point in civilization at which there will be peace on earth, it will come about by the inspiration of our religious tradition, elaborated into philosophic principles, and tested by the methods of the scientist.'

Fortunately, an opportunity also offered itself to George for recapitulating and expounding his views on art, criticism and aesthetics. 'I have been encouraged,' he writes, 'to re-enter the field by friends who seemed to be interested in my arguments. All that is needed for a man enamored of writing is but the slightest tap on the shoulder to send him back to his typewriter.' The typical self-depreciation of these remarks is not, of course, intended to conceal the strength of George's convictions and the thoroughness with which he prepared and argued his book *The Heaven of Invention* (1962). It is a book which aims at exploding the established myths of current critical schools and to clear the ground for rational, sober and sensible discussion of the arts and our reasons for enjoying them.

But, he knew very well that people do not want to be rational, sober and sensible, least of all when talking about art, and he resigned himself to being an outsider in a world where mumbo-jumbo so easily passes for profundity. His audience no doubt laughed delightedly at his sallies when he gave such irreverent talks as 'How to be an Art Critic'[24] or the one on 'Superstitions in Education' (1959), to which I referred, but they went on in their old ways, for a distrust of hedonism had been dinned into them from early on, and they preferred those who are solemn and wrong to a teacher who is light-hearted and right.

Three times he was lured to the typewriter to put his thoughts between covers and to tie up loose ends from his earlier researches. *The Cult of Childhood*, which the Warburg Institute was proud to publish in 1966, deals with one aspect of the history of Primitivism, *Vox Populi*[25] with another. Finally, I must mention his Introduction to the *History of Ideas*,[26] which not only surveys the method but exemplifies it by sketching three such ideas, The People, Monotheism, and The Microcosm. One cannot overlook the note of satire which unites all these books and studies; what Lovejoy had called the metaphysical pathos of ideas appeared to George as a regrettable weakness of the human mind, which so easily got drunk on words. Discussing the term 'unity', for instance, in his chapter on Monotheism, he first patiently explains the various legitimate applications of the term, unity of origin, of matter, of purpose or structure, and of destiny:

But the word 'unity' has a kind of emotional aura about it, so that if something is unified it is said to be better than it would be if disunified. Thus a novel or any other work of art is supposed to be unified if it is to be praiseworthy, and even people have been told to unify their lives, to give them one purpose, to hitch their wagon to a star, or to seek their identity, as if they must have one and not several. Hence, to find at the top of the pyramid the One, was to find there also the source of values.

No wonder he says in the Preface to that same book that

The person who would study the history of ideas must have a kind of curiosity about the human mind that is not common. He must be willing to treat ideas that seem silly or superstitious and that are perhaps obsolete with the same care as he would give to established truths. For the history of ideas tells us among other things how we got to think the way we do—and if that is not of importance, one wonders what is.

Here speaks the voice of sanity, a sanity so lucid and unpretentious that one cannot be surprised to find how often it was and is drowned out by more strident utterances. George often reminded me of the *philosophes* of the eighteenth century confronting superstition and fanaticism with the weapons of wit and logic. He knew it was a good fight, but he had no illusions about its chances. And like some erudite scholar of that period, he gladly withdrew from the market place into his library just to read, and read for fun, for that curiosity about the human mind of which he spoke never left him even when his health and strength were failing. When he had decided he would write no more, he set himself tasks of reading. His letters tell of his reading through Cicero's works on Moral Philosophy, through Maximus Tyrius and the ten volumes of Fabre's *Souvenirs Entomologiques*. During one of the regular visits my wife and I made to Ruxton he told us that he was reading through the whole Bible. He commented on its cruelty and exalted its beauty.

On a next visit it turned out that he was working through the whole Greek text of Stobaeus, a late antique compilation which is not usually considered light reading but is valuable for the fragments of earlier writers it quotes. George was enthralled by the miscellany of knowledge he found there and sorry when he was through with it, but he knew there were better things still. Let me quote a passage from a letter he wrote to me little more than a year ago, on 16 September 1979:

I have been reading Euripides in the morning and Dante in the

afternoon. I think I told you that I had read through the five volumes of
Stobaeus and it seemed foolish to stop there. My admiration for
Euripides has naturally grown since I have been reading him in Greek
and not in those prosy translations and I even grow enthusiastic over the
various 'Messenger' speeches. I begin to feel as if I were 18 rather than
88. I can't but wonder whether the invention of printing didn't weaken
the visual imagination of people instead of strengthening it. For the
narrative power of these speeches seems incomparable to me. But then I
am quick to fly off on some speculative trip leaving common sense and
perhaps scraps of historical knowledge behind.

Who would not want to get old in this way?

I hope I have not given the impression that at any period of his life George
neglected the here and now for his love of learning. Re-reading his letters, I
was deeply moved again and again by his profound concern for his fellow men
and women, by his generosity and the warmth of his interest. But I know he
would not have wanted me to dwell on these personal matters in public. For
when he spoke in memory of the sisters Cone (1955), he said: 'It is very easy to
slip into mawkish tributes to the dead. But they disfigure their characters and
betray their privacy. A minimum of reticence at least is desirable.'

It is not mawkish, however, to remind you that as a true philosopher he
would have forbidden us to regret his death. Among his poems there is a
memorable quatrain entitled 'Life Eternal':

> Ahasverus dashed from out the staring crowd
> And struck the son of God as He trudged slowly by;
> The punishment inflicted came speedily and loud:
> 'For this, Ahasverus, you shall never die.'[27]

But it is not on this stark note that I should like to close, for I remember his
reflections on death in the sonnet he called 'Serenade':

> Welcome the gracious evening as it comes
> Like a swan calmly gliding towards the shore.
> Stilled is the children's piping and the drums
> Of pounding trucks, stilled is the radio's roar.
> Let your thoughts simmer down to zero and your mind
> Drop to the nadir, liberate desire,
> Explore no possibilities, be deaf, be blind,
> Be nothing more than fuel to my fire.
> Night will bring both fulfillment and release

From the day's labyrinth of 'How' and 'Why'.
One road alone will lead us on to peace
Where there is heard no phrase, no word, no sigh,
No question, no conclusion, only the blood's pulsation,
As we sink slowly, gently, into annihilation.[28]

It is wonderful to know that his wish expressed in the sonnet was granted, and that this is how his life ebbed away on 17 March 1980, as our mutual friend Charles Singleton wrote to me:

Simone tells that he was lying back in his bed (he sat up while I was there, with the usual tank of oxygen supplying him through the nose) and she was sitting beside him as she often did, holding his hand in such a way as to be able to feel his pulse. George's eyes were closed; he seemed asleep, or almost, when gradually Simone began to feel his pulse rather suddenly grow weaker, but still it continued, slower and slower, until finally she felt that that brave and wonderful heart had stopped beating. Death had come, and a more peaceful way could not have been conceived: no utterance, no stir from George, a peaceful exit, a heart that had been beating eighty-eight years had finally stopped beating.

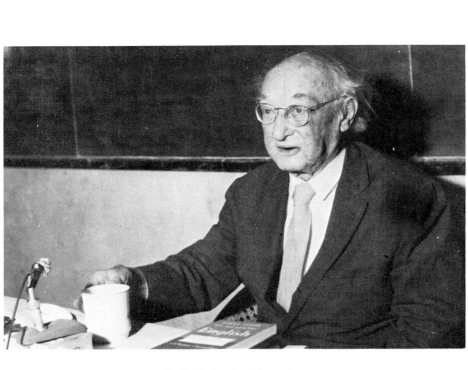

52. I. A. Richards giving a lecture.
1979. Photograph taken during his last visit to China

Ivor Armstrong Richards, the leading English critic of his generation, was born in Cheshire on 26 February 1893 and educated at Clifton and Magdalene College, Cambridge. Together with C. K. Ogden he advocated a scientific approach to the study of English literature, based on the results of linguistic and psychological theories. After his Cambridge years he went to Peking (1929–30), returning there for the last time shortly before his death. In 1939 he transferred to Harvard University, from which he retired in 1963, ultimately to settle in his old college in Cambridge. Having published many successful books on criticism he unexpectedly turned in his fifty-seventh year to the writing of verse. The insight he gained in this last phase (to which this essay is devoted) is best summed up in the reply he gave when complimented on one of his poems: 'It is all in the language.' He was a dedicated teacher, who pinned great hopes on the reform of the means of communication, and, like his wife Dorothea, a fearless mountaineer. He died in Cambridge on 7 September 1979.

The Necessity of Tradition

An Interpretation of the Poetics of I. A. Richards
(1893–1979)

1. AESTHETICS AND THE HISTORY OF THE ARTS

ANY art historian who likes to exchange ideas with colleagues in other departments of the Faculty of Arts will notice how many of the problems that he encounters in his field are also familiar to those who teach the history of music, or literature, or perhaps the dance. These historians all explore the history of traditions and conventions, because these alone permit them to assign a date or place to a painting, a building, a poem or a piece of music. Yet, when we enquire after a department in which these general questions are made the object of study, we may draw a blank. It is true that some philosophers may give courses on aesthetics, but they are more likely to discuss there the notions of beauty or of expressiveness than the more down-to-earth mechanisms of tradition.

Small wonder that many of the historians I have mentioned have little time or patience with the generalizations which they find in books on aesthetics. Frankly, I am also somewhat uneasy when I am confronted with disquisitions about 'the artist' or 'the work of art' without being told whether I am expected to think of the Temple of Abu Simbel or of a screenprint by Andy Warhol. Yet we historians of the arts would be lacking in gratitude if we ever forgot that our disciplines are in fact the offspring of aesthetics—whether or not the topic was known by that name or not. It is not long since the history of all the arts was conceived as the story of their beginnings, their rise, their efflorescence and their ultimate decline. The paradigm of that conspectus of aesthetics and the history of an art is of course Aristotle's *Poetics*, especially the pages devoted to the evolution of Greek tragedy from rude beginnings to the classic perfection of Sophocles, an evolution in the course of

The Darwin Lecture given at Cambridge University in November 1979.

which it revealed its intrinsic essence. Subsequent critics who accepted this reading were bound to regard any play which deviated from this model as decadent.

It was no doubt history which helped to soften the normative dogmatism of aesthetics and induced it to admit a plurality of values, which could encompass Shakespeare and even Kālidāsa without loss of status. But there came a moment, I believe, in which aesthetics took the initiative to expel the historians of the arts from its sacred precincts, at least those historians who concerned themselves with conventions.

I have a vivid personal memory of the intellectual crisis into which a great art historian was plunged by this move. I am referring to my teacher Julius von Schlosser,[1] whom even our fast-living times remember as the author of the standard work on the literature on art from antiquity to the end of the eighteenth century. Before he had become a university teacher relatively late in life, Schlosser had worked among the treasures of the vast Habsburg collections of sculpture and applied art at the Vienna Museum and many of his monumental papers on problems of late medieval art laid the foundation of much subsequent work. This erudite and sensitive practitioner, who was half Italian by birth, contracted a close friendship with the greatest aesthetician of his generation, Benedetto Croce, some of whose writings he translated into German. I cannot of course do justice to the philosophy of art which Croce championed with much verve and learning at the turn of the century in his *Estetica come scienza dell'espressione e linguistica generale*, a philosophy which found such a persuasive exponent in this country in R. G. Collingwood. I can only touch on the relation of this system of aesthetics to the history of the arts.

This relation could only be antagonistic, for though a brilliant historian himself, Croce had no use for the traditional Aristotelian view that the arts could be seen to have developed. He had to reject this whole approach and all its consequences, for he had come to the conclusion that art was pure expression. 'Since every work of art expresses a state of the soul', he wrote, 'and the state of the soul is individual and always new',[2] any attempt to classify these incommensurable expressions was doomed from the start. The division of the arts is without foundation. Any picture is as distinct from any other picture as it is from a poem. All that matters is what they can tell the spirit. There may be a craft of painting, as there is one of shoe-making, but its history belongs to what Croce called the practical, and not to the aesthetic sphere.

It was this radical doctrine which had such an unsettling effect on Schlosser as I knew him. He still felt entitled in his lectures to communicate his response to the great art of Piero della Francesca, but what should his attitude be to a master such as Uccello, who was celebrated for his obsession with perspective, if that was irrelevant to the history of true art?

I realize that the writings of Croce, Collingwood and even Clive Bell, who took a similar anti-historical line, are no longer much read, but I for one have continued to feel the dilemma posed by their challenge. On the one hand, I welcomed the individualistic implications of an approach which made short shrift of all versions of historical collectivism. I have always been on guard against the temptation to hypostasize the spirit of the age into a super-artist who expresses himself in the styles of painting, poetry or music. And yet I could not accept the dismissal of these styles and conventions as aesthetically irrelevant. Any system of aesthetics that has nothing to say about the place of conventions in the process of creation seems to me of little use to the historian of the arts.

2. I. A. RICHARDS

This being my conviction, I was very moved when I received from my revered and lamented friend Ivor A. Richards a copy of his Presidential Address to the English Association for 1978, entitled 'Prose versus Verse'; for he there reverses the verdict of Croce and, as he says, puts the responsibility for composing the poetry on the language, not on the intellect, feeling or wisdom of the poet. A language, he continues, has much stronger and broader shoulders than any poet.

It is not for me to comment on the trajectory of Richards' thought, but I think that the address testifies to a trait which made itself increasingly felt in his life after he had written *The Meaning of Meaning* (1923), an awareness of the mystery of language.

It was this awareness, I believe, which made him turn in his fifty-seventh year from the criticism and analysis of literature to the writing of poetry. He relates in his Address how he was writing a play which required 'some sort of song' and enjoyed 'the new exercise and its reward so much that the game became a habit, an addiction, call it what you please'. Let me quote from the cycle of sonnets which he called 'Ars Poetica'[3]—admitting characteristically that he was a bit taken aback at its audacity in assuming so ambitious a title—with which he concluded his moving lecture:

> Our mother tongue, so far ahead of me,
>   Displays her goods, hints at each bond and link,
>   Provides the means, leaves it to us to think,
> Proffers the possibles, balanced mutually,

To be used or not, as our designs elect,
  To be tried out, taken up or in or on,
  Scrapped or transformed past recognition,
Though she sustains, she's too wise to direct.

Ineffably regenerative, how does she know
  So much more than we can? How hold such store
  For our recovery, for what must come before
Our instauration, that future we will owe
  To what? To whom? To countless of our kind,
  Who, tending meanings, grew Man's unknown Mind.

It will be my task in this part of the lecture to spell out somewhat more fully the theory which Richards espoused, the theory that, as he put it, replaces Apollo as the source of the poet's inspiration by Language as his teacher and guide. I do not think he would have considered it offensive to hear it described in the terms of modern engineering as a theory of feedback. The language reacts back on the speaker. It is this important observation which puts any simplistic theory of self-expression in poetry out of court, precisely because it neglects the creative share language always has in any act of expression.

3. THE GRID OF LANGUAGE

I have no credentials, academic or otherwise, for discussing the mysteries of language except the credentials those of us have who had to switch languages relatively late in life. It was in this slow process that I learned to appreciate the meaning of I. A. Richards' image that language 'displays her goods, hints at each bond and link'. I found to my surprise that in describing the same painting in German and in English I had to take the goods which were on offer and thus had to single out different aspects of the same painting. Both descriptions, I hope, were corect, but they differed from each other in the elements they singled out from the infinite multitude of impressions. The grid or network of language we impose on the landscape of our experience will inevitably result in different maps. I need not go further than the topic of this lecture to illustrate this decisive point. My first subtitle, 'Aesthetics and the History of the Arts', could not be formulated in Latin, for Latin like Greek, notoriously lacks a term for art or the arts—or more exactly: the ancient term comprises a much wider category, as it still does in English idioms like the art of war and the art of love. Moving closer to our own day I find that a small coin of popular aesthetics, the term 'self-expression', cannot be exchanged on the Common Market, for there is no term in either German, French or Italian which corresponds exactly.[4] It is in the task of translating, not only poetry but even expository prose, that we learn that such a lack of exact correspondence is the rule rather than the exception. I believe it was also in this context of translation that the complexities of the issues first obtruded themselves on the thoughts of I. A. Richards; I am thinking of his book *Mencius on the Mind* (1931), which wrestles with the problem of rendering the system of a Chinese thinker into English. It is in such situations that we are forced to abandon the naïve idea of language as a set of labels or names affixed to existing notions—for language has created the notions which lose their existence when deprived of their names. We need not go quite as far in this approach to the creativity of language as the American linguist Benjamin Lee Whorf, who insisted that different languages fashion radically different mental universes which are mutually exclusive. We all live in the same world, but the accents we set, particularly the social values we experience, surely reflect language as much as language reflects them.

4. 'SECOND NATURE'

Considered in the light of anthropology rather than that of pure linguistics—if the two can ever be separated—the term 'self-expression' loses its validity not so much because of the theory of expression it implies—I shall come back to that—but because of its simplistic assumption that the self is an independent entity which does the expressing. What we know about human nature makes us question this idea, for we have all experienced how much man resembles that admirable creature, the chameleon. But he goes one better, he can change not only the colour of his skin, but even the cast of his personality. A telling idiom says that a given environment, social and psychological, can 'bring out' the best or the worst in us. The role which life assigns to us colours our personality to such an extent that we all recognize the typical don, the typical civil servant or hotel porter when he is presented to us on the stage or in a film. The language we adopt will mould our personality more subtly, but perhaps even more decisively. This language can become, as another splendid idiom has it, 'second nature'. When William of Wykeham said 'Manners maketh man' he certainly included language—public-school language.

Language may be described as a set of conventions and rules, but strangely enough you do not have to be aware of them to master the language. It certainly is not passed on in the culture as a skill which has to be learned by rote. The drill of imitation plays only a minor part in the language acquisition of the child. We have been frequently reminded of late, and rightly so, that the power of language does not reside in its vocabulary, but in its infinite flexibility. To learn a language is to learn to make statements which we have never heard before; language makes us creative without our being at all conscious of the miracle. Of course we do not acquire this instrument all at once, we learn, as we always learn, by feedback, by trial and error. We make mistakes and are corrected. But that is not the whole story. Somehow we must be capable after such a correction to generalize on the new rule we have learnt. If we could not transfer it to a whole family of utterances we could never make progress.

5. Perceptual Generalizations

We may envy children their pliability in casting their thoughts into these moulds, but for the student of language as a medium of literature and poetry, there are adult performances which are even more instructive. I mean the skill some people have for mimicry, parody or even forgery. On its lowest level it may be the skill of impersonating a teacher, which may blossom into a fine ear for mannerisms of speech and style and result in a *tour de force* of a page written convincingly in the style of a famous master. The reason why I am interested in this lowly art is precisely because I think it is not a matter of conscious effort. The parodist does not first sit down and tabulate the characteristics of the style he wishes to mimic. This would not get him very far. He rather acquires it by the direct method. He reads a lot and finds that gradually the mannerisms, rhythms and cadences of his prospective victim will come to him unsought. I do not know if any psychologist has devoted research to this capacity, which I would describe as that of perceptual generalization, the capacity not only to classify families of form but also spontaneously to produce fresh instances. It is this feat which the parodist performs when he learns to generate the style of an author, to the mortification of those who have valued the original effort as unique and inimitable. Again this process is not likely to succeed without trial and error; once in a while he will be tempted to use a word or phrase which on reflection he finds to be 'out of character'. How and why, it is hard to say, but it seems that people are still better at that kind of game than computers are—how long, I would not venture to predict.

I believe that if we knew more about these processes of generalizations which underlie the learning of language and the imitation of style, we would also come closer to understanding what interests the historian of the arts: the changes in style which all the arts have in common. Among the variety of forces which act upon language some may be called practical or functional, others aesthetic and social. The word 'feedback' belongs to the first category. It was coined when the engineers felt the need for a general term describing such effects as that of the governor of the steam engine or the thermostat. Strangely enough, ordinary language knew only of vicious circles, not of virtuous ones, but once a new term was launched, one wondered how one ever got along without it.

But the drifts of language also obey less tangible pressures of social preference and of fashion, a fact which we may deplore but can rarely avert. New ideals are imposed on speakers and writers which are frequently rules of avoidance rather than of use. Your style should not be stilted, precious or ponderous, and conversely it should not resemble colloquial style too much. The cumulative effect of these changes in use and in usage is a transformation of language and, given the creativity of the medium, also a transformation of what can and will be communicated.

6. THE DARWINIST APPROACH TO ART HISTORY

It may not be inappropriate for the Darwin lecturer to bring out this notion of creation without a creator which is implicit in Richards' 'Ars Poetica', all the less since Richards himself invoked the biological metaphor in earlier parts of the poem.

> Conceive your embryo at its earliest age,
>   The germ just entered the awaiting egg.
>   What were you then? And how has what ensued
>   Guided you since in all that you have done? . . .
>
> What guides this life to what it comes to be?
>   What led it through so blind a whirl of being?
>   What served throughout as substitute for seeing,
> Settled each loop and twist decisively? . . .

The answer given by Darwinism to these questions may be summed up, I take it, in the sobering terms 'random mutation and survival of the fittest'. It is this dual mechanism which has driven evolution forward, a creation without a creator, even, if one may so put it, a blind creation.

Transferred from the vast panorama of geological epochs to the narrow stage of human history, the mechanism goes under the name of trial and error. It was in particular Sir Karl Popper, the first Darwin lecturer, who convinced me that this formula throws light not only on the growth of science, but also on the evolution of art.

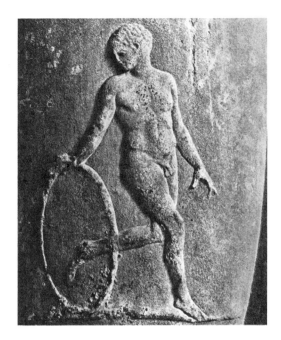

53. *Boy with a Hoop*. Greek marble relief. 5th century B.C.
Athens, National Archaeological Museum

I profited from his insight when writing my book *Art and Illusion* (1960) because it opened my eyes to the important fact that even the so-called imitation of nature cannot be achieved without the feedback principle. Even here there is an element if not of blind creation at least of groping. If I may quote my summing up from the last chapter of the book at some length:

> The history of art . . . may be described as the forging of master keys for opening the mysterious locks of our senses to which only nature herself originally held the key. They are complex locks which respond only when various screws are first set in readiness and when a number of bolts are shifted at the same time. Like the burglar who tries to break a safe, the artist has no direct access to the inner mechanism. He can only feel his way with sensitive fingers, probing and adjusting his hook or wire when something gives way. Of course, once the door springs open, once the key is shaped, it is easy to repeat the performance. The next person needs no special insight—no more, that is, than is needed to copy his predecessor's master key.
>
> There are inventions in the history of art that have something of the character of such an open-sesame. Foreshortening may be one of them in the way it produces the impression of depth; others are the tonal system

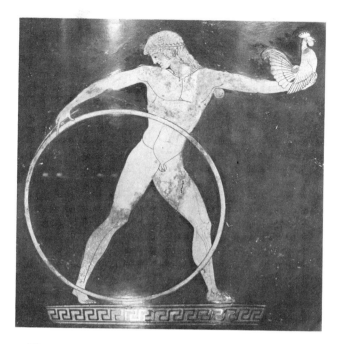

54. The Berlin Painter: *Ganymede with a Hoop*. Greek krater.
Early 5th century B.C. Paris, Musée du Louvre

of modelling, highlights for texture, or the clue to expression discovered by humorous art. . . . The question is not whether nature 'really looks' like the pictorial devices but whether pictures with such features suggest a reading in terms of natural objects. . . .

Leaving aside the art of burglary the paragraph states that the tricks of illusionistic representation could never have been developed simply by looking out of a window or going for a walk. They could only be found in the process of painting. For it was not at all easy for the Greek pioneers of the fifth century to predict that in representing a hoop as an oval (Fig. 53) rather than as a circle (Fig. 54) it would seem to extend in depth. It is tempting to say that hoops seen at an angle look like ovals, but this is a somewhat dubious assertion. Psychologists as sophisticated as J. J. Gibson would insist that they look circular because they are circular.

The same applies *mutatis mutandis* to the other means of naturalistic painting to which I referred. You might argue about whether a head painted in various tones of red and blue looks like a head, but it can certainly suggest one. The same applies to the suggestive power of tonal gradation from warm to cool tints which landscape painters exploited to great advantage for the rendering of distance.

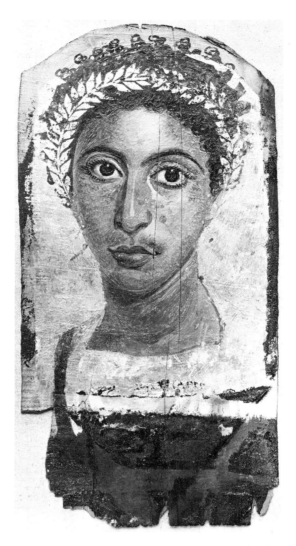

55. Hellenistic portrait from Egypt. *c.* A.D. 150. East Berlin, Staatliche Museen

I am confirmed in my conviction about the limits of introspection in these matters by the debate which was caused by my book on Art and Illusion. It seems difficult to arrive at an agreement among philosophers, psychologists and artists on what is actually their experience in looking at a representation. There are some who speak as if they simply saw a surface covered with pigments, while for me this is the hardest to see. I have frequently[5] reverted to the example of the rendering of eyes, particularly the magic of the white dot which simulates a highlight and imparts an added degree of intensity to the gaze of the Hellenistic portrait from Egypt (Fig. 55) I find hard to discount. I

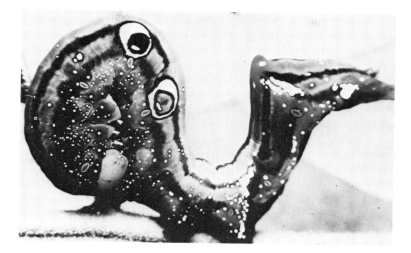

56. Larva of a noctuid moth. Photograph by Edward S. Ross

believe that our response to these experiences is too deeply rooted in our biological heritage to yield to conscious analysis. I have been much impressed in this context by the observation that long before art discovered the trick of eliciting this response nature had stumbled on it by random mutation and natural selection.[6] There is an incredible caterpillar (Fig. 56) which carries on its body two simulated pairs of eyes; together these suggest a threatening head, which the creature displays to deter predators, meanwhile curling up and hiding its real tiny head.

Evidently such forms would hardly have evolved if they did not provide the advantage to the species of triggering a response of fear in its natural enemies, presumably birds or reptiles. From ethologists we are learning more about the power of such trigger mechanisms, which release certain pre-programmed responses. Now I do not want to advocate the wholesale transfer of these modes of thought into aesthetics. We are not simple trigger mechanisms which react to given configurations in a predictable way. Not even animals are. Their reactions, as we know, are also governed by their past history. That intriguing phenomenon of 'imprinting' reminds us of the importance of what in humans we might call the most impressionable age. I would not be surprised if aesthetic effects we have experienced early in life determined our reactions in later years and if this might also help to explain the power of local traditions in the arts. To be sure, traditions can lose their hold and give way to new reactions, but I do believe that an awareness of our biological heritage should make the student of aesthetics pause before he undertakes to account for our responses to art.[7] Understandable as it is for us to ask of a work of art which moves us, 'why is this so beautiful? so exhilarating? or so heartbreaking?', I am not sure there will ever be an answer except the old one: that the artist has found the way to our heart. For if I am sceptical about the power of introspection in matters of representation, I am doubly so when it comes to our response to what is more specifically called expression.

Darwin himself, of course, devoted a book to the study of expression, his great work *The Expression of the Emotions in Man and in Animals*, which is mainly devoted to a minute examination of the facial symptoms of feelings, which are traced back to similar reactions in primates and other animals. But Darwin would not have been Darwin if he had remained unaware of what I have called the feedback principle, though he turns to it only in his concluding remarks. 'The free expression by outward signs of an emotion', he writes, 'intensifies it', adding a footnote on the effect of an actor's movements on the actor (which had actually been noticed by Lessing) and on the observation that 'passions can be produced by putting hypnotized people in appropriate attitudes'. 'He who gives way to violent gestures', Darwin says, 'will increase his rage; he who does not control the signs of fear will experience fear in a greater degree.' These are adumbrations of what became known as the James–Lange theory of expression, the intimate link between bodily and psychological states. It is an area which was of particular interest to Aby Warburg, the founder of the Warburg Institute, who was deeply influenced by Darwin's book on Expression.

7. GRIEF IN GREEK ART

I can think of no better illustration of this unity of experience and expression which concerned Warburg than the articulation of the feelings of grief and mourning which we owe to Greek art.

Geometric Vases of the mid-eighth century show us the ritual lament during the funeral ceremonies in appropriately schematic shapes (Fig. 57). We can

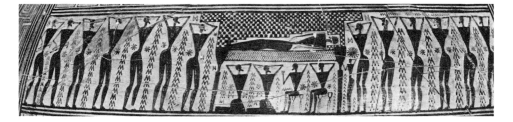

57. *The Mourning of the Dead.* From a Greek vase in the 'Geometric Style'. 8th century B.C. Athens, National Archaeological Museum

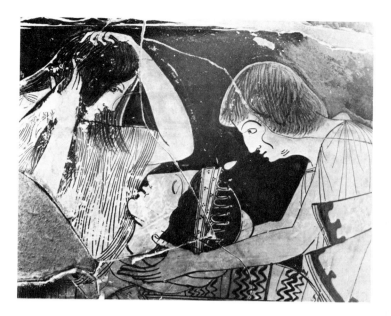

58. *Lamentation scene.* Greek red-figured vase. 5th century B.C.
Athens, National Archaeological Museum

infer nothing about the sentiments of those mourners, who clasp their hands to their heads, but then we might not have done so either if we had attended the funeral, for wailing is a ritual that has to be performed for its magic effect rather than for its expressive function.[8] Looking at a detail from a red-figured vase of *c.* 470 BC (Fig. 58) we feel in the presence of death; there is still the ritual gesture of tearing the hair, but the contrast between the impassive beauty of the dead woman on the bier and the grief-stricken man could not be more poignant. Around the middle of the fifth century, Attic painters began to articulate these feelings of mourning in representations of funeral rites on white-grounded *lekythoi*, small oil flasks for libations. They convey grief, not lament, a respect for the dead even shared by the genii or spirits of sleep and death as on this famous lekythos in the British Museum (Fig. 59). Attic sculptors of tombstones took part in this movement of crystallizing the valedictory mood. Instead of the loud lament you have the simple handshake of farewell, maybe of father and son, or of man and wife (Fig. 60). In some of the most moving of these monuments as in the example now in Berlin (Fig. 61) nearly all outward gestures are stilled, the family are together in silent mourning at the inevitable.

This is the time when Xenophon makes the Socrates of the *Memorabilia* ask the sculptor to render not only the movements of the body but also the workings of the soul, *tēs psychēs erga.*[9] It is hard to imagine that these

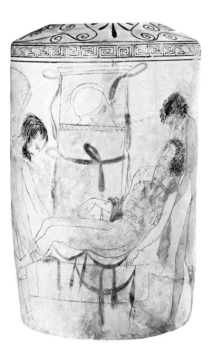

59. Lekythos. Greece, 5th century B.C. London, British Museum

articulations of human feelings did not affect those who visited these tombs. The convention, for it was a convention, must have helped them to bear their loss without denying their grief. Towards the end of that century Aristotle was to make his somewhat cryptic remarks about the effects of tragedy, the much debated notion of *katharsis*, the purgation of the emotions. It suits my argument that this term refers not to the feelings of the playwright, but to the experience of his audience. And as with the dramatist the feelings of the sculptor who was commissioned to carve these stelae do not come in. There is no reason to think that he felt sadder than did the wailing women of yore. And yet there is a difference. Whether or not he was affected by the death of that particular person, he must surely have known about the workings of the soul, he must have known about sadness. In arranging his figures and their poses he must have watched their effect on his own mood. Elsewhere[10] I have contrasted this idea of feedback with that of self-expression, which I have called a centrifugal theory since it regards the artist as a sender who transmits his own feelings to the beholder. Instead I have proposed a centripetal theory, which lays stress on the effects which the work has on the artist's own response to the conventions with which he operates. There are many ways of rendering the emotions of grief, but they may not all strike a chord in the

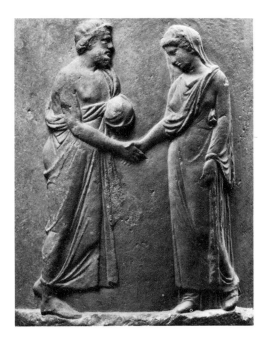

60. Attic tombstone. *c.* 440 B.C. Munich, Staatliche Antikensammlungen

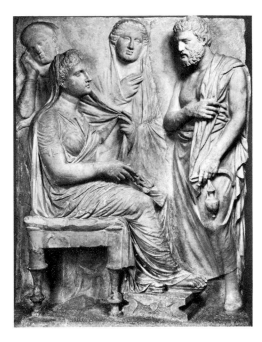

61. Attic tombstone. 5th century B.C. East Berlin, Staatliche Museen

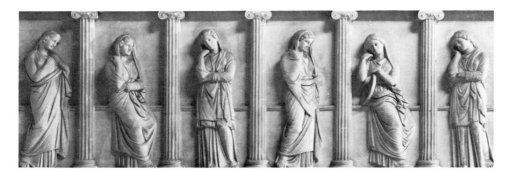

62. Sidonian sarcophagus. Mid 4th century B.C. Istanbul, Archaeological Museum

maker. Take another Greek work of the period, but from Asia Minor, the weeping women sarcophagus from Sidon (Fig. 62), which links once more with the theme of the ritual lament, but in a new style. It is a fine work in which the show of grief is fully humanized, but not all these figures are equally convincing, at least to me. Some are moving, others rather empty. The sculptor had failed to apply the test of my centripetal theory, not because he failed to grieve, but because he was less concerned with that authenticity which only his own reaction could confirm. Feeling alone will not produce a work of art, nor will a mastery of means, both have to be present in abundance.

8. MICHELANGELO'S MOSES

Nobody can talk about self-expression without thinking of that archetypal genius, Michelangelo, who imposed his personality on his creations. His *Moses* (Fig. 63) may well be the most famous instance of this unity between the maker and the work, the powerful prophetic figure with his formidable turn of the body and his fierce and dominating mien. But even this individual vision of prophetic might is not without precedent. Donatello's statue of St. John (Fig. 64) must have impressed itself on Michelangelo in his Florentine days. Some artists and critics flinch when they hear art historians talking about influence, as if we accused a genius of having pinched his ideas from someone else. But we have all pinched our ideas, because, as Richards reminded us, we owe our language 'to countless of our kind, who, tending meanings, grew Man's unknown Mind'. What inspired Michelangelo was the tradition he found most beautifully embodied in Donatello's majestic seated evangelist; it was a tradition which had blossomed forth in many great works throughout the centuries. Witness a prophet by that great artist born in the twelfth century, Nicolaus of Verdun (Fig. 65), perhaps the equal of Donatello and

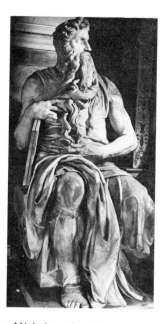

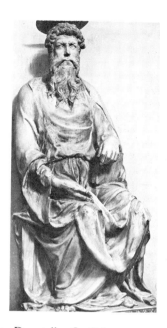

63. Michelangelo: *Moses. c.* 1515.
Rome, S. Pietro in Vincoli

64. Donatello: *St. John.* 1413–15.
Florence Cathedral

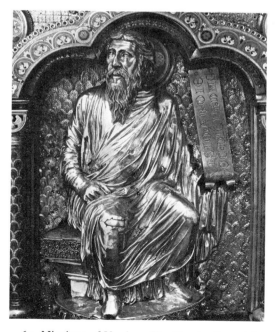

65. Nicolaus of Verdun: *The Prophet Jeremiah*
(from the 'Dreikönigsschrein'). Early 13th century.
Cologne, Cathedral Treasury

Michelangelo. It is next to impossible that the later artist can have known it. What he had inherited was the language, the conventions of Western sculpture in rendering figures of authority and power.

The needs for this mastery were manifold throughout the history of Christian art; let me only remind you of the convention of placing such prophets and apostles in serried ranks in the voussoir of cathedral porches like the one from Rheims (Fig. 66), which dates from around 1230. To be an artist in this tradition you had to be able to produce any number of variations on this theme. Today one has to go to architectural or decorative monuments to experience the range of inventiveness which allowed the artist to discover ever fresh potentialities of such a motif. Our museums have yielded to the pressure of hurried and bored visitors who shy away from such plenitude. To appreciate a work they want to see it in artificial isolation.

I suspect that this tendency also obscures for them what is such a vital characteristic of the arts in the past—the possibility of teamwork. I am not sure that in our individualistic age and with our individualistic aesthetics we can ever quite reconstruct the processes of collective creativity. It was one of the inestimable values of the rule of conventions that it made collaboration possible.

Take that beautiful monument of Florentine craftsmanship, Ghiberti's first door of the Baptistery (Fig. 67), showing eight panels of such seated figures, the four doctors of the Church and the four Evangelists. We know the names of a round dozen of assistants who worked in the workshop during the two decades or more the work was in progress, among them Paolo Uccello and Michelozzo, but we have little idea how the work was distributed. I think the temptation must be resisted to assign the portions we like best to the master and the parts which appeal to us less to a more menial hand. What I said about picking up and mimicking a manner and style of speech to the point of possible forgery must surely also have applied to the gifted members of a workshop. Working for so long and in such close association, they could probably do you a Ghiberti, that is to say, a figure of which Ghiberti would have approved. If he had not, he would have sent them away. He could always intervene at any stage as the leader of any team does, either by precept or demonstration. Like the producer of a play or of a film, he would remain in charge and take the credit. This is a point, I think, where art history can profit from the emphasis on feedback I am here advocating. It illuminates the possibility of creation by remote control.

Not all artists were equally suited for this method of teamwork. Michelangelo was not. His conception of creativity evidently excluded the kind of workshop which alone made the execution of major enterprises in sculpture

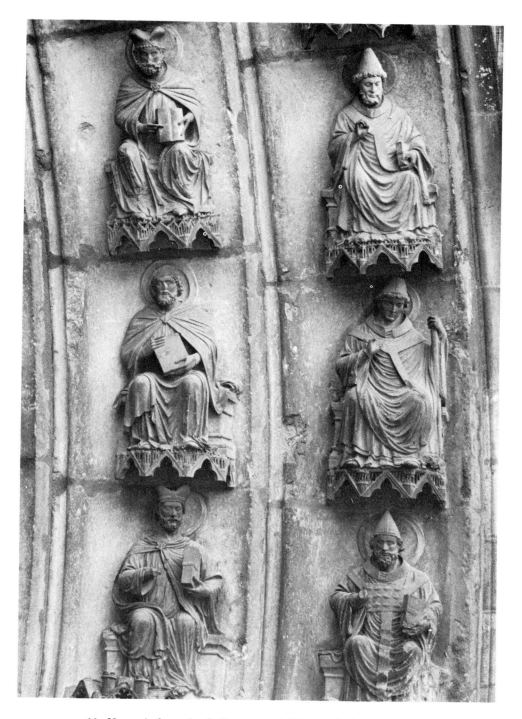

66. Voussoir from the Callixtus portal, Rheims Cathedral. *c.* 1230

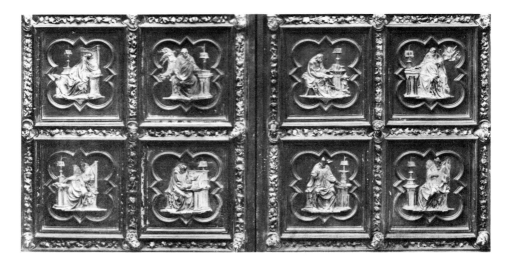

67. Lorenzo Ghiberti: *First Bronze Doors* (bottom eight panels). Completed 1424.
Florence, Baptistery

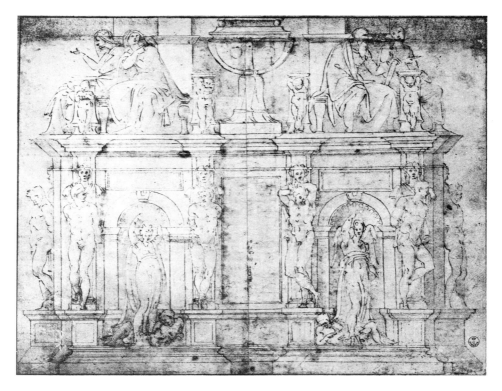

68. Andrea da Sangallo after Michelangelo: *Study for the lower part of the tomb of Pope Julius II*.
1513. Florence, Casa Buonarroti

possible. There is a famous drawing or copy of a drawing showing his original conception of the tomb of Julius II (Fig. 68), on which the Moses was to figure. It remained a torso. Only in the medium of painting could even the superman Michelangelo realize the potential of his immense creativity.

I have talked of Michelangelo because he became the archetype in Western thought of the Neoplatonic conception of genius, the visionary who rivals the demiurge in creating a world out of nothing by gazing at the realm of ideas. I do not deny for a moment that the very sublimity of this thought has added a new dimension to our ideas about art, but I also believe that for aesthetics this model was not wholly beneficial, and that it is time to redress the balance.

9. CHANGING AIMS

An apocryphal anecdote about Turner may serve as a convenient parable for the conception of creativity I have been advocating in this lecture. The painter is supposed to have 'got three children to dabble watercolours together till he suddenly stopped them at the propitious moment'. Judging by the size of the Turner bequest—almost 20,000 items in the British Museum alone—the children must have kept him pretty busy—that is, if they were children and not rather demons or angels.

Whatever may have been the intention of those who originally circulated this story, I certainly do not think that the element of feedback diminishes the dignity of genius. It may stand for what Karl Popper in his opening address of the Salzburg Festival of 1979 called 'Creative Self-Criticism in Science and in Art'.[11] Admittedly, there are vital differences in the two areas of human creativity. The aims of science are more easily formulated than those of art. Paul Ehrlich called the drug against syphilis he had developed Salvarsan 606 because he and his collaborators had tried out 605 compounds of arsenic before they found one they considered non-toxic for humans. This is an example of applied science where the criteria may be easiest to specify, but though there are no such clear-cut criteria of success or failure in art, the same forces operate which I have mentioned in relation to language. Use and purpose have had a vital influence on the development of artistic conventions and media, they have led to unintended discoveries which were embodied in creative conventions. Moreover in art various periods accepted what I called Principles of Exclusion which are enshrined in the so-called 'Rules of Art'. In poetry there may be the elementary demand of grammar or versification, in the painting of certain periods the laws of perspective or of anatomy, which might figure in criticism or self-criticism. But the point is precisely that criticism here can operate on any level of the creative process. If the children had been dabbling paint for Kandinsky, he would have stopped them at a different point. He would not have wanted a landscape to emerge, but rather a combination of colours to which he could attribute special spiritual significance. It is this change in the rules of elimination which largely constitutes the history of style. I remember an American artist telling me that he had started painting a picture of a girl taking off her shift when he saw a painting of the same motif in an art journal. To safeguard his originality he turned his painting upside-down and transformed it into an abstract. Needless to say a Russian icon painter would not have cancelled his painting on finding that it resembled another icon. He would have been more likely to have had second thoughts if he had found that what he had painted was without precedent and therefore without authority. There are less easily formulated grounds for criticism which still may be applied in this sifting process, the shibboleths of schools or of movements which help to guide the artist who is his own critic. But on a deeper level it must surely be the effect which the creation has on the maker himself which must be decisive for the real artist: the process I have called authentication. Trying out possibilities within his range and medium he will find that his self—and here I would like to speak of his 'self'— resonates to a particular configuration. It is this experience, I think, to which Picasso referred when he said proudly and justly 'I do not seek, I find'.

For there is one aim which has united the arts in many historical periods and which alone entitles them to the claim of creativity—the aim of novelty. A simple repetition of what has been done before falls outside this concept of art. I believe this creativity is inseparable from what I described as articulation. Just as language teaches the poet to articulate his experience, so the visual arts serve as instruments for the discovery of new aspects of the outer and inner world. Whether you think of Michelangelo or of Rembrandt, of Rubens or of Van Gogh, we know what we mean when we say that the visual and psychological experiences they embodied in their work only entered our heritage through their mediation.

10. INNOVATION AND REFINEMENT

There is one distinction here which I still like to introduce: creative articulation can take two almost opposite directions. The artist can strain the medium in an effort to extend its range and thus to discover novel possibilities at the extremes as it were. But he can also make discoveries by refining his medium, by introducing a more subtle calibration which permits him to bring out new shades and nuances never recorded or expressed before. Not that these two ways of enriching the language of art need be mutually exclusive.

The greatest masters were frequently creative in both directions. But it is in the nature of things that their more dramatic innovations are more easily described and appreciated than their miracles of refining.[12] I had a wonderful opportunity to reflect on the magic of artistic refinement when I was fortunate enough to visit the Chardin Exhibition in Paris in 1979. But the subtleties of tone and of texture which turn these paintings of simple kitchen utensils into the visual equivalent of great poetry do not survive the process of mechanical reproduction, let alone the change of scale and tonal range of the screen. I believe it is inevitable that these and similar limitations of our methods of communication have introduced a bias into the discussion of artistic achievements which is far from healthy.

There may be artistic traditions which depend even more on the need to appreciate such fine calibration than does our Western art. Compared to the masters of the Far East, our Western painters may sometimes look coarse. I lack the knowledge to substantiate this hunch, nor does it much matter in my present context, for I hope I can make the same point in turning in conclusion to the history of yet another art, that of music.

11. MUSIC

I know there are musicians who dislike any talk of the expressive character of music, but I think that their approach flies in the face of experience. At any rate, for the purpose of my exposition, I side with Plato, who stressed the ethical or psychological effects which music has on the hearer. Remember that he condemned the effeminating effects of the Lydian Mode and only wished to admit the invigorating Dorian Mode into his Ideal State. One is tempted to call this ancient approach to the arts, for which I have also quoted Aristotle, a magico-medical one, there are tranquillizing spells as in the lullaby and rousing ones as in the Bacchic dance. I should like to emphasize again that those affected in these and countless other ways need not know and possibly can never know how and why the spell works. They need not know about the secrets of music any more than the tea-drinker need know about the chemically active agents in 'the cup that cheers'.

There is a history of the spread of tea-drinking from China to Europe, but, I suppose, the effects of tea have remained very much the same. The effects of music have proved less stable. A pure trigger-theory of music will work as little as a trigger-theory of any other art, but though effects may change with training and habituation, no other art, not even poetry, may be more indebted to conventions which crystallized in a long tradition. What seems to me so characteristic of the great masters of the medium is the extent of their voyages of discovery throughout the length, breadth and depth of the tonal system they inherited. The mere sight of the collected works of Bach, Haydn, Mozart or Schubert is awe-inspiring even if you do not remember how short a lifetime was allotted to some of them. How did Schubert manage to write more than six hundred songs, in addition to all the piano works, chamber music, symphonies, abortive operas, Masses and choral compositions, in a period of some fifteen years? Surely only by letting music serve him, as he served music.

It seems to me that music must always have filled the minds of these masters, tunes and harmonies were always running in their heads, they were incessantly composing and what they left us are only the snatches they managed to write down when some commission or occasion prompted them to do so. I know that not only the very great exhibited this prodigious productivity. If you consult your *Grove* you will frequently find that the composer of whom you have heard for the first time wrote scores of Masses and dozens of operas. Many of these minor masters were also on intimate terms with their medium and thanks to the radio we can now sometimes enjoy their work. We will be struck at first by the kinship of their inventions with those of the masters, but after a time we will also frequently find that they fail to hold us because for all their euphony they offer far fewer surprises, far fewer riches than the canonic composers. Maybe they let the medium take over and failed to watch their own response. It is this evident danger which has given the term 'convention' a bad name. I have sufficiently explained why we cannot do without the creative potential of artistic conventions.

Of course, music like the other arts has come to rely among other effects on the effect of novelty, but here as elsewhere, there is always a danger that the craving for this stimulation swallows up all other charms music holds in store. In contemplating the situation in music as an outsider, it seems to me that the two contrasting possibilities of articulation which I discussed in relation to art, have come to dominate two entirely different branches of our musical life. Composers are understandably anxious to make an impact by extending the range of the medium by new inventions, but meanwhile the cultivation of subtle calibration has found its own place in the musical life of our century. I am referring to the art of performance. In this respect, I believe we must be living in a Golden Age. There must be more great pianists today than we could count on our fingers, masters of the keyboard who are outstanding not only as technical virtuosos but also as profound musicians who can give us the feeling that it is not they who play the music, but the music which plays them. Music lovers, and there are plenty of them, are avid for this experience, they flock to hear performances of the same compositions because they have become sensitive to the small and important range of legitimate variants in timing, touch and phrasing which reveal new facets of the great masterpieces. Music critics sometimes chide the public for their conservativism in the matter of programmes, but for me this developed sensitivity is a reassuring token of the continued vitality of the arts which no student of aesthetics should ignore. For if he accepts the insight of Ivor A. Richards that it is always the idiom which inspires the artist he will also be led to reflect anew on the relation between the forming and the performing arts.

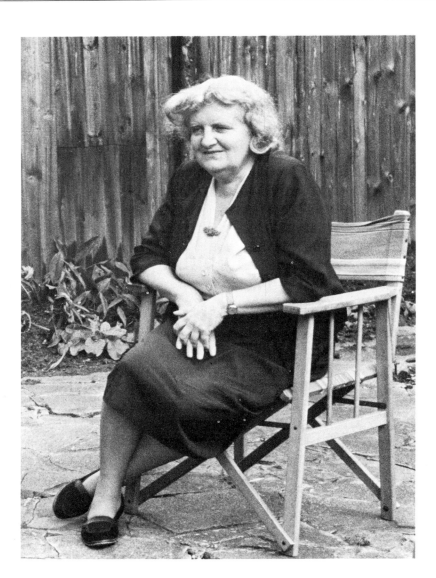

69. Frances A. Yates.
1958. Photograph by the author

Dame Frances Amelia Yates, an outstanding historian of Renaissance life and thought, was born on 28 November 1899 and educated at Laurel Bank School, Glasgow, Birkenhead High School and privately. She graduated in French from University College, London, in 1924, and then took an MA in 1926. After spending some years on private research, writing and teaching, she joined the staff of the Warburg Institute in 1939, remaining with this Institute even after her retirement in 1967. During her long life she was the recipient of many academic honours and many invitations to lecture in France, Italy and the United States. She died on 29 September 1981 at the age of eighty-one.

The Evaluation of Esoteric Currents

A Commemoration of the Work of Frances A. Yates
(1899–1981)

IT IS a comfort to me to think that the majority of those assembled here to pay tribute to the memory of Dame Frances Yates knew her as she was in life. For how could I possibly describe her presence, that sibylline figure with the leonine head, those shining eyes and expressive features which would look in turn visionary or kindly, eager or gloomy, but never, never arrogant or affected. We remember that almost childlike unworldliness which yet went together with a soundly practical common sense in her judgement of people and situations, her profound concern for her colleagues and her students, and that good-humoured laughter with which she reacted to the follies and pedantries of academic life.

Her intellectual formation was as unique as was her personality. Her father's position as a chief naval constructor necessitated frequent moves from shipyard to shipyard, and so she had little regular schooling. Instead she was mainly taught by her two remarkable elder sisters, Hannah, who was fourteen years older, and Ruby, more than twelve. The Yateses were certainly an unusual family, in which things of the mind counted for much more than worldly concerns. Hannah became a novelist of no mean gifts; Ruby, who had a talent for painting, became a missionary teacher in South Africa and described her dedicated life there in a book entitled *A Garland for Ashes*. A brother, James, ten years older than Frances, was killed in the war late in 1915. On our last visit to her house in Claygate my wife and I found Frances busy sorting the letters which her brother had written home week by week throughout his school and university years, and she remarked that the age reflected in these letters seemed to her as remote as that of Elizabethan England.

Memorial address given at the Warburg Institute in January 1982.

Frances took an external BA at University College, London, and though her MA was internal, her mind was never ground in the academic mill. I always attributed the complete originality of her approach to this happy escape, and I know that she thought so too. Not that she had not fully mastered all the techniques of research. Her first book, which she published at the age of thirty-four, the biography of John Florio, subtitled 'The Life of an Italian in Shakespeare's England', certainly succeeded in what she described in the Preface as 'an attempt at reconstructing, from material collected from many and varied sources, the life and character of Florio as contemporaries saw him'. Reading with the knowledge of hindsight we can discern in these modest words the first adumbration of her aims as an historian. She saw the past in terms of living human beings rather than of impersonal forces, and it was the way people and events were reflected in the minds of contemporaries that she strove to reconstruct through her indefatigable labours. What counted most for her in this work of reconstruction were human contacts and relationships, the network of friendships and hostilities that makes up the living fabric of a culture, and it was in following one of Florio's contacts that she found the theme which was to become decisive for her life and work.[1] I am of course speaking of Giordano Bruno, whom Florio met in Oxford in the spring of 1583, and whom she describes as 'this slender little man with the large dreamy eyes and the chestnut-brown hair'. Florio figures in Bruno's *Cena de le ceneri* (The Ash Wednesday Supper), recounting Bruno's clash with two Oxford pedants, ostensibly over the interpretation of the Copernican theory.

I say ostensibly, for the more Frances tried to penetrate this turbulent story in order to reconstruct the way it may have been read by contemporaries, the less could she accept the conventional reading of the clash as a conflict between a champion of modern science and medievalizing bigots. She had formed the plan of publishing a translation of this crucial text, but evidently felt hampered by the complete isolation in which she worked. In 1936 she put an advertisement in the *Times Literary Supplement* about her project. This brought a response from Dorothea Waley Singer, the wife of Charles Singer, the historian of science, a response which was decisive for her life and for ours. For the Singers invited her to their house at Par together with Edgar Wind, who brought her into the circle of the Warburg Institute, then recently arrived from Hamburg. The experience of meeting this small band of refugee scholars who had brought Aby Warburg's library and ideas to these shores must have struck a chord in her, and her loyalty to this Institute never wavered, as she so nobly showed in her will.

In some of her contributions to the first numbers of our journal she set out her new interpretations of Giordano Bruno's attitudes and aims. She argued that the Oxford pedants he attacked were not the medievalizers but the anti-scholastic grammarians, and that for him the doctrine of Copernicus was a Pythagorean mystery which pointed the way to a spiritual renewal. This lapsed Dominican who had been sent to Elizabethan England with a letter from the King of France was revealed as the champion of the movement of the *'politiques'* who hoped to heal the religious divisions of Europe by opposing both the Protestant radicals and the Catholic fanatics.

It was clearly incumbent on her to trace the ramifications and manifestations of this movement. This she did in her monumental study of *The French Academies of the Sixteenth Century*, which came out in 1947[2] but is reported as complete in the first *Annual Report* of this Institute, covering the year 1940–1.

In this great book, which testifies to her staggering erudition, she gave a further indication of how she conceived of her work as an historian. I refer to the opening paragraph of the tenth chapter, which I had rather quote than paraphrase:

> The political and religious history of the sixteenth century in France is usually written from the point of view of its disunity; the wearisome story of the campaigns of the religious wars has been told again and again, and the fanatical hatred animating the opposing parties has been painted in the darkest colours. Such a picture is a true reflection of the grim events which actually occurred. Nevertheless, history as it actually occurs is not quite the whole of history, for it leaves out of account the hopes which never materialised, the attempts to prevent the outbreak of wars, the futile efforts to solve differences by conciliatory methods. Hopes such as these are as much a part of history as the terrible events which falsify them, and in trying to assess the influence of their times upon idealists and lovers of peaceful activities such as our poets and academicians the hopes are perhaps as important as the events.

No wonder that hard-headed historians, reading such words, did not quite know at first how to place her. No Board of Studies, as far as I know, has ever introduced 'hopes' among the options, and so her pursuit of hopes and dreams seemed to place her outside the pale of orthodox studies. But no wonder either that, after thirty more years of unceasing work among the texts and documents, she was recognized as the pathfinder she was; her books had made her famous, she had vindicated her faith in the historical importance of dreams and dreamers for the course of civilization.

Dreams are notoriously hard to explain to the wide-awake mind; their images are elusive and fragile, like the wings of a butterfly. It was precisely here that Frances Yates found she could profit from her contact with the Warburgians, who had always urged the relevance of visual evidence for the study of cultural history. She gave a new emphasis and a new twist to this approach by concentrating on those ephemeral images which only the historical imagination can reconstruct, the pageants and festivals, the masques and ballets, designed to entertain, and to instil in the minds of the mighty a glimpse of higher values, of possibilities beyond the reach of conventional argument. She was to make these mute images yield their secret message, as she did in *The French Academies* and in the dazzling interpretation of the Valois tapestries. She paid equal attention to the verbal images of rhetoric, propaganda and poetry of the Elizabethan age and she studied the dream of a world empire that had been adapted and sometimes perverted by the newly emergent nation-states but still held the promise for war-torn Europe of a return to chivalry and noble deeds.

Since I had come to the Institute early in 1936 I must have been there at the time of her first visits, but frankly I do not remember them, nor do I have very vivid memories of her from the time when she had joined the commune of Warburg scholars evacuated to the Lea near Denham and had taken charge of the Institute's publications.

It was different when I returned after the war late in 1945. At that time the Institute was housed in South Kensington, in the former Senate and Library premises in the Imperial Institute Building, and there I was privileged to experience the triumph of mind over matter. There was a self-service canteen in the dark and dismal basement which served some of the vilest food on offer even in those days of austerity. Not all my colleagues braved these horrors of dubious mince-meat, soggy greens and mashed potatoes made of 'pom', but I do not think that Frances Yates or Rudi Wittkower ever noticed what they were eating. I did, but I often sat down with them and sometimes with Charles Mitchell at one of the long tables to listen to their inspiring conversations. The depressing surroundings were turned as by magic into one of those academies which were the topic of Frances's research.

The Warburg Institute never was, and I trust will never be, a mutual admiration society. We did not necessarily agree with each other, and in those early years Frances had to submit to a good deal of criticism, especially from the instinctive scepticism of Fritz Saxl and the more measured probing of Gertrud Bing, who always read her drafts and returned them with her polite but unsparing comments. Frances was to pay a moving tribute to the role of this catalyst in the preface to her *Art of Memory*.[3]

But though she was always ready to accept criticism in matters of detail and presentation, she generally stood her ground when it came to larger issues. Rather than give up her interpretation she would go on rooting among the sources till she found another text or image that seemed to her to clinch the argument. There can be few of us who have not occasionally felt a little giddy when trying to follow her reading of the evidence, but in the course of the years I have come to think that there is a quality in her historical intuition which we disregard at our peril. I mean the rapport she had established with the people of the past. She had always been a reader of primary rather than of secondary sources and though her disregard of established views would make one pause, one had to concede that she had come to understand the mentality of past ages with greater immediacy than most of us.

When, in discussing Baïf's Academy, she writes, for instance, that 'all hope is not lost of finding some healing way of mediation with which to soothe the agony of Europe's soul' we sense that she is giving voice to an authentic feeling which contemporaries could not have dared to formulate quite in that way but which they would have recognized as their own. If she appeared on occasion to dig in her heels under attack it was because she felt it her duty to lend a voice to such hopes and longings of a tormented age.

The mad and maddening writings of Giordano Bruno still challenged her understanding and demanded that she should appreciate his dream of supernatural powers to be achieved through spiritual techniques. Once more her interest in the visual image bore fruit, for that art of memory which Bruno taught in England turned out to rely on the manipulation of such images, a tradition expounded by Frances in what is perhaps the most original of all her original books. She found this art to be linked in Bruno's mind and practice with the Great Art, the *Ars Magna* of the thirteenth-century Catalan philosopher and mystic Ramón Lull, with which she wrestled in years of truly heroic study. But for her the turning-point came when it dawned on her quite suddenly, as she wrote, that the long-sought clue to the enigma of Bruno was to be found in the esoteric writings attributed to Hermes Trismegistus (Fig. 70). To these pseudo-Egyptian texts, which were regarded with awe in the Renaissance, she was to add that other mystical current, the Jewish Cabbala, as another source of insights.

What attracted her in these newly found trends was again the element of hope, the hope cherished by some of the best minds of the age, of healing the agonies of a divided Europe by rising beyond dogma to a higher truth, the hope which made Bruno write that 'true religion should be without controversy and dispute'. His vision of the dawn of a coming age of the sun blended with the old dreams of a beneficent world ruler. Frances Yates became increasingly absorbed in the various manifestations of this current, but she made no concessions herself to occultism of any form. In her interpretation, which she presented in her riveting book, *The Rosicrucian Enlightenment*,[4] it was the rational scientific revolution of the seventeenth century which reaped the harvest of these fantastic dreams.

But while science was in need of rationality, poetry was not. 'Looking back, it seems to me', she once wrote, 'that I always had behind me or within me the thought of Shakespeare.' She had followed her book on Florio with one on *Love's Labour's Lost*,[5] but it did not satisfy her. In her essay on 'Elizabeth as Astraea' she hinted that the key to Shakespeare might be found in the very tension between the optimistic imagery of the age and its terrible realities. No wonder that she scrutinized the tradition of Hermeticism and that of the art of memory for further clues towards an understanding of Shakespeare's mind and thought. In *Theatre of the World*[6] she tried to forge such links through the figure of John Dee, magician and Vitruvian, and through Robert Fludd, whose memory theatre she wished to connect with Shakespeare's Globe. But only when she was invited to give the Lord Northcliffe Lectures in 1974 did she venture into the open in her interpretation of the last plays, which she sees as manifestations of the hopes aroused by what she calls the Elizabethan revival under James I, another hope cruelly dispelled by the death of Prince Henry and the re-orientation of British policy. In her last book, *The Occult Philosophy in the Elizabethan Age*,[7] she wished to give yet further substance to that vision of a reformist movement based on the Christian Cabbala.

It would be hybris and folly for me to attempt an evaluation of any of these works or indeed even of any of her individual themes and theories. What I want to bring out in conclusion are the moral qualities of her personality, qualities which must surely figure prominently in any future study of her life and work. The first is her uncompromising sense of values, the second her intellectual courage.

I have said enough about the first to have made it clear that hers was not the cool detachment of the academic historian who tries to chronicle past events for their own sake. She made no secret of who were her favourites and who her villains. One need only look at the moving last chapters of her book on the Valois tapestries[8] to find her sympathies and hatred splendidly engaged, as when she castigates the cold egotism and overweening vanity of the impossible Duke of Anjou, or read in her Shakespearian lectures how bitterly she regretted the role England played or refused to play in the tragedy of the Winter King. Cruelty, intolerance, bigotry and pedantry were responsible for what she sometimes called the 'lost moment in history'.

When I mentioned her courage I was thinking not only of her willingness to make a stand for any value she believed in, but also of that intrepid

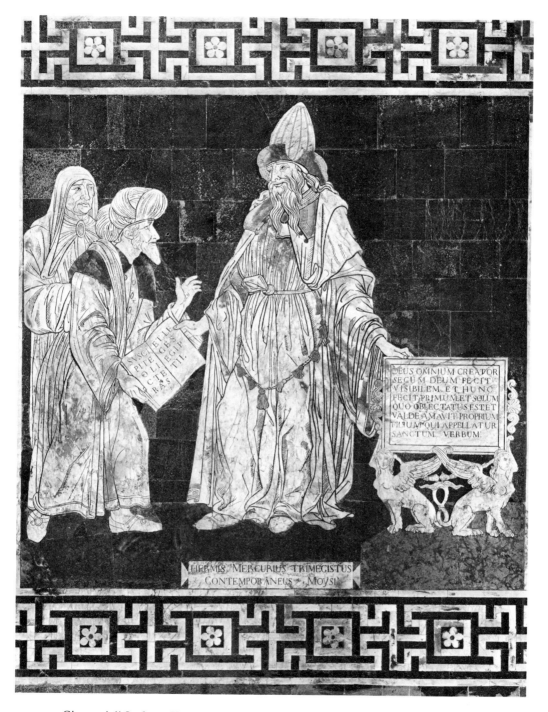

70. Giovanni di Stefano: *Hermes Trismegistus*. 1488. From the pavement of Siena Cathedral

determination with which she threw herself into problems of research which had daunted all her predecessors and colleagues. No doubt her intelligence, her independence and her immense capacity for work gave her confidence. I remember that when she became interested in Lullian or pseudo-Lullian astrology she told me that there was an unpublished fourteenth-century manuscript in Catalan in the British Museum which she would have to read. She never had formally studied medieval Catalan, and the book was in a difficult script, but being Frances she ploughed through the whole codex to gain a better picture of what Lullian astrology was like.

Not that she would claim to have mastered it in one go. It was part of her unconventional courage that she was never afraid of telling the reader of her failures to understand a particular text or doctrine. She wanted neither to abandon her quest nor to pretend to know more than she did. She wholly lacked false modesty and false pride. In a characteristic passage from the final pages of her astounding study of the art of Ramón Lull you will again hear her authentic voice, and though it is not short I should like to quote it:

This article has concluded nothing, for it is not an end but a beginning. The Lullian Art still looms in mystery like some huge unclimbed mountain. One might call the present effort a reconnaissance expedition searching out new routes for some future attempt on the summit. Only a beginning has been made at trying to clear the entrance to some long forgotten tracks of ascent and descent and it would be futile to speculate on the nature of the mountain as a whole until these have been further pursued. They lead into country much of which is unexplored, the mass of the unpublished works of Ramón Lull, and the mass of his published works which is almost equally unexplored from the points of view here suggested. The task of going through all this material is one of extreme difficulty, labour and complexity, needing expert knowledge in many fields, and I publish the present attempt at mapping out some of the routes in the hope of enlisting co-operation. My aim has been to re-open the problem of Ramón Lull and his Art through suggesting some fresh ways of approaching the problem. To prove these suggestions either right or wrong will involve stirring up, sifting, and bringing to light the Lullian material, and that is bound to be an instructive and illuminating process. Lullism is no unimportant side-issue in the history of Western civilization. Its influence over five centuries was incalculably great.[9]

Reading this heartfelt appeal, penned in 1954, in the situation of today, one cannot help asking, 'But who will be equipped in the future to carry on with this work of exploring and sifting material of such extreme difficulty? Who will be allowed to acquire that expert knowledge in many fields to prove her suggestions either right or wrong?' I hope these need not be idle rhetorical questions. I believe that if we wish to honour her memory we just must not allow her life and times to represent yet another lost moment in history.

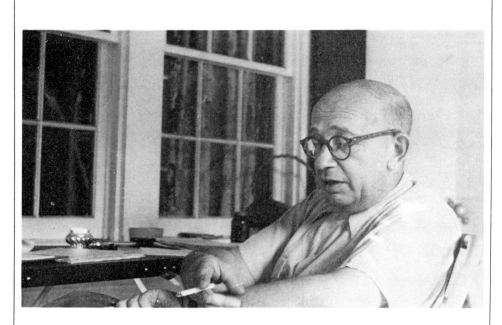

71. Ernst Kris.
1951. Photograph by the author

Ernst Kris, art historian and psychoanalyst, was born in Vienna on 26 April 1900. He graduated in 1922 in the History of Art from Vienna University and joined the staff of the Kunsthistorische Museum of Vienna as a curator of the collection of Sculpture and Applied Art. In 1927 he became an associate member of the Vienna Institute for Psychoanalysis and combined these two areas of interest until his emigration to England in 1938. In 1940 he went to the United States where he devoted his attention to the psychology of propaganda. After the war he directed various research projects for Yale University. He died in New York on 27 February 1957.

The Study of Art and the Study of Man

Reminiscences of Collaboration with Ernst Kris (1900–1957)

A WELL-DOCUMENTED biography of Ernst Kris would surely make absorbing reading, not only because of the acuteness of his intellect, but also because of the influence he exerted on so many fields in the course of a relatively brief career. The purpose of these pages is much more modest: to offer a brief account of my personal recollections gathered during the twenty-two years I had the privilege of working with him, first as his assistant and later as his friend and co-author of a book that was never published. Given the circumstances of our collaboration, my view of him will inevitably be fragmentary. Others who knew him—his professional colleagues and his patients—must have seen different sides of his rich personality.

The career of Ernst Kris was unusual from the beginning. When he was still a schoolboy the shortages of the war years made it necessary for the Gymnasium he attended in Vienna to work in rotating shifts so as to save coal. Certain mornings, therefore, the pupils were free; some probably used this opportunity for sport or pleasure. Kris discovered that it was possible on these mornings to smuggle himself into the University, passing himself off as a student. He must have developed his interest in art history very early, for it was to lectures in that subject he went. Thus he followed several courses of lectures given by Max Dvořák, the pioneer of *Geistesgeschichte*. Later in life he liked to imitate the intense manner in which that champion of Mannerism and Expressionism would present an imaginary encounter on the steps of St. Peter's in Rome between Michelangelo and Ignatius of Loyola. Though Kris, in his youth, might have found Dvořák's bias for the Counter-Reformation acceptable, he soon distanced himself from this current and turned with sympathy and understanding to the teaching of Dvořák's successor at the

Based on the Introduction to the Italian edition of Ernst Kris's Psychoanalytic Explorations in Art, *1967.*

University of Vienna, Julius von Schlosser. It was under Schlosser, the great humanist, friend of Benedetto Croce and explorer of the *Letteratura Artistica*, that Kris took his doctorate, and Schlosser always used to refer to him as '*mein Urschüler*' (my arch-and-original pupil). Indeed, even during dark days of the war, when Kris lived in exile, Schlosser went out of his way to pay tribute to his former student in a footnote to his book on Ghiberti.

It must have been through Schlosser that Kris turned his interest to those sections of the Vienna collection which the older scholar had tended with such loving care, the collections of sculpture and applied art with their treasures of Renaissance bronzes, of goldsmith work, of Gothic statuary and Renaissance *Kleinkunst*. The bronzes were in good hands with the appointment of Leo Planiscig, the connoisseur of Italian Renaissance sculpture, and so it was natural for the junior scholar to busy himself with the remainder of that fabulous princely collection. He became Keeper of that section in his early twenties, and his bibliography shows that he started publishing monographic studies of individual pieces by the goldsmith Jamnitzer and the Augsburg sculptor Daucher as early as 1921/22. At the same time he prepared the publication of his doctoral thesis, a study of the *Stil rustique*[1] (1926) which led him far beyond questions of connoisseurship to face the problem of naturalism in its extreme form, the casts which Wenzel Jamnitzer and Bernard Palissy made of real insects and animals for decorative use in their products (Fig. 72). The borderland between Renaissance science and Renaissance art was explored in this fertile paper, which dealt with a current of the sixteenth century that had long been neglected. Kris continued to publish monographic studies of interesting items in the collection and strengthened his knowledge of late medieval sculpture. But the main need was for a scientific catalogue of those riches of the Habsburg Collection which did not much appeal to contemporary taste but were of unique historical importance, the goldsmith work and the engraved gems. Before he had reached his thirtieth year Kris had made himself into an international authority in these intricate and remote fields of study. He did documentary research in Italian archives about the families of craftsmen who excelled in these techniques, he examined the treasures of the old princely and ecclesiastical collections. I remember him telling how he was working among the church plate and reliquaries of the *tesoro* of St. Peter's when a large group of cardinals passed by and began first to watch and then to question him till he felt proudly that he was receiving these dignitaries in audience—no doubt responding in faultless Italian. He was called to New York to catalogue the post-classical cameos of the Milton Weil Collection, having published the standard book on the *Meister und Meisterwerke der Steinschneidekunst in der italienischen Renaissance*.[2] He

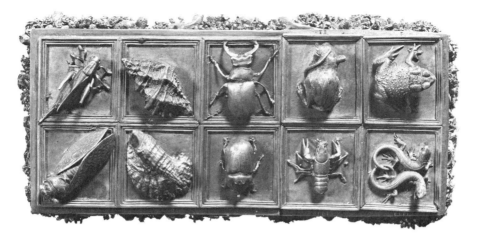

72. Wenzel Jamnitzer (1509–1585): *Writing-box*. Vienna, Kunsthistorisches Museum

and Planiscig formed a splendid team and enjoyed their expertise. They had developed a private code for discussing works of art submitted to their opinion and if they suspected a fake they would ask each other whether it should not be attributed to 'Maledetto da Maiano'. It was Planiscig, by the way, who in one of these situations first unmasked a forgery by Dossena, an incident which led to the forger's downfall.

It was in that period, around 1931, that I first met Ernst Kris in his offices in the Kunsthistorische Museum. Nine years younger than he, I was then a student, in my third year, of Art History and Archaeology at the University of Vienna under Julius von Schlosser. Schlosser liked to teach at the Museum and to select for his seminars some puzzling objects, which he asked his students to investigate. I had been assigned the study of a medieval ivory and had to apply to Ernst Kris for permission to examine it in my hands. I remember that this first encounter was not propitious. Kris was not encouraging. He thought there was no chance for me to find out anything which Goldschmidt, the great authority, had not observed before. But though he was critical of the project, he was interested in the student. Indeed, as I had to repeat these visits to his office, he suddenly warmed to the task of opening my eyes to the problems of the calling I had apparently selected in my foolish ignorance. 'Why', he burst out, 'do you want to study the history of art?' And as I presumably looked rather sheepish, he started on a long and logical indictment of such a career.

Do you want to be a dealer? Do you want to write expert opinions for collectors? If not, why are you here? To say you like art is no sufficient reason. If you do and can afford it become a collector yourself. But if your interest is intellectual, you must realize that you have chosen the wrong field. We really know too little about art to make any valid statements. The best our colleagues can do is to escape to some more advanced branch of study; they want to draw on psychology, but really psychology is not yet sufficiently developed to help the art historian. Take my advice, and change your subject.

I confess that I was too determined or too lazy to take his advice. But it certainly impressed me to hear such a successful specialist speak with such lack of respect of his own achievements. I tried to laugh it off at the time, and when we produced our annual comedy at the University in 1932 I put these words of Ernst Kris (comically versified) into the mouth of the personification of Doubt, a tempting demon eager to divert the student from his path. Kris was in the audience, and his reaction was characteristic: 'Tell me', he said, 'why do you really study the history of art, if you can write such plays?' He never retracted, and I now know that this little interview must indeed have had a lasting effect on my development. I never became the kind of art historian Kris wanted to castigate in his homily, indeed I never became the expert and master of a field such as Kris had become before he was thirty.

Of course I did not know then that the advice Kris had been trying to give to the young student reflected a profound crisis in his life. He himself toyed at the time with the idea of giving up art history because of his increasing absorption in psychoanalysis.

The reasons for this change of interest were originally biographical. After a long courtship Kris had married in 1927 Marianne Rie, the daughter of an intimate friend of Sigmund Freud, who was also the family doctor of the Freuds and Freud's regular partner in the weekly card game (*Tarockpartie*). Marianne was a young psychoanalyst. Freud suggested that in the circumstances it would be wise for her fiancé to undergo analysis, which he did in 1924. But maybe it was one particular incident which turned the mind of Ernst Kris away from the orthodox method of studying works of art, which he had practised with such skill and success. Having become interested in Baroque sculpture he once visited the Vienna Belvedere, where the long series of physiognomic studies by Messerschmidt is exhibited, to which he was later to devote two important studies. It was Marianne who asked him in front of these busts whether Messerschmidt had been insane. She felt intuitively that there was a psychotic element in the grimacing faces (Figs. 73 and 74). Looking into the master's biography Kris found her intuition confirmed. He began to work on a detailed monographic study of these heads for the *Jahrbuch* of his

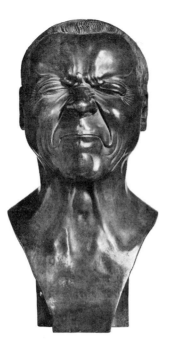

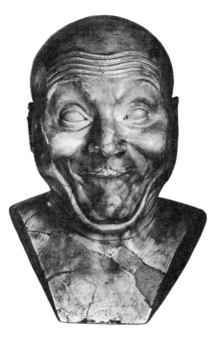

73. Franz Xaver Messerschmidt:
The Morose Man. c. 1770. Vienna,
Österreichische Galerie, Lower Belvedere

74. Franz Xaver Messerschmidt:
The Buffoon. c. 1770. Vienna,
Österreichische Galerie, Lower Belvedere

museum, and in it for the first time he combined his mastery of historical insight with the results of psychoanalysis. As an historian he was able to place the interest in physiognomic expression firmly into its eighteenth-century setting, giving a masterly sketch of the development of physiognomic studies from Le Brun to Darwin.[3] As a psychologist he could show why this fashionable branch of study attracted the psychotic artist and in what way he transformed it to serve his private delusions. The paper was published in 1932. In writing it for an audience of art historical experts Kris had felt for the first time that he was inhibited from discussing purely psychoanalytic problems. He had to reserve these for a paper destined for a more specialized readership.[4] These, then, were inevitably years of decision for Kris. The wish to abandon the confining milieu of pure museum studies and to join in the intellectual adventure of psychoanalytic research became overwhelming and prompted the desire to abandon art history for medicine. But a better solution of this conflict offered itself; Sigmund Freud invited Kris to become an editor of *Imago*, the journal which had been specifically founded to provide a meeting-ground between psychoanalysis and the study of cultural subjects. If I remember rightly, Kris told me that Freud at that time urged him to continue his Museum work and to complete the catalogue of goldsmiths' work in the collection under his care. He probably wanted him to have a foot in both camps.

Through this appointment Kris moved right into the centre of the psychoanalytic movement in Vienna and actually began to practise psychoanalysis. When I got to know him better I learned that he had two patients in the morning before going to his office in the Museum. He also saw patients in the evening. His capacity for work was astounding. He did not stop publishing art historical studies nor did he stop advising collectors. But it was clear to him that he could not fully use the potentialities of his intellect without some research assistant who would help him collect material and work in libraries while he was confined to the Museum or the consulting room. His first assistant in these years was one of my fellow students at the University who was my senior by one year, Otto Kurz. Kris had conceived the idea of investigating the myth of the artist and his magic powers and of collecting the typical anecdotes told about artists for what they revealed of the artist's psychology. In Kurz he found a collaborator of prodigious learning who much to the delight of Kris collected sources from all over the world. The result was a book *Die Legende vom Künstler*[5] and, as in the earlier instance, an article on the subject for *Imago*. But Kris was insatiable in his work. The one research project did not suffice for his energy. And so Kurz suggested myself as an assistant to test another of Kris's ideas which had grown out of the Messerschmidt studies. The varied reactions to these expressive heads had posed the problem in his mind how far our reading of the facial expression in works of art is reliable. With his marvellous eye for suitable material he suggested a study centring on the thirteenth-century statues of founders in the Cathedral of Naumburg. These lifelike but imaginary portraits (Figs. 75 and 76) appeared to be so full of expression that a whole drama had been woven around them. Ciceroni had developed the legend that all these figures were participants in a story of conflict and murder. Doubting the possibility of such an interpretation of early Gothic sculpture, Kris hoped to prove that the complexity seen in the expression of these figures was not entirely due to the intention of the artist. The artist had only sought means of bringing the portraits to life. But their expression was more intense than clear. It thus clamoured for explanation and rationalization and the complicated story was the result. In order to test his hypothesis Kris wanted to arrange a series of psychological experiments which I was to help to organize. We showed various subjects the photographs of these statues and asked them to interpret their expressions. We also showed them only the upper or the lower half of the face and we compared these results with the reaction of the same people to

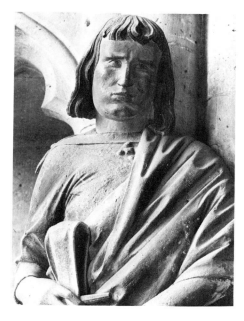

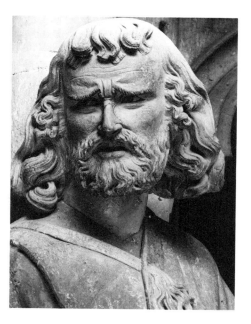

75. Head of one of the founders
of Naumburg Cathedral. *c.* 1260

76. Head of one of the founders
of Naumburg Cathedral. *c.* 1260

works by later artists, such as Bernini. In these experiments Kris established contact with the academic department of psychology in Vienna under Karl Bühler, who was at that time studying the theory of human expression and writing the history of these theories.[6] A number of Bühler's assistants and collaborators were invited to Kris's house to act as subjects in these experiments and I, in my turn, served as subject for similar studies done in Bühler's seminar.

It was by no means a matter of course that a member of the psychoanalytic circle thus collaborated with the circle of Bühler, who was known as a critic of Freud. But even then Kris had a bent for academic diplomacy. He saw it as his role to mediate between psychoanalysis and other disciplines and he took this role seriously.

It was certainly not easy to be a diplomat and a mediator in these darkening years of the early 1930s. It was particularly difficult for a person of Jewish descent. Kris was deeply aware of all the undercurrents of resistance he had to encounter within the Museum and in the University. Unlike many who were in the same situation he did not close his eyes to these dangers. On the contrary, he kept them wide open. He made a point of reading the *Völkische Beobachter* and he had no illusions. In Austria itself the scene had also darkened with the abolition of Parliament and the establishment of a dictatorship. It was when telling an anti-government joke at the office and being met with frozen stares that Kris began to reflect on the instability of the effect of the comic. The invitation to share in a mild form of aggression had led to embarrassment all round.

This sense of isolation aroused in Kris a true concern and solicitude for those in a similar situation. A career in Austria had become an impossibility for Jewish scholars and thus he did everything to help find alternative employment for his young colleagues. He procured a position for Otto Kurz at the Warburg Institute, then still in Hamburg, and thus I became his principal research assistant.

But with that sense of urgency and that absorption in his interests that characterized Kris at all times, he decided that we were not now going to continue the study of facial expression in art. That could wait. The study of Messerschmidt had pointed to the common area between unconscious fantasies and the comic which Freud had explored in his famous study of the Joke.[7] It was tempting to approach this area more closely by studying the graphic joke, the caricature. It was in this project that I was to become his collaborator. He offered me the wonderful opportunity of writing a book on the subject with him. I collected the material and we would sit together several times a week in the evening drinking black coffee, discussing, planning, and ultimately writing. It was during our joint work in 1934–5 that I first came very close to him. It was and remains a miracle to me how one man could do so much work on such a level. Although occupied with his psychoanalytic practice and with editorial duties on *Imago*, he by no means neglected his duties to the Museum. On the contrary, in these very years the opportunity arose of putting into practice a plan that he and Planiscig had worked out earlier for completely reorganizing the collection of sculpture and applied art in the Vienna Museum.

Instead of continuing the old-fashioned arrangement according to materials and media, they decided to show the growth of this extraordinary accumulation of treasures in terms of the collectors who had assembled them. There was to be a hall devoted to the Burgundian heritage of the Habsburgs, a large group illustrating the patronage and collection of the Emperor Maximilian I, and so, through the centuries, presenting a panorama of dynastic history and cultural developments. To handle the precious jewellery and glass was not a task that could be left to assistants. Kris carried these objects himself to the showcases and arranged them according to his sensitive taste. I well remember visiting him in the Museum in those days when he was physically so tired from standing on his feet all day that he was close to collapsing, but he not only carried on, but would rush home in a taxi to receive the evening's patients.

After a rapid supper I would then come at about nine o'clock and we often sat together till midnight talking about caricature and about many other things as well. When it came to writing we really wrote together, he sitting on one side of the desk and I on the other. Usually it was he who held the pen but we would jointly formulate every sentence before he wrote it down. During this joint work I learnt something about the workings of his extraordinary mind. It was a complex mind, fond of complexities. I began to sense a rhythm in his scientific imagination which accounted for a contradiction that had at first baffled me. For there was a marked contrast in these working sessions. There were the thrilling evenings when Kris let himself go; he would sit back, relaxed, and open up the most astonishing vistas on the development of the human mind and the position of art in the household of the human psyche. He would fluently sketch a breathtaking theory which seemed to illuminate the whole growth of human culture. Suddenly everything seemed clear and simple and we agreed that the history of caricature should be presented as a facet of this great evolution. But soon I knew that my next visit might find him in a very different mood. When I reminded him of his bold theory, he would shrug it off and insist that we knew so very little about these matters. He would seek to qualify any sweeping statement we had sketched and would reorganize the whole book to suit a more cautious and more modest mood.

This rhythm of advance and withdrawal may be shared by many imaginative scientists, but I believe that with Kris there were special circumstances which contributed to this caution. One was his absolute and unconditional allegiance to Freud. He did not feel entitled to advance an apodictic statement which might be found not to be in accord with Freud's theory. Moreover he was quite genuinely convinced that any new idea he would think he had conceived, would and could be found anticipated somewhere in the collected works of Freud. Indeed, one of the forms his withdrawal would take, then and later, when one reminded him of the vistas he had opened, was to say with a shrug, there is nothing new in this, everybody would know it if people only knew how to read Freud. This attitude also accounted for the second motive of those partial withdrawals. There was nothing he abhorred more than the oversimplified and vulgarized versions of psychoanalysis which had become the small coin of cocktail party conversations. I well remember wanting to show him later in our friendship an article on art and psychoanalysis in which every picture was predictably interpreted as a representation of the sexual act. I could not make him read it, he found all this too embarrassing and too irrelevant. One of his reiterated warnings was increasingly: 'it is all much more complicated much, much more complicated. Why should it be simple?'

It cannot be denied that this constant awareness of the complexity of problems, together with his desire never to appear disloyal to the legacy of Freud, occasionally inhibited the free flow of his style. I remember teasing him about his predilection for qualifying clauses and hints of possible reservations by composing a doggerel poem which never came to saying anything because everything had to be hedged in with cautionary 'ifs' and 'buts'. Of course he took it in good part, because he was well aware of his weakness, if weakness it was.

This is not the place to tell in any detail why our book on the History of Caricature ultimately remained unpublished. The dates tell their own story. Aware as he was of the Nazi menace Kris urged me also to leave Vienna as soon as possible, and by the end of 1935 had found a position for me at the Warburg Institute, which had meanwhile emigrated from Hamburg to London. He himself did not want to move. He was determined to stay as long as Freud stayed in Vienna. But he knew very well that time was running out and used his diplomatic skill to make contacts abroad. Thus he arranged a Daumier Exhibition in Vienna to help us with our researches, but also to have the pleasure of displaying subversive cartoons and to collaborate with French colleagues. His initiative earned him the *Légion d'Honneur*, which he valued as a safeguard.

What he valued even more, however, was another link with French culture; on the suggestion of Charles de Tolnay he was invited to join the annual meetings held at Pontigny, where, among other leading members of French intellectual life, he met the novelist Martin du Gard, with whom he formed a permanent friendship.

He had visited England in the spring of 1937 and there read a paper to a psychoanalytic audience on 'Ego Development and the Comic'.[8] He was moving with increasing determination in the direction of pure psychological theory. The visual arts no longer hold the centre here, the interest shifts to those problems of 'meta-psychology' which were then particularly topical in psychoanalytic debates. While many English analysts, following Melanie Klein, were mainly intent on exploring the unconscious fantasies of the psyche, Kris, who was so close to Freud and to his daughter Anna, came here and elsewhere increasingly to stress the area called 'ego psychology', the factors of defence and control, which are so frequently underrated in those vulgarized accounts he so disliked.

Thus when Kris finally emigrated and moved to London in 1938 he came as a psychoanalyst who had made his important contribution to a topical debate. The history of art, at that time, held little attraction for him. He had come to see in aesthetics a field of research in which certain general propositions of psychoanalysis could best be developed and illustrated.

But he could never forget the political situation and the coming war for a moment. He was acutely aware of the terrible danger in which so many of his Viennese and German friends were at that time, he was convinced of the need to combat the apathy and false optimism he found only too frequently in England. When the war broke out he had already made contact with like-minded people interested in propaganda and psychological warfare. He became an adviser to the British Broadcasting Corporation and analysed the trends and tricks of Nazi propaganda, incidentally recommending me, his erstwhile assistant, for a post in the 'Monitoring Service' (Listening Post), where I remained throughout the six years of the war. Kris did not remain in England. Freud had died early in the war, and there was nothing to keep him. In 1940 he accepted the mission of organizing the analysis of wartime propaganda in Canada and then he moved to New York, where he remained in close contact with the British Broadcasting Corporation.

I cannot write of his war-time activities, for though we worked in the same set-up, we could not, in the nature of things, communicate much about our work. I know that he was able to convince the highest American authorities of the value of his contribution and that even Roosevelt took notice. He had completely moved away from art and art history, and organized since April 1941, together with Hans Speier, a research project on totalitarian propaganda at the New School of Social Research in New York, where he became a visiting Professor. The result was a book on German radio propaganda published in 1944. He also lectured at the New York Psycho-Analytic Institute and at the College of the City of New York. In 1946 he became an American citizen. By then his position in the intellectual world of New York and indeed far beyond that circle was secure. He was recognized as one of the leading expositors of Freud's theoretical ideas and he spent much of his time and his energy in safeguarding the heritage of Freud.

In 1949 Kris procured for me a Rockefeller Fellowship to come to the United States for a few months and to resume our collaboration. These were happy months after the years of tragedy and anxiety we had both gone through. I well remember how eager he was to take me out, immediately on arrival, to show me that wonder of American life, the drug store, where he insisted on my eating a 'banana split'. He was now a greatly respected psychoanalyst, working too many hours a day, as he had always done, but enjoying the respect in which he was universally held. I had always admired his versatility and capacity for concentration, but even I was astounded when I attended one of his Seminars at the New School of Social Research, where a paper on child psychology was presented. The quickness of his formulations of intricate questions, the uncanny mastery of a vast bibliography in this technical subject explained the awe with which he was regarded by members of the group. It was a true virtuoso performance at the top of his form. When I asked him how he could keep up with the bibliography of such a subject he told me that he did not need much sleep. He was often awake at night and during these hours he read the many periodicals to which he subscribed. When he was tired, he put out the light and slept again.

He would still sometimes tease me for my continued interest in the history of art. 'Who wants to know these things?', he would repeat, and remember with a mixture of amusement and incredulity that he had once expended so much energy in disentangling the various members of the Miseroni family of glass cutters. Sometimes, perhaps, he protested a little too much. He could not forget his eminence in what he looked upon now as a former life. He enjoyed beautiful objects and he longed to show Italy to his growing daughter and son. Occasionally, I believe, he would even be consulted by specialists in the Metropolitan Museum of Art, but he did not like to talk about this.

The problems of aesthetics had become somewhat marginal to his interests, as compared with the theoretical questions he encountered in his practice. He was mainly engaged in supervising and training analysts, and the issues of technique and of interpretation that came up in his daily work fascinated him. But even more was he attracted by the possibility of observing this process in an actual life situation and so testing Freud's conception of human development. He accepted the invitation to organize a research project of his own at the famous Child Study Center at Yale University which appointed him to a Professorship. Heading a team which included his wife he set out to engage in what is called a 'longitudinal' study of child development, the recording of the various stages of growth and the interaction of the child with his family. At the same time he proposed to study the problem of 'sublimation' in the painting of nursery-school children in Yale, and accepted the responsibility for a research project on Gifted Adolescents in the Psycho-Analytic Institute of New York.

It would be very misleading, however, to imagine that this turn of events had changed Kris into a cold and tough-minded scientist. I well remember a talk we had when I naïvely asked why the answer to a certain question could not be found in these investigations, and he replied with passion 'because these are human beings'; he would not tolerate their being submitted to any test or treatment which offended their human dignity.

I was fortunate to see Kris often in those years, whenever I came to the States or he to England. I often enjoyed his hospitality in the country retreat he had bought about one hour's drive from New York in the hilly woodlands of Connecticut. A good deal of ground belonged to the house and he developed a passion for improving the lay-out, planting trees, clearing away brushwood and growing flowers. He once confided to me that for him this relaxation replaced the concern with beautiful things he had enjoyed in the Museum. For he was deeply responsive to beauty. He liked to tell that when he was courting Marianne, who was then studying in Berlin, he had so impressed a florist where he had selected a bouquet, that he had been offered employment as a flower-arranger.

His attachment to the piece of ground he owned even increased, perhaps, after he had suffered a heart attack. He had never been robust, and he often predicted that he would not live long. He knew that the exercise on the land did him good, but he would not otherwise make any concession to the demands of his doctors, who advised him to cut down his activities. When I once urged him to reduce the number of his patients, he assured me that analysing was his life, that he did not want to spend fewer hours on that pursuit, because he felt he was learning so much in every analytic hour. He would miss this intellectual stimulation so much that life would not be worth living.

This answer was characteristic of the man, of his zest, his energy, his unwillingness to give in. He had no time for the usual social duties, he rarely saw people except professionally, he had few relaxations except his grounds. Those who did not know him intimately might well have found him remote and tense. Only a few were allowed to know how much he cared for the happiness of others, and how little for his own.

When he suffered his second and fatal heart attack in February 1957 his one concern was for his patients. He calmly went through the list with his wife and suggested to which colleagues they should be sent if he did not survive. His ashes were scattered in the grounds of his Connecticut house.

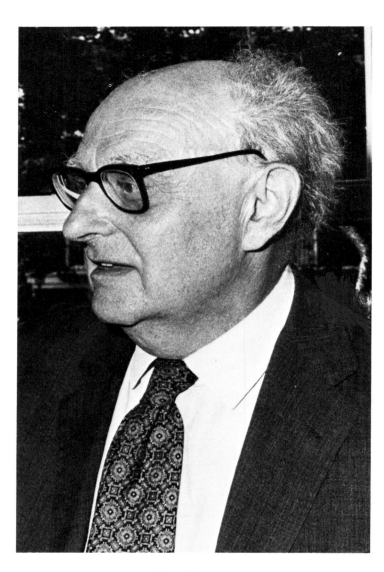

77. Otto Kurz. *1977*

Otto Kurz, art historian and polymath, was born in Vienna on 26 May 1908; he died in London on 3 September 1975. After graduating from Vienna University in 1932 he joined the staff of the Warburg Institute, which was then still based in Hamburg, and soon followed it to London. From 1943 to 1965 he was its librarian and then taught there as Professor of the Classical Tradition with special reference to the Near East until his death. He also did several spells of teaching at the Hebrew University of Jerusalem.

The Exploration of Culture Contacts

The Services to Scholarship of Otto Kurz (1908–1975)

IN THE province of the Republic of Letters in which the Warburg Institute is situated, Otto Kurz had become a legend in his lifetime as a polymath, a wit and a scholarly oracle always willing to be consulted.

I was fortunate to have worked side by side with him during most of the forty-six years from 1929, when we became fellow students, to 1975, when he died as my colleague at the Warburg Institute, but time and again I could only marvel at the speed and accuracy with which he located, absorbed and retained information, and the utter selflessness with which he shared his knowledge with others.

Not that he was easy to know. His life was overshadowed by tragedies, but he never liked to talk about himself and he never complained. Only his intimates realized that, exceptional as he was as a scholar, he was even more so as a human being.

Otto Kurz was born in Vienna on 26 May 1908, the only child of Dr. Max Kurz and his wife Anna, née Mandl. His parents both came from the small-town Jewish communities of Moravia, that corner of the Austro-Hungarian Monarchy which also produced Sigmund Freud and Gustav Mahler. Max Kurz was a respected general practitioner in the service of the Austrian Tobacco Monopoly but also had a private practice. He evidently had many interests, and a delightful picture-book he drew for little Otto, which is still extant, testifies both to his talents and to his human warmth. Even later in life Otto Kurz often quoted the views and sayings of his father, with whom he was perhaps on closer terms than with his mother. Otto Kurz had the conventional education of his class, he attended the Humanistisches Gymnasium and, like so many other boys, eagerly collected stamps and coins.

Memoir from the Proceedings of the British Academy, *1979.*

One of the few little incidents he ever told from his school days suggests that even then his exceptional knowledge had been noticed. When he was set an essay on the joys of winter, he had cheekily written the single sentence, 'Winter has no joys for me.' Asked whether he was punished, he reluctantly admitted that his knowledge of German Renaissance literature made him proof against retribution. It was another boy who got it in the neck for imitating the performance when a similar theme was set.

He never had much respect for the traditional methods of his school. I remember him making fun of the way he was supposed to learn Latin. He wondered, he said, how many applications he would receive if he announced somewhere that he was willing to teach a language, one hour every weekday for eight years, to a standard enabling his pupil to translate easy texts with the aid of a dictionary.

Since school could not satisfy his thirst for knowledge, Kurz volunteered at that time to work part-time in the Library of the Österreichisches Museum für Kunst und Industrie, the counterpart of the Victoria and Albert Museum. The early items in his bibliography were in fact written before he ever got to university. The first is a publication with commentary of the Catalogue of the Vienna Art Exhibition of 1777 (published in 1927); the item had been considered lost, but Kurz tracked it down in the Vienna Nationalbibliothek among the many entries under 'Catalogue', neither inflating nor dismissing the relevance of the little find, which listed the exhibits of many artists and showed (as Kurz recognized) the co-existence of Baroque, Rococo and Neo-Classical trends in the Vienna of that year. Much weightier was the brief note 'A contemporary reference to Dürer' (published 1928) which the schoolboy found in Johannes Cochläus' 1512 edition of Pomponius Mela's *Cosmographia*. The proof of the popularity of Dürer's prints in Portugal at comparatively so early a date foreshadows a lifelong interest in the dissemination of cultural achievements. The knowledge he stored at that time of German humanist literature also remained readily available to him when his interests had long turned elsewhere. When, in 1964, I was looking for evidence of the influence of the invention of printing on the awareness of progress, he asked, 'Is this not quite common in the Latin school comedies?', and instanced a play by Nicodemus Frischlin (of whom I had never heard), in which Cicero is mocked for his ignorance of the new art. He had probably not read it for some forty years.

When early in 1929 I was admitted to the seminar of Julius von Schlosser (the Zweites Kunsthistorisches Institut) of Vienna University, Kurz, who was a year ahead of me, was already the acknowledged star of his generation. I believe the first report I heard him give in the Kunsthistorisches Museum dealt with the board game by the German Renaissance carver Hans Kels and impressed his teacher no less than his fellow students for the range of its erudition. From that time on I counted him as one of my teachers. Our ways home from the University coincided for a considerable stretch and where they divided we used to stand for a long time while he expounded some piece of out-of-the-way lore. Nor was it all erudition. We had a great deal of fun together, sampling lectures on literature or on vulgar Latin and sometimes—I fear—giggling at what seemed to us like pedantry or vacuity. But Kurz was no rebel against authority. He had the profoundest respect for real scholarship, a respect which he preserved throughout his life. Two of his teachers had a lasting influence on his outlook: first and foremost Julius von Schlosser (whose life-work, *Die Kunstliteratur*, Kurz was to keep up to date in the Italian editions of 1937, 1956 and 1964), and to whom he devoted a penetrating and moving memoir, *'Julius von Schlosser, personalità, metodo, lavoro'*, published in 1955,[1] one of the most personal of his writings. It was from Schlosser that he learned how to combine the curiosity of an antiquarian browsing in old guide-books with the wide horizon of a true historian. The rival Chair in Art History (Erstes Kunsthistorisches Institut) was held by Josef Strzygowski, who advocated a global outlook and the recognition of Asian influences on Western art. Kurz never subscribed to his theories, but he was certainly impressed by the problems he encountered in these lectures and in a later *curriculum vitae* he enumerated Strzygowski among his teachers. The closest personal ties, however, developed with Hans Tietze, who was something of an outsider and merely held an *ad personam* chair. The author of many volumes of Austria's *Kunsttopographie* and of an important book on the Methods of Art History, Tietze was an encyclopedist, whose immense bibliography (together with that of his wife Erica Tietze Conrat) Otto and Hilde Kurz were later to compile for the *Essays in Honor of Hans Tietze*.[2] It may well have been his example which determined Kurz to choose for his dissertation that most unfashionable figure Guido Reni, for Tietze had pioneered the study of the Bolognese with his article of 1906 on Annibale Carracci's Galleria Farnese.

Collecting material on a neglected artist who had once enjoyed such fame was a pleasure to Kurz; I recall a joint expedition to a church outside Bologna, to which we lugged his heavy camera and tripod to photograph an unpublished altar piece, but I also recall the comic despair with which he would repeat 'how does one write a dissertation?' He claimed to have looked for models and found that writers of monographs never stuck to the point. Writing about one painting they would enlarge on the subject-matter, the next would give them a pretext to discuss the life of the donor, the third the pedigree, and the fourth the style. This could not be right. Having finally submitted in 1931 his terse draft on 'The early works of Guido Reni' to Schlosser, he found in the margin a number of pencil-marks which he took for signs of criticism. So he promptly omitted the relevant paragraphs and shortened his piece even further. The marks had in fact been Schlosser's way of expressing his approval, but nothing untoward happened, since the final version was never read.

Such anarchic conditions may well cause a modern reader to shake his head, but our studies at that time were wholly unstructured. There was no art historical syllabus and no examinations except the final *rigorosum*, which was an oral. Lectures were hardly more important than they are at Oxford or Cambridge, but instead of regular tutorials there were only the reports for seminars, many of which were expected to demand several months of preparation and to continue over more than one meeting. These tasks were the main topics of conversation among students and it was here that the advice and guidance of Kurz was most frequently asked and received.

Unhappily the situation was also anarchic in a more sinister sense. The University enjoyed 'extraterritorial' immunity from police interference, a fact which led to a reign of terror by Nazi thugs. Kurz was among the victims of their brutal violence when he was assailed in the University library and hit over the head with a steel truncheon. After his recuperation he was welcomed back by Schlosser to his seminar with a line from Schiller: *Monument von unserer Zeiten Schande* (Reminder of the disgrace of our time), but Schlosser had no more power or determination to put an end to this disgrace than had the other members of the professorial body.

These were tense and unhappy times in Austria as in the rest of Central Europe, and the chances of employment for a young scholar were exiguous in the best of cases, and non-existent for students of Jewish extraction. The suffering and heartbreak of the situation should not be minimized, but there was one side-effect which at least benefited those whose parents were able to support them for a while—lacking any prospect of an ordinary career they just continued to study. Thus Kurz and I took lessons in Chinese with a kind missionary at the Ethnological Museum. Our teacher's passion was the diversity of tones used in various Chinese dialects, a subject more confusing than enlightening to beginners; neither of us stayed the course for long, but Kurz returned at various periods of his life to the study of the language, which certainly enabled him to make out titles and simple inscriptions.

On the advice of Schlosser, Kurz also attempted to improve his prospects by enlisting in the course of the Österreichisches Institut für Geschichtsforschung, an institution modelled on the Ecole des Chartes, the graduates of which enjoyed a high prestige among prospective employers. For his entrance examination Kurz submitted a paper on the later works of Guido Reni, which again cost him agonies to write. He was altogether unhappy in the uncongenial atmosphere of the place, but a fortunate constellation of circumstances in which Schlosser still had his share led to a turning-point in his life. He had written a paper on Vasari's Life of Filippo Lippi (published 1933), demonstrating that certain romantic motifs which also occurred in one of Bandello's novels were derived by both authors from an unknown source. It was thus, so it seems, that he came into contact with Ernst Kris, an art historian, eight years his senior, who was keeper in the Collections of Sculpture and Applied Arts of the Kunsthistorisches Museum.[3] Kris had been the first student to graduate after Schlosser had transferred from the Museum to the University and had earned the respect of his teacher. Now Kris was looking for an *amanuensis* to help in an ambitious project that had grown out of his work on Messerschmidt. It had turned out that the biography of that artist written in the eighteenth century contained several stereotypical anecdotes also told of other artists. Through his marriage Kris had by then come into contact with the circle of Sigmund Freud and had not only undergone analysis but had also applied psychoanalytic insights to the study of artists. He realized that it was not enough for the historian merely to reject the typical legends told about artists as untrue; their very persistence and popularity suggested that they expressed a widespread reaction to the mystery of artistic creation. In proposing to collect such motifs from all over the world as a contribution to the psychology of art Kris could not have found a more suitable helpmate than Kurz, whose wide reading had by then extended beyond the horizon of Western culture and included Byzantine, Islamic, Central Asian and Chinese sources. Moreover, the interests of the two young scholars (Kris was in his early thirties, Kurz in his twenties) were complementary; where Kris looked for psychological symptoms, Kurz enjoyed tracing the migration of motifs in the light of those culture contacts which remained his overriding concern throughout his life.

Kris had also been drawn into an enterprise which concerned cultural history. The Warburg Library in Hamburg, the only institution devoted to this subject, had begun to compile a *Kulturwissenschaftliche Bibliographie zum Nachleben der Antike*, for which a large number of collaborators were enlisted. It was natural that Kurz should also join this team (the first volume of 1934 contains twenty-five contributions by him) and providential that Kris recommended his admired young colleague to Fritz Saxl, the Director of the Warburg Library, as an ideal research assistant. True, the situation in Germany had, if anything, become worse than that in Austria. In January 1933 Hitler had been appointed Chancellor, but the consequences were not yet fully realized. Kurz was to remark later that he must have been the only Jew to immigrate into Germany at the time of the Nazis. Perhaps immigration is too strong a word. When he came to Hamburg in the spring of 1933 he was not offered fixed employment but was asked to help with a variety of tasks, including the organization of the Library's neglected photographic collection and research assistance to a variety of visiting scholars.

The most immediate and the most permanent gain for Kurz was the contact he made with the Library, its staff and its users, first and foremost among them Fritz Saxl, a congenial scholar whose versatile mind encompassed the study of Rembrandt, of Mithraic monuments and of the history of astrological imagery, a subject inherited from Aby Warburg[4] which fitted in so well with the interests of Kurz in the transmission and dissemination of motifs. No less important, from the human point of view, was the friendship of Saxl's helpmate Gertrud Bing, which lasted throughout their lives. There were plenty of projects at the Warburg with which Kurz could and did help, but there also was unfinished business in Vienna, which prompted his return. He still had to undergo the torture of eleven examinations at the Institut für Geschichtsforschung (which he did in December 1933), and most of all to complete the book on the *Legende vom Künstler* (published 1934), which was dedicated to the Warburg Library. Meanwhile, however, the situation in Germany had grown increasingly menacing and it was decided to accept the invitation of an *ad hoc* committee to transfer Warburg's Library to London. The books arrived in London in December 1933 and were temporarily accommodated in Thames House.[5]

Kurz was most eager to rejoin the Institute and in April 1934 Saxl wrote that he needed his help. The financial situation, however, was precarious and all Saxl could do was to procure a one-year grant from a member of the Warburg family for Kurz, in support of another joint project with Ernst Kris—research into 'the magic of effigies and the prohibition of images'. Once arrived, however, Kurz was soon drawn into other projects in which the Institute had become involved. There was first of all the second volume of the *Bibliography*, for which he read and discussed an even wider range of publications, but above all there was the ambitious project of a new and scholarly edition of Marco Polo's *Description of the World* by Paul Pelliot and A. C. Moule, which was sponsored by Sir Percival David, the great collector of Chinese art. The enthusiasm and impatience of Sir Percival is delicately characterized in the preface to that work where it is mentioned that one of the editors received no fewer than four letters and one long message from the sponsor on a single day. Saxl, who looked for opportunities of proving the usefulness of the unknown Institute to his English colleagues, also offered help, and so the resources of the Library and the staff were placed at Sir Percival's disposal. At one point Kurz was ordered to go to Venice to meet Sir Percival at the Hotel Danieli, a meeting which necessitated his travelling for two nights, with Saxl wishing him to charge no fee, only expenses. Sceptical as Kurz was about the value of some of these feverish activities, the subject itself was close to his heart since it involved the contact between China and Europe across Central Asia. He developed a lifelong admiration for the two great scholars who prepared this model edition.

But another fortunate circumstance prevented Kurz from abandoning his erstwhile field of Bolognese painting for the lure of the Far East. He was recommended as a guide and interpreter by the German art historian Heinrich Bodmer to a young Englishman who did not have much Italian but wished to do research in Italy on Guercino. That student was Denis Mahon, and the close ties which developed between him and Kurz in the course of their long travels became of benefit to both scholars, who may be said to have jointly revived interest in Italian Seicento painting.

It was during their frequent journeys between Bologna and Cento (Guercino's birthplace), as Kurz once told me, that he worked through the whole text of Vasari's *Lives* for any mention of drawings, a labour which resulted in the subsequent publication of Vasari's *Libro dei Disegni* (published 1937). The study of art historical sources and drawings altogether looms quite large in his bibliography of that time, the most important being his 'Contribution to the History of the Leonardo Drawings' in the Royal Collection of Windsor (1936), which helped to establish the pedigree of that great corpus. But he was also extending his feelers towards the East, studying a leaf from an insular pattern-book which has a bearing on the much debated history of Psalter illustrations in Byzantium.

The generosity with which the English world of learning received and supported the many refugees from Nazi persecution can never be sufficiently appreciated, but for the individual arrival whose special field was rather remote from ordinary university curricula the situation could not possibly be easy, either financially or psychologically. Kurz did some teaching at the Courtauld Institute soon after its establishment but this could not provide a living wage, and Saxl was only able, in 1935, to secure a grant for another year from an anonymous donor. Without the continued association with Denis Mahon, whom he accompanied on his travels (including a trip to Russia), the situation might well have been desperate. Yet Kurz was certainly not a gloomy companion during the spring of 1936, when we lived in the same boarding-house and jointly prepared our meals on the gas-rings of our bedsitters.

Unsettled as was his life, and uncertain as was his future, he still decided to marry, late in 1937, his former fellow-student of the University of Vienna to whom he had been deeply attached for many years, Hilde Schüller, who shared so many of his interests. The Institute at that time was homeless, having had to leave Thames House in the spring of 1937, and the preparation of alternative accommodation in the Imperial Institute Buildings dragged on till early 1938. In March 1938 Hitler occupied Austria, in September of that year there followed the Munich crisis. The anxieties for relatives and friends still left at the mercy of their persecutors and the dread of the devastation that would accompany the almost unavoidable war created a nightmare situation which even those of us who lived through it find hard to recapture, let alone convey. Kurz had managed to arrange for his father to join him in England, but his mother had wished to stay close to her own mother and ultimately perished at the hands of the Nazis. It was a blow which he never mentioned even to his friends.

And yet life had to go on and work had to continue. Expanding Saxl's work on the history of star imagery in Western manuscripts, Kurz drew up a project for a book on classical book illustration and its survival in secular literature. Though he later hoped to complete it jointly with Byvanck, the rich material he had collected unfortunately remained in his drawer. Another joint enterprise succeeded better, the Handlist which he compiled at that time with Hugo Buchthal, of illuminated Oriental Christian manuscripts (published 1942). The pull of the East was strong. He wanted to take a course in Japanese to master the literature on Eastern art, but lacked the money to do so. Instead he and I accepted a commission from T. S. R. Boase, the Director of the Courtauld Institute, to write bibliographical introductions for students of the new subject of art history, the first to be devoted to iconography (where Kurz undertook the sections on portraiture and on Christian art).

In 1939 Saxl staved off our financial worries by securing a two-year grant for both Kurz and myself from Sir Percival David on condition that we would find a permanent job at the end of that period. The outbreak of the war upset all these arrangements. The books of the Institute were again packed into cases and evacuated, but Saxl kept its activities alive by arranging photographic exhibitions on various themes. After the fall of France and the threat of invasion in the spring of 1940 Kurz was interned as an 'enemy alien'. He took his fate philosophically and liked to joke, later, about the 'old camp tie' which linked a number of Central European intellectuals in permanent friendship. His daughter Erica, his only child, was born while he was away.

On his release he was engaged to do some more teaching for students of the Courtauld Institute in Surrey. Towards the end of 1940, however, another

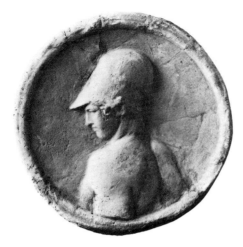 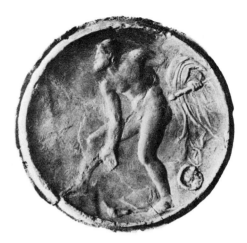

78. Plaster model for silverwork found
in Begram, Afghanistan. 1st century A.D.
Paris, Musée Guimet

79. Plaster model for silverwork found
in Begram, Afghanistan. 1st century A.D.
Kabul Museum

strange concatenation of fate gave him the opportunity to work in the field which had interested him for so long, the culture contacts between East and West. One of the photographic exhibitions organized by the Institute was a display of illustrations of Indian Art belonging to Stella Kramrisch. It was this event which led in turn to a visit of the great French archaeologist Joseph Hackin, then a member of the Free French Forces, who was invited to lecture on the finds he had made in the service of the French Government in a series of seasons in Afghanistan, including the depot of a trading-post at Begram, which yielded a group of objects of Hellenistic, Indian and Chinese origin (Figs. 78 and 79). He discussed his ideas and plans with Saxl and Kurz and was obviously so impressed by their interest and knowledge that he decided to leave all his material in their charge before he left England, never to return. Understandably this decision did not remain unchallenged, involving as it did the rights of two rival Government authorities. It is all the more gratifying to record that the disinterested services of Saxl and of Kurz ultimately received unqualified recognition in the official account as it appeared years later in the *Mémoires de la délégation archéologique française en Afghanistan*, Tome XI, *Rencontre de trois civilisations Inde—Grèce—Chine (Nouvelles recherches archéologiques à Begram)*.[6]

Admittedly this happy consummation was not reached before some fourteen years had passed, but it seemed right to interrupt the chronological sequence of this account to document one of the main research projects which occupied Kurz during and after the war. He made himself at home in the history of Hellenistic and Roman glass and silver; in other words, he added classical archaeology to his previous accomplishments.

Meanwhile the war had also claimed other victims. The Institute's Librarian Hans Meier had been killed in an air-raid in April 1941 and with him the whole material for the third volume of the *Bibliography*, which he had in his flat, had been destroyed, together with essential parts of the Institute's equipment, in the same night. It was decided to remove the Institute's staff to the Lea, a country house near Denham, which was run more or less like a collective farm. The Kurz family did not join for some time but preferred greater privacy in another house near London. Kurz continued to teach some students of the Courtauld Institute but he also worked on a book on fakes, which had been commissioned by Faber and Faber (published 1948). Unlike most authors writing on that subject he shunned sensational accounts and anecdotes, offering strictly what the title promises, a Handbook for Collectors. Only in an addition to the second edition (1967) did he give rein to satirical humour in the discussion of forged medieval frescoes allegedly uncovered in Germany after the war (Fig. 80); in fact, few of his writings so preserve the flavour of his style as a raconteur as this record of gullibility.[7] He was still not allowed to forget Bologna. At the suggestion of Anthony Blunt he began in 1943 to catalogue those holdings of Bolognese drawings in the Royal Collection at Windsor Castle which remained after those by the Carracci, by Domenichino and by Guercino had been allocated (published 1955). In the same year he was at last given an official post and function on the staff of the Warburg Institute, being appointed Assistant Librarian. In the next year—in November 1944—the Warburg Institute itself found a safe anchorage in the University of London and with the end of the war books could be brought out of storage and normal life resume.

Rich and varied as his publications remained in the subsequent years— including his surveys of recent research in the *Burlington Magazine* (1948– 60)—it was in the Library that he found the true scope for his talents, particularly after his appointment as Librarian in 1949. The limited budget of the Institute demanded utmost concentration on essentials. As he once said to me: 'It is really very simple, at the beginning of the financial year we can buy any book we want—but then we cannot buy another one.' He always knew how to select the one significant title from any field of study which would enable the prospective user of the Library to orient himself about the state of research and find his way to other information. He could not have offered this guidance to users of the Library if he himself had not been an experienced scholar. As such he had always found it hard to understand how specialists ever managed to stop short at the frontiers of their so-called field. Whatever

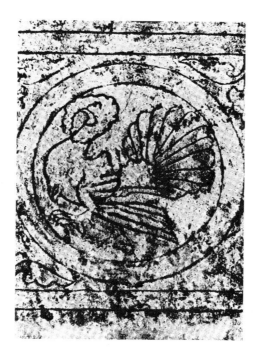

80. *The 'Schleswiger Truthahnbilder'.*
Fake medieval mural showing picture of a turkey

question he felt tempted to explore, he said, the search for an answer inevitably led him across these artificial frontiers. A drawing by Dürer of a sleeping nymph could only be explained through the history of a pseudo-classical inscription '*Huius nympha loci*' (1953); a group of Florentine drawings for an altar demanded for its elucidation an understanding of the liturgical problem of where to keep the consecrated wafer (1955). At the same time the skill with which he had learned to master new subjects also made him impatient of the specialist's claim that one could not possibly 'keep up' with the bibliography of more than one limited area. What were they talking about? Granted that, say, in a 'Rembrandt year' a mass of literature on that artist came out—would it really take more than a week to sort the wheat from the chaff and read anything of significance of which a Rembrandt specialist had to take note?

His clear vision of what the Library had been and what it should be made him rarely hesitate about purchases. He gave priority to texts over secondary literature, to original works over translations, and ignored inflated pot-boilers. He was aware of the obligation the librarian had to maintain the subject areas which had been cultivated in the past, but also to expand into new fields of studies. Together with Gertrud Bing, with whom he travelled to Italy in 1953, he established a system of exchange which greatly benefited the Italian holdings of the Library. Few users of the Institute's resources who knocked at his door to consult him did not emerge with a long list of titles of works in their special field of which they had never heard. The number of books in which he is thanked in the preface testifies to the range and value of his contribution. But he not only gave advice, he gave encouragement and something of his own enthusiasm. Nobody expressed this inspiring character of his companionship more charmingly than Beryl Smalley in the Preface to her book on *The English Friars and Antiquity* (Oxford, 1960): 'Dr. Otto Kurz ordered me to turn a forty-minute paper into a book, and I obeyed him.'

Few of those who consulted him as an oracle knew that in May 1957 he had been visited by a terrible tragedy. His wife had to undergo brain surgery and emerged from the operation half-paralysed and without speech. Refusing the pessimistic prognosis of the specialist who advised permanent hospitalization, Kurz took her home and nursed her back to something like normal life, later aided by the therapeutic skill and devotion of Nurse Irene Wilkinson. Yet despite this burden he carried on in the Library and even continued to write and to publish.

In fact, it was in this period, during the last eighteen years of his life, that his work expanded organically, not into one, but into two fields he had previously merely reconnoitred. The first of these was the field of Islamic art, its sources, and its influences. Three scholars should here be mentioned who may have encouraged this interest: Paul Wittek, the historian of Turkey and a frequent visitor to the Warburg Library, D. Storm Rice, of the School of Oriental Studies, and, later, Richard Ettinghausen, whose work he especially esteemed. Again external circumstances may have provided the final impulse. In the summer term of 1962 he was given leave of absence for six weeks to go to Jerusalem. He had been invited by the Salomons Foundation, because the eminent Orientalist, the late Professor L. A. Mayer, had wished him to complete a project of long standing, the *Bibliography of Jewish Art and Archaeology*. Though a librarian, Kurz was never an enthusiast for large bibliographical compilations, but he carried out this demanding task with his customary attention to detail (published 1967). The real gain of the visit, however, was his involvement with the L. A. Mayer Memorial Institute and its magnificent collection of Islamic art, in the administration of which he was asked to take a share. He never did things by halves. In the years which remained to him he tried to see as many of the chief monuments of Islamic art as were within his reach; he took his wife, despite her partial disablement, to Anatolia, to Granada and Cordoba, and acquired sufficient Arabic at least to read inscriptions and book-titles. When, in pursuit of his overriding interest in culture contacts, he went to Rome in 1963, to examine the voluminous correspondence of the seventeenth-century Jesuit polymath Athanasius Kircher in the Gregoriana, he told me on his return that many of the scholar's Orientalist correspondents had written to him in Hebrew or Arabic. 'I did not know you could read Arabic', I said. 'I don't', he replied, 'but that much anyone can read.'

When in the early months of 1964 he returned to Jerusalem I was not surprised to hear that he would give a lecture course on 'Islamic art in its foreign contexts'; but even I had not expected that he had proposed a seminar on eighteenth- and nineteenth-century art which he intended to open with a discussion of the design of the Museo Clementino of the Vatican and its importance for the history of Neo-Classical architecture. He had also collected notes over the years on Heine's *Salons*, which he would use for later meetings.

In 1965 Professor Hugo Buchthal resigned his personal Chair in the History of Byzantine Art at the Warburg Institute to accept a position in the United States and Kurz was asked whether he would exchange the Library for a teaching post. He had developed an enthusiastic interest in the Institute's new teaching programme, through which he hoped to make its position as a centre for cultural history better known and understood. Yes, he said in his paradoxical way, there was one topic he really would like to teach—the history of maize. And, becoming serious, he explained that the aspect of the history of civilization which was most in need of cultivation was the transmission of food plants and of other materials across the globe. It was a facet of culture-contact which had fascinated him ever since his concern with East–West relations had acquainted him with the researches of Berthold Laufer, the German Sinologist who worked at the Field Museum in Chicago. (He once remarked to J. B. Trapp that what he would want to be written on his tombstone was: 'He did everything wrong, but he bought the works of Berthold Laufer.')

While he was preparing this course he participated in the Institute's teaching on the Renaissance by giving classes on geographical discoveries, to which he brought many otherwise neglected accounts by humanists on exotic countries, and on astrology (in which he spent two classes casting my horoscope according to the strict rules of the game). The official title of the Chair which he took up in October 1965 was 'Professor of the History of Classical Tradition with special reference to the Near East'; and he did justice to this designation by giving regular classes, jointly with his colleague A. I. Sabra and Dr. R. Walzer of the University of Oxford, on 'The Sources and Legacy of Islamic Civilization'. But he never dropped any problem that had once attracted his attention, and so he continued to accumulate notes on an ever-widening range of topics.

Since neither writing nor lecturing much appealed to him he only accepted such tasks to oblige or to intervene in a worthwhile debate (as in the National Gallery cleaning controversy of 1961–2). He never believed that a fact had to be published merely because it had escaped the attention of others. One example must suffice. I had come across evidence that Bosch's famous Triptych in Madrid known as the *Garden of Earthly Delights* had once belonged to Henry III of Nassau. As was my invariable rule, I submitted it to Kurz, who opened a drawer in his desk and produced a voluminous folder about the history of this and other works of Bosch which confirmed my hypothesis. He had never thought seriously of publishing these notes on 'Four Tapestries after Hieronymus Bosch' and only wrote them up for the *Journal of the Warburg and Courtauld Institutes* to oblige me. The same number of the *Journal* (xxx, 1967) also contains his article on 'A Volume of Mughal Drawings and Miniatures' which he had discovered or rediscovered in the Vatican Library. Glancing at the bibliographical footnotes of these two articles, which extend from folklore to the history of the 'Royal Umbrella', gives an idea of the effortless virtuosity with which he could play on the instrument of the Library.

Having been inured to lecturing by a third visit to Jerusalem, Kurz allowed himself to be persuaded—however reluctantly—to accept the Slade Professorship at the University of Oxford in 1970, where he lectured on 'Islamic Art between East and West'. It is hoped that these lectures, which were much admired, will ultimately be published. Apart from a number of articles reflecting his concern with the cultural relations between East and West— 'Relations between Prague and Persia at the time of Rudolf II' (1966), 'A Gold Helmet made in Venice for Sultan Suleyman the Magnificent' (1969), 'The Turkish Dresses in the Costume-Book of Rubens' (1972) (with Hilde Schüller Kurz), 'Folding Chairs and Koran Stands' (1972), 'Lion Masks with Rings in the West and in the East' (1973), 'The Strange History of the Alhambra Vase' (1975)—the main fruit of his preoccupation with this topic was his dazzling book on *European Clocks and Watches in the Near East* (1975), which grew out of a lecture he gave at the Warburg Institute in 1973. The subject had attracted his attention through the collection of watches which forms part of the L. A. Mayer Memorial Institute.

But these later studies were only fragments of the larger design he was planning. In the last year of his tenure of the Chair (1974–5) he felt sufficiently prepared to attempt a series of classes on the problem area really closest to his heart: on what he called 'material culture'. Moving from the history of plants such as millet, corn, coffee to that of spices, sugar and fruits, he ended his last class with an unforgettable justification of these studies. Reminding us of the horrors that so often accompanied the clash of cultures he wanted us to regard the resulting benefits through the exchange of goods and of knowledge as a redeeming feature of the tragic history of mankind.

At the party given in his honour to mark his retirement he spoke of his plan to move with his invalid wife to Jerusalem, where the Salomons Foundation had offered them a comfortable service flat. He said without apparent regret that he had done with research—for clearly, in giving up his instrument, the Library, he had no choice but to renounce his mode of life. He died suddenly in his room at the Warburg Institute on 3 September 1975, a few weeks before his official career would have come to an end.

Kurz was of medium height and, as a young man, light of build. Later in life he had become somewhat portly but he remained lively and quick in his movements. His speech, on the other hand, had always been slow, and whether the language was German, English or Italian it almost resembled a somewhat monotonous chant. Once he had embarked on a topic he was hard to interrupt or to deflect. He had little small talk and either gave a delightful performance or fell silent, unless he had thought of a witticism which summed up his opinion of a person or a situation. Like all good jokes, these epigrams sprang from the context and do not retain their flavour in cold print, depending as they did on the dead-pan manner with which they were delivered. The opening words of a lecture he gave on book illustration in classical antiquity provide as good an example as any of this effect: 'The main centres of book illustration in antiquity', he began gravely, 'are Athens, Alexandria, Antioch, Rome, and Princeton. In the course of this lecture I shall show examples of each of them.' But it was not the quip which counted, but the impressive way in which he subsequently discussed the reconstruction of ancient books proposed in Kurt Weitzmann's *Roll and Codex*, published in Princeton.

In the last analysis his public *persona* was little more than the shell he had developed to protect his vulnerable and almost childlike self. He was as helpless in practical matters as the popular stereotype of the learned professor has it. Wherever he encountered aggressiveness, ignorance or pomposity, he shrugged his shoulders and withdrew into his own world. His manners, like those of many shy persons, were somewhat formal and even slightly awkward, but his tact was flawless. His human warmth expressed itself in his love of children and animals, and in his profound response to great art and great music, particularly the music of Mozart and Haydn. His sense of values was incorruptible and his friendship immutable. There can never be many like him.

Notes

FOCUS ON THE ARTS AND HUMANITIES

1. Chicago, 1967.
2. See also my essay on Warburg in this volume, pp. 117–37.
3. London, 1949.
4. London, 1966.
5. London, 1975.
6. London, 1958.
7. *The Savage Mind*, 1966, p. 247.
8. 'Eine verkannte karolingische Pyxis im Wiener Kunsthistorischen Museum', *Jahrb. d. Kunsthist. Sammlungen in Wien*, N.F. 7, 1–14, 1933.
9. 'Zum Werke Giulio Romanos', *Jahrb. d. Kunsthist. Sammlungen in Wien*, N.F. 8 and 9, 1934 and 1935.
10. See my paper on Kris in this volume, pp. 221–33.
11. *Computers and the Humanities*, November 14, 1980, pp. 187–96.
12. *On Poetry and Poets*, London, 1957, p. 114.
13. In a subsequent discussion, Thomas Kuhn remarked that he also acknowledges the possibility of scientific progress.
14. New Haven, 1967.

THE DIVERSITY OF THE ARTS: G. E. LESSING

Readers who have no German can only have a limited access to Lessing's œuvre. A selection exists in Everyman's Library (ed. W. A. Steel) containing *Laocoon, Nathan the Wise* and *Minna von Barnhelm*. There are also various translations of his play *Emilia Galotti*. Translations of other of his prose works which are quoted here are mentioned in the notes. A recent monograph is H. B. Garland's *Lessing the Founder of Modern German Literature* (London, 1962). There is an exhaustive bibliography listing publications in all languages by Siegfried Seifer, *Lessing Bibliographie* (Berlin and Weimar, 1973).

1. F. Nicolai, *Anhang zu Schillers Musenalmanach für das Jahr 1797*; cf. B. Rosenthal, *Der Geniebegriff des Aufklärungszeitalters* (Germanische Studien, Heft 138), Berlin, 1933, pp. 97, 181.
2. Gotthold Ephraim Lessing, *Sämtliche Schriften*, herausgegeben von Karl Lachmann. Dritte, auf's neue durchgesehene und vermehrte Auflage, besorgt durch Franz Muncker. Leipzig–Stuttgart, 1886–1924 (subsequently quoted as L.M.), x. 209–10.
3. J. G. Robertson, *Lessing's Dramatic Theory*, Cambridge, 1939, pp. 116 f.
4. Nicolai to Ramler in 1765, see Waldemar Oehlke, *Lessing und seine Zeit*, Munich, 1919, i. 246.
5. F. Horn, quoted in F. v. Biedermann, *Lessings Gespräche*, Berlin, 1924, p. 268.
6. L.M. viii. 41.
7. A. Aronson, *Lessing et les classiques français*, Montpellier, 1935, pp. 94–146.
8. *Der Freygeist*, 4. Aufzug, 3. Auftritt, L.M. ii. 98.
9. Lessing to Gleim, 16 Dec. 1758, 14 February 1759, L.M. xvii. 155–9:

251

Ernst und Falk (translated as *Masonic Dialogues* (1927)), ii. L.M. xiii. 356. On this aspect see F. Mehring, *Die Lessinglegende*, Berlin, 1906.

10. *Hamburgische Dramaturgie*, 81, L.M. x. 127–8 (for English translation see E. C. Beasley and H. Zimmern, *Selected Prose Works*, London, 1908).

11. *Wie die Alten den Tod gebildet*, L.M. xi. 3. English translation by E. C. Beasley and H. Zimmern, New York, 1966.

12. *Ueber eine zeitige Aufgabe*, L.M. xvi. 293–4.

13. C. N. Naumann, quoted by Oehlke, op. cit., i. 236.

14. Oehlke, op. cit., i. 238; F. Horn in Biedermann, op. cit., p. 273.

15. L.M. xvii. 3.

16. 21 October 1757, L.M. xvii. 125.

17. L.M. viii. 41.

18. L.M. x. 232.

19. *Goezes Streitschriften gegen Lessing*, herausgegeben von Erich Schmidt, Stuttgart, 1893, p. 78.

20. *2nd Anti-Goeze*, L.M. xiii. 149.

21. *8th Anti-Goeze*, L.M. xiii. 191.

22. 2. Aufzug, 1. Auftritt, L.M. iii. 41.

23. J. G. Robertson, op. cit.; René Wellek, *A History of Modern Criticism 1750–1950*, i. London, 1955.

24. Folke Leander, *Lessing als aesthetischer Denker* (Göteborgs Högskolas Årsskrift, xlviii, 1942–3), Göteborg, 1942, p. 37.

25. Arthur von Arx, *Lessing und die geschichtliche Welt*, Frauenfeld/Leipzig, 1944, pp. 69 ff.

26. L.M. xvi. 535.

27. *Ergänzungen des Firmicus*, L.M. xii. 275.

28. *Ehemalige Fenstergemälde im Kloster Hirschau*, L.M. xii. 38.

29. Ibid. and *Selbstbetrachtungen*, L.M. xvi. 539.

30. Nicolai to Gebler, 1779, Biedermann, op. cit., p. 218. See also Lessing to Mendelssohn, 5 November 1768, L.M. xvii. 270; to Heyne, 17 November 1770, L.M. xvii. 349; and *Hermäa*, L.M. xiv. 290.

31. This essay is included in the *Selected Prose Works* translated by E. C. Beasley and Helen Zimmern, London, 1908, etc. For a recent assessment of Lessing's theory see Jörgen Birkedal Hartman, 'Die Genien des Lebens und des Todes', in *Römisches Jahrbuch für Kunstgeschichte*, XII, 1969, 11–38. The winged twins representing Sleep and Death are shown on the funeral lekythos in Fig. 58 of this volume.

32. Hugo Blümner, *Lessings Laokoon*, Berlin, 1880; W. G. Howard, *Lessing's Laokoon*, New York, 1910; F. O. Nolte, *Lessing's Laokoon*, Lancaster, Pa., 1940; René Wellek, op. cit., and the London MA thesis by Charles R. Bingham, *Lessing's Laocoon and its English Predecessors*, 1938.

33. *Œuvres*, ed. J. Assézat, Paris, 1875, i. 385; Lessing's review, L.M. v. 95.

34. A. Frey, *Die Kunstform des Lessingschen Laokoon*, Stuttgart, 1905; Lessing's tribute to Diderot, L.M. viii. 288. See also L.M. xiv. 440.

35. *Polymetis*, London, 1747, p. 67 (I have reversed the sequence of the passages, which are discussed in detail in Bingham, loc. cit.).

36. *Tableaux tirés de l' Iliade...*, Paris, 1757, p. xxxiii. Blümner, op. cit., fails to refer to this parallel, and E. Schmidt in his standard biography of Lessing, Berlin, 1909, i. 529, is less than frank about it. S. Rocheblave, in his *Essai sur le Comte de Caylus*, Paris, 1889, pp. 218–20, exaggerates in the other direction.

37. I have discussed some aspects of this problem in my books *Art and Illusion*, London and New York, 1960, *The Sense of Order*, Oxford, 1979, and *The Image and the Eye*, Oxford, 1982.

38. A. Frey, op. cit., pp. 13 f.; F. O. Nolte, op. cit.; W. Rehm, *Winckelmann und Lessing*, Berlin, 1941. For additional evidence see Lessing's scathing remarks on artists quoted by H. Schneider, *Lessing*, Berne, 1951, p. 50.

39. *Ueber eine zeitige Aufgabe*, L.M. xvi. 296.

40. *Laokoon XI*, L.M. ix. 80.

41. *Laokoon VIII*, L.M. ix. 65.

42. 13 April 1769, L.M. xvii. 287.

43. *Vom Wesen der Fabel*, L.M. vii. 429.

44. See my 'Icones Symbolicae', in *Symbolic Images*, London, 1972.

45. *Vom Wesen der Fabel*, L.M. vii. 476.

46. *Laokoon IX*, L.M. ix. 65–67.

47. Three years later J. G. Herder, *Kritische Wälder*, iii. 1769, writes in a similar context: *Ein Kunstwerk ist der Kunst wegen da*. See my 'The Renaissance Conception of Artistic Progress and its Consequences', in *Norm and Form*, London, 1966.

48. 12th *Literaturbrief*, L.M. viii. 27.

49. *Laokoon II*, L.M. ix. 13.

50. L.M. vii. 68.

51. Lawrence Marsden Price, *English Literature in Germany*, Berkeley, 1953, pp. 228 f.

52. Lessing's translation of Dryden's *Essay of Dramatick Poesie*, L.M. vi. 249–94.

53. Lessing's note for the *Laokoon*, L.M. xiv. 387.

54. *Die Freyheiten der englischen Bühne*, Lessing to Nicolai, 21 Jan. 1758, L.M. xvii. 133.

55. Preface to *Oedipe*, 1719; *Œuvres*, Kehl, 1784, pp. 68 and 71.

56. R. Petsch, *Lessings Briefwechsel mit Mendelssohn und Nicolai über das Trauerspiel*, Leipzig, 1910.

57. Dec. 1756, L.M. xix. 56. For the context see Petsch, op. cit., pp. 62 ff.

58. Lessing on Hogarth, L.M. v. 368, 405, 422.

59. Lessing on Burke (whom he intended to translate), L.M. xiv. 220. For Burke see also my essay on Freud in this volume, p. 94.

60. L.M. xiv. 355.

61. *Laokoon I*, L.M. ix. 10.

62. I find a negative confirmation in F. O. Nolte, op. cit., p. 137, who writes: 'although Lessing, by the vigorous and somewhat dramatic tone of his argument would make it appear so, there was no urgent call for *Laokoon as it is orientated* at the time it appeared.'

63. *Laokoon XXVI–XXIX*, L.M. ix. 156–77. We know from the drafts (L.M. xiv. 379, 411) that Lessing merely used an effective literary device when he pretends that Winckelmann's *History* had just appeared when he wrote the last sections.

64. *Lectures on Painting by the Royal Academicians*, ed. R. N. Wornum, London, 1889, pp. 402 f.

65. *3. Stück*, L.M. ix. 195 anticipates the James-Lange theory of expression.

66. Oehlke, op. cit., i. 384.

67. Op. cit., p. 343 ff.

68. H. H. J. Peisel, *Die Lebensform Lessings als Strukturprinzip in seinen Dramen* (Dissertation, University of Pennsylvania), Philadelphia, 1941, esp. p. 53.

69. L.M. xvi. 422.

70. Oehlke, op. cit. i. 8 f.; Peisel, op. cit., pp. 5 f.

71. Wittenberg, 1714.

72. L.M. xiv. 135–42.

73. K. G. Lessing in Biedermann, op. cit., p. 8.

74. 30 May 1749, L.M. xvii. 19. For Lessing's early maturity see F. O. Nolte, *Grillparzer, Lessing und Goethe*, Lancaster, Pa., 1938, pp. 101–4.

75. *Der junge Gelehrte*, 2. Aufzug, 4. Auftritt, L.M. i. 319. For Lessing's self-satire see the letter to his mother 20 January 1749, L.M. xvii. 8.

76. Letter to his father, 28 April 1749, L.M. xvii. 16.

77. Hans Leisegang, *Lessings Weltanschauung*, Leipzig, 1931, pp. 27–55.

78. *Die Religion*, L.M. i. 265.

79. *Rettung des Cardanus*, L.M. v. 323.

80. See Robertson, op. cit., p. 348.

81. F. O. Nolte, op. cit., and H. B. Garland, *Lessing*, Cambridge, 1937, pp. 117–23. For a contrary estimate see Otto Mann, *Lessing*, Hamburg, 1948, pp. 224 ff.

82. This trait has provoked much puzzled criticism: Oehlke, op. cit., i. 184; W. Dilthey, *Das Erlebnis und die Dichtung*, Leipzig, 1910, p. 83. There are similar variations on the father-child relationship in *Philotas*, who asks the image of his father to enter his soul and help him commit suicide (4. Auftritt), L.M. ii. 362, and in such dramatic fragments as *Giangir* with its Oedipus paraphrase (L.M. iii. 251), *Das Horoscop* (L.M. iii. 371), another Oedipus story, and *Kleonnis* (L.M. iii. 364), where the father is jealous of his son.

83. F. Mehring, op. cit., pp. 322 f. For a neat summary of the plot see Kuno Fischer, *Lessing*, Stuttgart, 1881. The interpretation of O. Mann, op. cit., p. 207, that Tellheim is a victim of peace deserves to be quoted.

84. *Rettung des Horaz*, L.M. v. 272.

85. To Eva König (about Sonnenfels) 8 January 1773, L.M. xviii. 72.

86. *Rettung des Lemnius*, L.M. v. 41 ff.

87. L.M. xii. 38 and 159 ff.

88. 11 Nov. 1774, L.M. xviii. 117. For Lessing's increasing aversion to the stage see F. Horn in Biedermann, op. cit., p. 267; To Karl Lessing, 25 February 1778, L.M. xviii. 265; For his theology see Dilthey, op. cit., pp. 85–120, C. Schrempf, *Lessing als Philosoph*, Stuttgart, 1906, P. Lorenz, *Lessings Philosophie*, Leipzig, 1909, Leisegang, op. cit., and H. Chadwick, *Lessing's Theological Writings*, London 1956.

89. Letter to Nicolai, 25 August 1769, L.M. xvii. 298; *Bibliolatrie*, L.M. xvi. 475; *Ueber eine zeitige Aufgabe*, L.M. xvi. 295–6.

90. Letter to Karl Lessing, 2 February 1774, L.M. xviii. 101; *Des Andreas Wissowatius Einwürfe wider die Dreieinigkeit*, L.M. xii. 96/98; *Von der Duldung der Deisten*, L.M. xii. 271; *Aus den Papieren des Ungenannten*, L.M. xii. 431–5, 442–3.

91. *Leibnitz von den ewigen Strafen*, L.M. xi. 461 f.; *Des Andreas Wissowatius, &c.*, loc. cit.
92. Naumann in Oehlke, op. cit., i. 236. On Bayle and historical Pyrrhonism see Arnaldo Momigliano, 'Ancient History and the Antiquarian', *Journal of the Warburg and Courtauld Institutes*, xiii, 1950, which contains much material not discussed by A. von Arx, op. cit.
93. *Absagungsschreiben*, L.M. xiii. 103.
94. *Eine Duplik*, L.M. xiii. 24.
95. Ed. cit., p. 88.
96. K. R. Popper, *Logik der Forschung*, Vienna, 1935, pp. 208–9; London, 1959.
97. 'When I make the statement that "all mercury evaporates over fire" I am under no obligation to bring together all mercury existing in nature for the sake of anyone who objects to the generality of my assertion, and to make it evaporate in front of his eyes. Rather than do so I would simply tell him: "My dear fellow, all the mercury I ever placed over fire actually evaporated. If you know any that does not evaporate, bring it along so that I can also get to know it, and thank you for it."' *Axiomata*, L.M. xiii. 108.
98. Oehlke, op. cit., i. 46.
99. *II. Literaturbrief*, L.M. viii. 25; *Vom Wesen der Fabel*, L.M. vii. 477.
100. Letter to his mother, 20 January 1749, L.M. xvii. 9.
101. *Aus einem Gedichte an den Herrn M.*, L.M. i. 243. For Lessing's scientific temper see Folke Leander, op. cit., p. 13.
102. *Dass mehr als fünf Sinne für den Menschen seyn können*, L.M. xvi. 522. For the aesthetic application of the mind's limited capacity see *Hamburgische Dramaturgie*, 70, L.M. x. 82.
103. The earlier literature is reviewed in Martha Waller, *Lessings Erziehung des Menschengeschlechts* (Germanische Studien, 160), Berlin, 1935; subsequently

see Arx, op. cit., pp. 125 ff.; Mann, op. cit., pp. 345 ff.; Schneider, op. cit. (for having laid the ghost of Thaer's alleged authorship); and Chadwick, op. cit. (note 88), pp. 40 ff.
104. L.M. xiv. 382.
105. For this reason Lessing would have rejected Hegel (whose precursor he has so often been called) no less violently than Hegel was to dissociate himself from Lessing (Arx, op. cit., p. 56).
106. *Das Testament Johannis*, L.M. xiii. 15. English translation in Chadwick, op. cit.
107. Oehlke, op. cit., ii. 413 f.
108. 3. Aufzug, 7. Auftritt, L.M. iii. 95.
109. To Gebler, 13 August 1779, L.M. xviii. 323.
110. For a contrary opinion see Garland, op. cit., p. 145.
111. 3. Aufzug, 8. Auftritt, L.M. iii. 98.
112. In his biographical essay, F. O. Nolte, op. cit., p. 139, expresses misgivings about twisting the scalpel in Lessing's wound but still finds something like a confession of guilt in Lessing's tragic outburst to Eschenburg (31 December 1777, L.M. xviii. 259); 'I, too, wanted something of the good things of life, like other people.' Is not the real tragedy that Lessing had even to see this misfortune as a punishment for jealousy?
113. Letter to Eschenburg, 26 October 1774, L.M. xviii. 115. For Lessing's unexpected defence of *Werther* see R. Schneider, op. cit., p. 37.
114. Letters to Karl Lessing, 30 April and 11 November 1774, L.M. xviii. 109 and 117. See also B. Rosenthal, op. cit., and F. O. Nolte, op. cit., pp. 116–17.
115. J. H. F. Müller, quoted in Biedermann, op. cit., p. 155.
116. *An Göthe* (1800) provides a moving epilogue to the drama in which Lessing had been the protagonist.
117. Letter to Karl Lessing, 30 April 1774, L.M. xviii. 109.

'THE FATHER OF ART HISTORY': G. W. F. HEGEL

All Hegel's major works have been translated into English, some of them several times, and can easily be traced in the catalogues of major libraries. There is a useful selection, *The Philosophy of Hegel*, edited with an introduction by Carl J. Friedrich. Since Hegel was and remains such a controversial figure, whose writings influenced the political thought of both Marxism and Fascism, the literature pro and con his philosophy would fill a library. See also my essay 'In Search of Cultural History' in *Ideals and Idols*, Oxford, 1979.

1. AI, p. 92. I quote from the edition *Hegels Werke in zwanzig Bänden*, Suhr- kamp Verlag, Frankfurt-am-Main, 1970. The abbreviation AI refers to the

first volume of the Lectures on Aesthetics, AII to the second volume, and so on.

2. See my lecture series, *The Ideas of Progress and their Impact on Art*, published by Cooper Union, New York, 1971 (privately circulated). Published in German as *Kunst und Fortschritt*, Cologne, 1978.

3. Ed. cit. p. 529.
4. Ed. cit., para. 462.
5. AIII, p. 573.
6. AI, p. 30.
7. AI, p. 56.
8. I am grateful to Alex Potts for referring me to Herder's *Plastik* (1778).
9. AI, pp. 24–5.
10. See my 'The Use of Art for the Study of Symbols' in J. Hogg (ed.), *Psychology and the Visual Arts*, Harmondsworth, 1969.
11. AI, pp. 456–7.
12. AI, p. 465.
13. AII, p. 286.
14. In 1817 Goethe wrote to Heinrich Meyer about the Elgin Marbles: 'the continent will soon be swamped by these magnificent forms like cheap cotton goods'. See John Gage, *Goethe on Art*, London, 1980, pp. 89–94. See also: J. Rothenberg, *Descensus ad terram: The Acquisition and Reception of the Elgin Marbles* (Columbia University thesis, 1967), New York and London, 1977.
15. AI, p. 431, and AII, p. 434.
16. AIII, p. 17.
17. AIII, p. 20.
18. AIII, p. 68.
19. AIII, p. 99.
20. AII, p. 227.
21. AII, p. 226.
22. AII, p. 226.

23. AI, pp. 42–3.
24. In *Ideals and Idols*, Oxford, 1979, pp. 24–59.
25. K. R. Popper, *The Open Society and its Enemies*, London, 1945; *The Poverty of Historicism*, London, 1957; *The Logic of Scientific Discovery*, London, 1959.
26. Manfred von Eigen and Ruthild Winkler, *Das Spiel—Naturgesetze steuern den Zufall*, Munich, 1975, p. 197.
27. I quote from Karl Rosenkranz, *Friedrich Georg Wilhelm Hegels Leben*, Berlin, 1844, p. 335.
28. Julius von Schlosser, ' "Stilgeschichte" und "Sprachgeschichte" der bildenden Kunst', in *Sitzungsberichte der Bayr. Akademie der Wissenschaften, Phil-Hist Abt*, 1935, I. See also my 'Art History and the Social Sciences', in *Ideals and Idols*, Oxford, 1979.
29. See my 'Art History and the Social Sciences' op. cit.
30. AI, p. 50.
31. Karl Rosenkranz, op. cit., p. 229.
32. Ed. cit., p. 46.
33. Renato Poggioli, *Teoria dell'arte d'avanguardia*, Bologna, 1962. Poggioli does not refer to Hegel in this context.
34. *The Ideas of Progress*, op. cit. (note 2).
35. Printed in *Manifeste*, 1905–33, Diether Schmidt, Dresden, 1964, p. 290.
36. Ibid., p. 238.
37. See *Journal of the Royal Institute of British Architects*, December 1976.
38. J. M. Richards, 'The Hollow Victory, 1932–1972', in the *Journal of the Royal Institute of British Architects*, May 1972.
39. *Die Religion innerhalb der Grenzen der blossen Vernunft*, II Abschn, II Teil, 4 Stück, par I, *Werke*, Berlin, 1914, Bd VI, p. 318.

NATURE AND ART AS NEEDS OF THE MIND: LORD LEVERHULME

An Exhibition with the title *Lord Leverhulme, A Great Edwardian Collector and Builder* was held in the spring of 1980 at the Royal Academy of Arts, London. The catalogue of the Exhibition can be consulted for illustrations and bibliography. The Leverhulme Trust Fund continues to support education and research.

1. Catalogue of the Lord Leverhulme Exhibition, Royal Academy of Arts, London, 12 April to 25 May 1980.
2. See my *Symbolic Images*, London, 1972, pp. 165–7 and note. See also *Critical Inquiry* special issue on metaphor, Vol. 5, No. 1, Autumn 1978, with supplementary articles in Vol. 6, No. 1.
3. William Hazlitt, *Selected Essays*, edited by Geoffrey Keynes, Nonesuch Press, 1948, pp. 3–8.

4. Harold G. Henderson, *An Introduction to Haiku*, New York, 1958.
5. Lady Murasaki, *The Tale of Genji*, a novel in six parts translated from the Japanese by Arthur Waley, London, 1935.
6. William Wordsworth, *The Prelude, or Growth of a Poet's Mind*, text of 1805 edited by Ernest de Sélincourt, Oxford, 1933.
7. See my 'Art and Scholarship', in

Meditations on a Hobby Horse, London, 1963.
8. See note 1, above.
9. *The Times*, 21 February 1981.

10. *The Story of Art*, London, 1950, 13th edition 1978.
11. See my essay on Warburg in this volume, pp. 117–37.

VERBAL WIT AS A PARADIGM OF ART: SIGMUND FREUD

Freud's collected works (*Gesammelte Werke*), edited by Anna Freud, were published in eighteen volumes in Frankfurt am Main (1940–68); the English standard edition in twenty-four volumes was published in London (1953–74). Ernest Jones's biography, *The Life and Work of Sigmund Freud*, appeared in three volumes from 1953 to 1957. A more recent monograph, with ample bibliography, is Frank J. Sulloway, *Freud, Biologist of the Mind* (1979), in which also the editions of Freud's Correspondence are listed.

Freud's attitude to art and artists, which is the subject of this essay, has given rise to much comment. In his biography Ernest Jones writes that both Ernst Kris and Freud's architect-son had tried to dissuade him from dealing with this topic since Freud lacked an organ for art. Jones felt compelled to concede that Roger Fry was right in stating that the few words which Freud devoted to the motivations of artists in his *Introductory Lectures on Psychoanalysis* (1917, XXIII) were neither just nor adequate (I have not referred to these remarks in my essay). The thorough book by Jack J. Spector, *The Aesthetics of Freud, A study in Psychoanalysis and Art* (1972), contains a detailed bibliography. The author's criticism of my evaluation of Freud's book on the Joke has not, however, convinced me.

1. M. H. Abrams, *The Mirror and the Lamp*, 1953. See also my article 'Four Theories of Artistic Expression' in *Architectural Association Quarterly*, 1980, Vol. 12, No. 4.
2. Letter, 1 November 1914.
3. *Gesammelte Werke*, XIV, p. 91.
4. 'Freud's Aesthetics', *Encounter*, XXVI, January 1966, 30–40.
5. Letter, 8 July 1915.
6. 26 December 1922.
7. See my paper on Kris in this volume, pp. 221–33.
8. 'ist das nicht der rote Fadian, der sich durch die Geschichte der Napoleoniden zieht?'
9. *Ges. W.*, VI, p. 204.
10. *Ges. W.*, p. 146.
11. Letter, 16 April 1909.
12. *Ges. W.*, X, p. 172.
13. Letter to Lou Andreas-Salomé, 10 July 1931.
14. Letter, 20 July 1929.
15. Letter, 24 September 1907.
16. 'Warum kann der lebendige Geist dem Geist nicht erscheinen? *Spricht* die Seele, so spricht, ach! schon die *Seele* nicht mehr.'
17. Interestingly enough the Russian novelist knew how to have it both ways. He knew that the type was prefigured in art, and so he continued his description of Leonardo's mother quoted above as follows: 'Once, in Florence, in the museum of San Marco, in the gardens of the Medici, he saw a statue which had been found in Arezzo, an olden city of Etruria, a little copper Cybele, the immemorially ancient goddess of the Earth, with the same strange smile as that of the young village girl of Vinci—his mother.' Merezhkovsky, *The Romance of Leonardo da Vinci*, 1903. In this way Walter Pater's famous description of the *Mona Lisa* as 'older than the rocks' could be effortlessly fitted into the story of Leonardo's life.
18. Ernest Jones, Vol. 3, p. 441.
19. Letter, 7 November 1914.
20. *Ges. W.*, XIV, pp. 437–8.

THE AMBIVALENCE OF THE CLASSICAL TRADITION: ABY WARBURG

All Warburg's published works were collected in the German edition of his *Gesammelte Schriften* (2 volumes, 1932), but none of them has been translated into English. His lecture on Serpent Ritual was published in an English translation in *The Journal of the Warburg Institute* in 1939. Extensive summaries and extracts from his published and unpublished writings are included in my monograph, *Aby Warburg, An Intellectual Biography*, London, 1970, with a bibliographical appendix. I have therefore not included all these individual references in my essay.

1. Anton von Werner (1843–1915) was President of the Prussian Academy of Art and favourite court painter of Kaiser Wilhelm II. In his day he was well

known for his paintings of ceremonial military scenes and for his meticulous observance of uniforms and costumes.

2. Thomas Mann, 'Die Stellung Freuds in der modernen Geistesgeschichte' in *Die psychoanalytische Bewegung*, Vienna,

1929, pp. 8–32. Reprinted in *Gesammelte Werke*, Frankfurt-am-Main, 1974, Vol. 10, p. 256.

3. *Introductory Lectures on Psycho-Analysis*, 1917, XXIII.

4. *Die Mneme*, 1908.

THE HIGH SERIOUSNESS OF PLAY: J. HUIZINGA

Huizinga's collected works, *Verzamelde Werken*, were published in Dutch in nine volumes (1948–53). His principal works exist in English: *The Waning of the Middle Ages*, 1924, *Erasmus of Rotterdam*, 1924, *In the Shadow of Tomorrow*, 1936, *Homo ludens*, 1949. Two important selections of his essays are also available in English: *Men and Ideas*, translated by James S. Holmes and Hans van Marle, Meridian Books, 1959, and *Dutch Civilization in the Seventeenth Century and other essays* selected by Pieter Geyl and F. W. N. Hugenholtz, London, 1968, which also includes Huizinga's autobiographical sketch, 'My Path to History'. References given in brackets after the quoted text in my essay are to his collected works.

1. *Art and Illusion*, New York and London, 1960.

2. 'Personification', in R. R. Bolgar, ed., *Classical Influences on European Culture*, Cambridge, 1971, pp. 247–57, and my 'Icones Symbolicae', in *Symbolic Images*, London, 1972, pp. 123–95.

3. See my *The Sense of Order*, Oxford, 1979.

4. I have normally quoted from the text of the English edition (London, 1949) 'prepared from the German edition published in Switzerland, 1944, and also from the author's own English translation of the text which he made shortly before his death'. The English translator F. Hopman says that 'comparison of the two texts shows a number of discrepancies and a marked difference in style' and expresses the hope to have achieved 'a reasonable synthesis'. I have checked the extracts against the Dutch original cited in the references. In the case of relevant divergencies I have either substituted my own translation or drawn attention to the differences.

5. G. J. Heering, *Johan Huizinga's religieuze gedachten als achtergrond van zijn werken*, Lochem, 1948.

6. 'Het is een hachelijk pogen, om in een oude, ver van ons gelegen letterkunde aan te wijzen, waar de grens ligt tusschen het ernstig en het niet-ernstig bedoelde. Het is zelfs dikwijls nutteloos en verkeerd, om met een onbescheiden naarstigheid die bewuste onderscheiding in twee staten van uitdrukking, buiten den kring onzer eigen ideeën te willen toepassen. Want juist om, zelf onbewust, die beide staten saam te houden en te vermengen tot de aandoenlijkste uiting van de innigste gedachten, is het vermogen van enkelen die in evenwicht van doen en denken leven in den vollen bloei van een cultuurtijdperk.'

7. 'The Aesthetic Element in Historical Thought' (Huizinga's inaugural lecture of 1905) in *Dutch Civilization in the 17th Century and other essays*, ed. Pieter Geyl and F. W. N. Hugenholtz, London, 1968, especially p. 242.

8. Karl J. Weintraub, *Visions of Culture*, Chicago, 1966, pp. 228–9.

9. See my 'In Search of Cultural History', in *Ideals and Idols*, Oxford, 1979.

10. E. Rosenbaum, 'Johan Huizinga', *Die Zeitung*, London, 11 May, 1945.

11. The passage is omitted from the English translation, on which see Weintraub, op. cit., p. 212.

12. 'In Search of Cultural History', op. cit.

13. P. Geyl, 'Huizinga as an Accuser of his Age', *History and Theory*, II, 1963, iii, 231–62, 275. (No source is given.)

14. Ibidem.

15. 'Johan Huizinga and the Task of Cultural History', *American Historical Review*, LXIX, 1964, iii, 607–30.

16. See my *Aby Warburg, An Intellectual Biography*, London, 1970, p. 9.

17. My quotations are generally from the English translation by J. H. Huizinga, London, 1936, but references here as always are to the *Collected Works*.

18. Quoted by Geyl, 'Huizinga', op. cit.

19. The word 'Marxism' is added in the English edition.

20. English translation, London, 1932, after the Spanish original, chapters IX and X.

21. I am indebted to Prof. A. Momigliano, who made me see the importance of this shift.

22. The last sentence only in the English edition.

23. K. R. Popper, *The Poverty of Histori-*

cism, London, 1957, pp. 27 ff., and *The Open Society and its Enemies*, London, 1945, Chapter XI, p. 2.

24. I quote from the English translation by J. S. Holmes and H. v. Marle in *Men and Ideas*, Meridian Books, 1959, p. 74.

25. English edition p. 6.

26. L. Wittgenstein, *Philosophische Untersuchungen*, Oxford, 1953, pp. 31 ff.

27. Konrad Lorenz, *Das sogenannte Böse. Zur Naturgeschichte der Aggression*, Vienna, 1963.

28. N. Tinbergen, 'On War and Peace in Animals and Man', *Science*, CLX, 28 June 1968, 1411–18.

29. W. H. Thorpe, 'Ritualization in ontogeny, I, Animal Play', in J. Huxley, ed., *A Discussion on Ritualization of Behaviour in Animals and Man*, Philosophical Transactions of the Royal Society of London, Series B. No. 772, CCLI, 1966.

30. Thanks to the kindness of the editor of the Oxford English Dictionary Supplement I have been allowed to see their collection of references, from which it appears that the German term *Hackliste* was used by T. J. Schjelder-Ebbe in *Zeitschrift für Psychologie*, LXXXVIII, 1922, 227. The earliest non-scientific usage there recorded is in

A. Huxley, *Point Counter Point*, 1928, p. 48. Could the novelist have taken it over from his brother, the biologist? W. C. Allee, *Animal Aggregations*, Chicago, 1931, and *The Social Life of Animals*, London and Toronto, 1938, appears to have made the term more popular, though its real vogue dates from the post-war period.

31. J. S. Bruner, 'Nature and Uses of Immaturity', *American Psychologist*, XXVII, 8 August 1972, i–22, which also offers an excellent point of entry into the bibliography of the problem of play. See also Maria W. Piers, ed., *Play and Development*, New York, 1972.

32. K. R. Popper, *Objective Knowledge, an Evolutionary Approach*, Oxford, 1972 (see Index under Reduction).

33. M. Peckham, *Man's Rage for Chaos. Biology, Behaviour and the Arts*, Philadelphia and New York, 1965, and my review in *The New York Review of Books*, 23 June 1966.

34. I. Heidemann, *Der Begriff des Spiels*, Berlin, 1968, and Volker Harms, *Der Terminus 'Spiel' in der Ethnologie*. Arbeiten aus dem Institut für Völkerkunde der Universität zu Göttingen, Band 4, Hamburger Philosophische Dissertation, 1969.

THE HISTORY OF IDEAS: GEORGE BOAS

A Select Bibliography of the works of George Boas was compiled by Dr Richard Macksey and published in connection with this essay in the *Journal of the History of Ideas*, 1981, pp. 352–3.

1. *The Limits of Reason*, New York, 1961, p. 51.

2. *The Inquiring Mind*, La Salle, III, 1959, p. 18.

3. *The Story of Art*, 1950, 13th edn., Oxford, 1978.

4. 'A Fourteenth Century Cosmology', *Proceedings of the American Philosophical Society*, 1954, Vol. 98, No. i, 50–9.

5. *A Sudden Thought*, Salisbury, Md, 1968, I.

6. *The Limits of Reason*, op. cit., p. 58.

7. 'Superstitions in Education', *The Johns Hopkins Magazine*, April 3–8, 1959, 3.

8. 'The Problem of the Humanities', *The Journal of General Education*, 10 October 1957, 209.

9. 'Superstitions in Education', op. cit.

10. *The Inquiring Mind*, op. cit.

11. *The Heaven of Invention*, Baltimore, Md, 1962, p. 7.

12. University of California Publications in Philosophy, Vol. 2, no. 6.

13. *Never Go Back* (*A novel without a plot*), New York and London, 1928.

14. *The Datum as Essence in Contemporary Philosophy*, Niort, France, 1927.

15. *The Major Traditions of European Philosophy*, New York and London, 1929, p. 327.

16. Review of J. H. Randall, Jr., 'The Career of Philosophy', *Journal of the History of Ideas*, 24 April 1963, 287–92.

17. Ibid., p. 292.

18. *The Heaven of Invention*, op. cit., p. 16.

19. 'The Cones', *Handbook of the Cone Collection*, Baltimore, 1955.

20. Translated by George Boas, New York, 1950.

21. *Journal of Higher Education*, 22 May 1951, 229–35.

22. *Dominant Themes of Modern Philosophy, A History*, New York, 1957.

23. New York and London, 1960.

24. 'Annual Members Dinner. The Walters Art Gallery', 21 May, 1962, duplicated.

25. *Vox Populi: Essays in the History of an Idea*, Baltimore, 1969.
26. *The History of Ideas: An Introduction*, New York, 1969.

27. *A Sudden Thought*, op. cit., p. 17.
28. Ibid, p. 13.

THE NECESSITY OF TRADITION: I. A. RICHARDS

The publications of I. A. Richards, CH, Litt.D., FBA, include the following: *Foundations of Aesthetics* (with C. K. Ogden and James Wood), 1921; *The Meaning of Meaning* (with C. K. Ogden), 1923; *Principles of Literary Criticism*, 1924; *Practical Criticism*, 1929; *Mencius on the Mind*, 1931; *Interpretation in Teaching*, 1938; *How to Read a Page*, 1942; *Basic English and its Uses*, 1943; *Goodbye Earth and Other Poems*, 1959; *Design for Escape: World Education through Modern Media*, 1968; *Internal Colloquies*, 1972; *New and Selected Poems*, 1978; *Verse versus Prose*, Presidential Address, the English Association, 1978.

1. For a portrait of Schlosser see also my essay on Otto Kurz in this volume, pp. 235–49.
2. Benedetto Croce, *The Breviary of Aesthetics*, originally published in 1915. My quotation, No. 4, Vol. 2, p. 47.
3. 'Ars Poetica' in *New and Selected Poems*, Manchester, 1978.
4. See also my first essay in this volume, 'Focus on the Arts and Humanities', pp. 22–3.
5. See my 'Illusion and Art' in R. L. Gregory and E. H. Gombrich, *Illusion in Nature and Art*, London, 1975.
6. See also my 'Visual Discovery Through Art' in *The Image and the Eye*, Oxford, 1982, especially p. 25.
7. This is also discussed in my essay 'Reason and Feeling in the Study of Art' in *Ideals and Idols*, Oxford, 1979.
8. For more on this subject see my 'Ritualized Gesture and Expression in Art' in *The Image and the Eye*, op. cit. (note 6).
9. *Memorabilia*, III, x, 8.
10. See my essay 'Freud's Aesthetics' in *Encounter*, January 1966, XXVI, 1, pp. 30–40.
11. *Encounter*, LIII, 1979, pp. 10–14
12. Lorenz Eitner, 'Art History and the Sense of Quality', *Art International*, May 1975.

THE EVALUATION OF ESOTERIC CURRENTS: FRANCES A. YATES

The memorial pamphlet dedicated to Frances A. Yates published by the Warburg Institute, London 1982, from which this Tribute is taken, also included the entry from *Who's Who* and a list of Dame Frances Yates's writings. Two volumes of her *Collected Essays* have meanwhile been published in 1982 and 1983.

1. *Giordano Bruno and the Hermetic Tradition*, London, 1964.
2. *The French Academies of the Sixteenth Century*, London, 1947.
3. *The Art of Memory*, London, 1966.
4. *The Rosicrucian Enlightenment*, London and Boston, 1972.
5. *A Study of Love's Labour's Lost*, London, 1936.
6. *Theatre of the World*, London, 1969.
7. *The Occult Philosophy in the Elizabethan Age*, London, 1979.
8. *The Valois Tapestries*, London, 1959.
9. *Journal of the Warburg and Courtauld Institutes*, 1954, reprinted in *Collected Essays*, London, 1982, a volume which also includes her lively articles on Bruno mentioned in this essay.

THE STUDY OF ART AND THE STUDY OF MAN: ERNST KRIS

A list of the art historical writings of Ernst Kris was compiled and duplicated by the New York Psycho-Analytic Institute in 1963 and contains fifty-nine titles (excluding book reviews). His *Psychoanalytic Explorations in Art*, a collection of articles, some of which were originally published in German, appeared in 1952 under the imprint of the International Universities Press; both contain extensive bibliographies. A further collection of *Selected Papers* was published in 1975 by the Yale University Press.

1. 'Der stil rustique' in *Jahrbuch der Kunsthistorischen Sammlungen in Wien*, 1926.
2. Vienna, 1928.
3. 'Die Charakterköpfe des Franz Xaver Messerschmidt' in *Jahrbuch der Kunsthistorischen Sammlungen in Wien*, 1932.

4. *Imago*, xix, 1933. Reprinted in English as chapter 4 of *Psychoanalytic Explorations in Art*, 1952.
5. Vienna, 1934. A revised English translation was published by Yale University Press, 1979, under the title *Legend, Myth and Magic in the Image of the Artist*, to which I contributed a Preface.
6. Karl Bühler, *Ausdruckstheorie*, Jena, 1933.
7. See my paper on Freud in this volume, pp. 93–115.
8. *International Journal of Psycho-Analysis*, xix, 1938. Reprinted as Chapter 8 of *Psychoanalytic Explorations in Art*, 1952.

THE EXPLORATION OF CULTURE CONTACTS: OTTO KURZ

Two selections of studies by Otto Kurz have been published in reprint, the first, under the title *The Decorative Arts of Europe and the Islamic East*, by the Dorian Press, 1977 (with a bibliography of all his writings), the second, under the title *Selected Studies*, by the Pindar Press, 1982. Together they contain fifty-one articles. For the book he published jointly with Ernst Kris see note 5 under Kris.

1. In *Critica d'Arte*, 1955, 2, 402–19.
2. Published by the *Gazette des Beaux-Arts*, 1958.
3. See my paper on Kris in this volume, pp. 221–33.
4. See my paper on Warburg in this volume, pp. 117–37.
5. A factual account of this move can be found in the *Annual Report of the Warburg Institute*, 1952–3.
6. Paris, 1954.
   'De vifs remerciements doivent être adressés au Warburg Institute de Londres, ainsi qu'à M. Otto Kurz, de cet Institut. Lorsqu'en 1941, J. Hackin s'éloigna de Londres pour une mission qu'il savait périlleuse, et où il devait trouver la mort, il confia au Warburg Institute les documents concernant Begram et approuva le travail que M. Otto Kurz entreprit alors, étude comparative entre les objets découverts à Begram et les objets gréco-romains analogues déjà connus. Après la libération de la France, quand le Musée Guimet put reprendre la publication concernant Begram, la totalité des documents lui fut remise et M. Otto Kurz, d'accord avec M. Saxl, alors directeur du Warburg Institute, accepta de continuer à consacrer une très grande partie de son temps aux recherches commencées. Il entreprit plusieurs voyages d'enquête à cet effet et parvint ainsi à réunir un ensemble de comparaisons remarquables. Sa contribution aux études dédiées à la mémoire de J. Hackin est très importante. Nous tenons donc, en terminant cet avant-propos, à souligner le rôle du Warburg Institute de Londres.'
7. 'One of the frescoes at Schleswig shows "Herod and the Murder of the Innocents" and beneath it—also in the style of the thirteenth century—a frieze of eight medallions with turkeys. In due course it was pointed out that the turkey is an American bird and was unknown in Europe before the sixteenth century. How could it have been known in Schleswig in the thirteenth century? The answer was very simple: long before Columbus the Vikings had reached America. Nothing was hitherto known about Viking journeys to America in the thirteenth century, but it could easily be assumed that they had continued their expeditions through the centuries. Moreover, they might well have taken live turkeys into their boats, thus providing themselves with fresh meat for the long journey home. Not all the turkeys were eaten; a few were brought alive to Schleswig, where they were much admired and depicted on the walls of the cloisters.

   'There was great rejoicing about this discovery which proved that regular trade relations between America and Northern Germany already existed in the thirteenth century. There were, however, a few discordant voices, and among them that of the painter August Olbers, the man who had restored the frescoes in the late nineteenth century. He declared that he had painted the much discussed turkeys. Inasmuch as no traces of the original frieze below the "Murder of the Innocents" had been preserved, he painted four foxes and four turkeys as animals which would symbolize the character of Herod. Olbers' testimony was brushed aside with scorn. Who would trust the memory of a very old man? Had not Fey declared that the turkeys—which in the meantime had multiplied from four to eight—were undoubtedly painted in the thirteenth century?'

Bibliographical Note

Details of the previous publications of the papers in this volume are as follows:

FOCUS ON THE ARTS AND HUMANITIES. One of a series of addresses delivered as part of the Bicentennial Programme, 'Unity and Diversity: The Life of the Mind', at the American Academy of Arts and Sciences in May 1981 and published in the *Bulletin of the American Academy of Arts and Sciences*, XXXV, January 1982, No. 4, pp. 4–24.

THE DIVERSITY OF THE ARTS. Lecture given under the title 'Lessing: Lecture on a Master Mind' at the British Academy, Henriette Hertz Trust, in May 1956 and published under that title in the *Proceedings of the British Academy*, XLIII, 1957, pp. 133–56. © The British Academy 1957.

'THE FATHER OF ART HISTORY'. Lecture delivered in February 1977 on being awarded the Hegel Prize of the City of Stuttgart and originally published as 'Hegel und die Kunstgeschichte' in *Die Neue Rundschau*, 88, 1977, II, Heft. 202–19. The English translation by Angela Wilkes (revised by the author) was first published in *Architectural Designs*, LI, 1981, pp. 3–9. © *Architectural Design*, London.

NATURE AND ART AS NEEDS OF THE MIND. The Fourth Leverhulme Lecture given at Liverpool University in February 1981 and published in the same year by the Liverpool University Press. Copyright © The University of Liverpool 1981.

VERBAL WIT AS A PARADIGM OF ART. Lecture given under the title 'Sigmund Freud und die Theorie der Künste' at Vienna University in May 1981 to celebrate the 125th anniversary of Freud's birth and published under that title in the *Sigmund Freud House Bulletin*, V, No. 1, Summer 1981, pp. 11–24.

THE AMBIVALENCE OF THE CLASSICAL TRADITION. Address given under the title 'Aby Warburg zum Gedächtnis' at Hamburg University in June 1966 on the occasion of the centenary of Warburg's birth and published under that title in *Jahrbuch der Hamburger Kunstsammlungen*, XI, 1966, pp. 15–27.

THE HIGH SERIOUSNESS OF PLAY. Lecture given under the title 'Huizinga's *Homo ludens*' during the celebrations of Huizinga's centenary at Groningen University in December 1972 and published under that title in *Bijdragen en Mededelingen betreffende de Geschiedenis der Nederlanden*, 188, No. 2, 1973, pp. 275–96 (also available as a separate volume on Huizinga, edited by W. R. H. Koops, E. H. Kossman and Gees van der Plaat, published by Martinus Nijhoff, The Hague, 1973). Reprinted in the *Times Literary Supplement*, 4 October 1974.

THE HISTORY OF IDEAS. A lecture delivered under the title 'In Memory of George Boas' at Johns Hopkins University, Baltimore, in October 1980 and published in the *Journal of the History of Ideas*, 1981, pp. 335–54, and under separate cover. Copyright by Journal of the History of Ideas, Inc., 1981.

THE NECESSITY OF TRADITION. The Darwin Lecture given at Cambridge University in November 1979 under the title 'Aesthetics and the History of the Arts'. Not previously published.

THE EVALUATION OF ESOTERIC CURRENTS. Address given at the Warburg Institute of the University of London in commemoration of Dame Frances Yates in January 1982 and published that year by the Institute in a memorial pamphlet. Reprinted in the *New York Review of Books*, 3 March 1982, pp. 11–13.

THE STUDY OF ART AND THE STUDY OF MAN. Paper based on the Introduction to the Italian edition of Ernst Kris's *Psychoanalytic Explorations in Art*, Turin, 1967.

THE EXPLORATION OF CULTURE CONTACTS. A Memoir of Otto Kurz, originally published in the *Proceedings of the British Academy*, LXV, 1979, 719–34. © The British Academy 1981. Reprinted as an Introduction to Otto Kurz, *Selected Studies*, II, London, 1982.

Sources of Photographs

The publishers would like to thank all the private owners, institutions and museum authorities who have kindly allowed works in their collections to be reproduced. Every effort has been made to credit all persons holding copyright or reproduction rights.

The works of Dali (Fig. 25), Picasso (Fig. 50) and Matisse (Fig. 51) are © S.P.A.D.E.M. Paris, 1984.

Figs. 1, 5: Courtesy, Museum of Fine Arts, Boston: Residuary Fund (Fig. 1), Francis Gardner Curtis Fund (Fig. 5); Fig. 2: Courtesy, Emerson Memorial Association, photo courtesy Frick Art Reference Library; Fig. 4: Courtesy of the Fogg Art Museum, Harvard University, Purchase – Alpheus Hyatt Fund; Figs. 6, 7: Herzog August Bibliothek, Wolfenbüttel; Fig. 9: Fotosammlung des Stuttgarter Stadtarchivs; Fig. 12: Staatliche Kunstsammlung Dresden, Gemäldegalerie, Alte Meister; Fig. 13: Reproduced by permission of the Trustees of the Wallace Collection, Crown Copyright; Figs. 14, 15: Photos courtesy of Walker Art Gallery, Liverpool; Fig. 16: With thanks to the Unilever Information Librarian; Fig. 17: The Tate Gallery, London; Figs. 18, 39, 59: Reproduced by courtesy of the Trustees of the British Museum; Fig. 20: Mary Evans/Sigmund Freud Copyrights; Figs. 23, 65, 75, 76: Bildarchiv Foto Marburg; Fig. 25: Photo courtesy of Museum Boymans-van Beuningen, Rotterdam; Figs. 27, 29: Historisches Museum der Stadt Wien; Fig. 31: Öffentliche Kunstsammlung, Kunstmuseum Basel; Figs. 38, 40, 67: Soprintendenza alle Gallerie di Firenze; Figs. 41, 43, 70: Alinari, Florence; Figs. 50, 51: The Baltimore Museum of Art; Figs. 55, 61: Staatliche Museen zu Berlin; Fig. 56: Edward S. Ross, Curator of Etymology, California Academy of Science; Figs. 63, 64: Photo – Ilse Schneider-Lengyel; Fig. 66: © James Austin, FIIP; Fig. 78: Cliché des Musées Nationaux, Paris.